Routledge Revivals

Pethick-Lawrence

First published in 1963, *Pethick-Lawrence* is a detailed biography of the life and career of Frederick William Pethick-Lawrence.

Written by Vera Brittain, a close friend of Pethick-Lawrence during the last twenty-five years of his life, the book is a thorough and affectionate record of his personality and achievements. It makes extensive use of Pethick-Lawrence's well-organised personal papers to provide a detailed account of his activities, both public and private, and traces his life from birth, through his schooling, his meeting with Emmeline and involvement with the suffrage movement, his political career and role as Secretary of State for India, his marriage to Helen, and his death in 1961.

Pethick-Lawrence is a personal view into the life of Frederick William Pethick-Lawrence, and twentieth-century society and politics.

Pethick-Lawrence

A Portrait

By Vera Brittain

First published in 1963
by George Allen & Unwin Ltd

This edition first published in 2021 by Routledge
2 Park Square, Milton Park, Abingdon, Oxon, OX14 4RN
and by Routledge
605 Third Avenue, New York, NY 10017

Routledge is an imprint of the Taylor & Francis Group, an informa business

© 1963 Vera Brittain

All rights reserved. No part of this book may be reprinted or reproduced or utilised in any form or by any electronic, mechanical, or other means, now known or hereafter invented, including photocopying and recording, or in any information storage or retrieval system, without permission in writing from the publishers.

Publisher's Note
The publisher has gone to great lengths to ensure the quality of this reprint but points out that some imperfections in the original copies may be apparent.

Disclaimer
The publisher has made every effort to trace copyright holders and welcomes correspondence from those they have been unable to contact.

A Library of Congress record exists under LCCN: 63024260

ISBN 13: 978-0-367-68996-4 (hbk)
ISBN 13: 978-1-003-13995-9 (ebk)

Pethick from the painting by John Baker at Dorking

Pethick-Lawrence
A Portrait

By VERA BRITTAIN

London
GEORGE ALLEN & UNWIN LTD
RUSKIN HOUSE   MUSEUM STREET

FIRST PUBLISHED IN 1963

This book is copyright under the Berne Convention. Apart from any fair dealing for the purpose of private study, research, criticism or review, as permitted under the Copyright Act, 1956, no portion may be reproduced by any process without written permission. Enquiries should be addressed to the publisher.

© George Allen & Unwin Ltd 1963

FOREWORD

Though Fred Pethick-Lawrence belonged to my father's now almost vanished generation, in a quarter of a century of stimulating friendship I never found him anything but contemporary. Nor was his self-identification with younger generations confined to the one which followed his own.

In his autobiography, *Fate Has Been Kind*, published in 1943, he writes of 'misunderstandings between young and old' as one of the unnecessary barriers which divide human beings into conflicting camps. He displayed as much interest in the life and work of my daughter — who once called his conversation 'animated history'—as he had always shown in mine. During the General Election of May 1955, when he was eighty-four and she, at twenty-four, had been selected as Parliamentary Labour candidate for the Harwich Division of Essex, he spoke for her twice and stayed overnight in her constituency, though she had not the smallest chance of winning the campaign.

I have never been sure whether this ability to remain on the scene however much it changed was due to a remarkable power of adjustment or to a conscious intellectual effort. In his book *Votes for Women*, Roger Fulford, who clearly admired him, tells us that Pethick-Lawrence 'was once described as having for part of his religion "conscious unity with the entire sentient creation".' Certainly Pethick identified himself with the second-class citizens of his first forty years—women, workers, and the members of subject races—by deliberately helping to put them in a position where they could become first class if they chose.

From his youth he was always to be found well to the left of centre on the side of the oppressed, though his consistent and courteous equanimity would not have suggested a revolutionary temperament to those unaware of his affiliations. His once considerable private fortune was largely expended in promoting revolutions and sustaining the rebels. This passion for justice and equality took him into the militant suffrage movement, in which his first wife Emmeline was a popular leader and his second wife Helen an intrepid young campaigner, and subsequently led him into the equally significant struggle for Socialism. More recently, as Secretary of State for India from

1945-7, he played a decisive part in the events, both exhilarating and tragic, which gave political independence to India's submerged millions.

In retrospect his long career, always conducted at a high level of integrity, appears to have had two major peaks. He climbed the first in brilliantly conducting his own defence at the Old Bailey Conspiracy Trial in 1912, and the second when he took the historic Cabinet Mission to India in 1946. Fortunately, the series of affectionate letters between him and Emmeline which cover these vital months have survived to add their note of humanity to the complex political tangle.

As Fred's life lengthened, his capacity for analyzing and clarifying a complex series of events remained unimpaired, and in his eighties he appeared physically more vigorous than he had been in his seventies. The numerous obituary articles which followed his death nearly all treated him as an active figure in current politics. When we spoke together at the farewell luncheon of the National Union of Women Teachers in April 1961, seven months before the ninetieth birthday which he just failed to reach, he showed me his pocket diary. It was closely booked for weeks ahead with public engagements.

This short biography is a modest endeavour to give vitality to his memory, and thus to pay the tribute due to him from the former underdogs of both sexes who advanced from subjection to independence in the tremendous century almost spanned by his life. When I began to record it I was uncertain how to describe him, so I turned up a letter which he wrote in 1951: 'Don't you think the time has come when we can be less formal in approach? My staff call me "Lord P.-L.", my M.P. friends call me simply "Pethick", my intimate circle "Fred". Take your choice and please err on the side of intimacy.'

Thenceforth he was 'Pethick' to me for a time, and subsequently 'Fred'. I have, however, called him 'Pethick' after the opening chapters of this story because (though it was never part of his name until his first marriage) he was most widely known by it, and it was the one used at his crowded Memorial Service in St Margaret's, Westminster, on November 2, 1961.

ACKNOWLEDGMENTS

I am gratefully indebted to Lady Pethick-Lawrence, and to Miss Esther Knowles and Miss Gladys Groom [former secretaries to Lord and Lady (Emmeline) Pethick-Lawrence and now their literary editor and executor] for the use of Lord Pethick-Lawrence's private papers, letters and broadcasts. This book is largely based upon them, in addition to his published autobiography *Fate Has Been Kind* (Hutchinson 1943) and several shorter books, essays and pamphlets, and to Emmeline Pethick-Lawrence's autobiography, *My Part in a Changing World* (Gollancz 1938).

I have also made considerable use of material on the Suffragette Movement in the London Museum, and of books and documents in the India Office Library of the Commonwealth Relations Office relating to the Cabinet Mission led by Lord Pethick-Lawrence as Secretary of State for India and for Burma in 1946, and to the transfer of power from Britain to India in 1947. To spare the reader too many wearisome references to footnotes, I have included in my Appendix a list of the main sources used for Part III.

My especial gratitude is due to Earl Alexander of Hillsborough, C.H., for so kindly sharing with me his personal recollections of the Cabinet Mission and for facilitating my use of the India Office Library; and to Mr Frank Turnbull, C.B., C.I.E., now Secretary of the Office of the Minister for Science, who was Private Secretary to Lord Pethick-Lawrence when he was Secretary of State for India and also Secretary of the Cabinet Delegation to India, for his expert and generous assistance in interpreting the work of the Cabinet Mission. I am most grateful for his kindness in reading the relevant chapters of this book, for filling in gaps in my knowledge, and for salutary criticisms which were all constructive and helpful.

My thanks are also due to Mr S. C. Sutton, chief Librarian at the India Office Library; to Mr John Hayes of the London Museum; to the staffs of both libraries for their help and courtesy; and to Miss Vera Douie of the Fawcett Library for kind and willing assistance.

I am indebted to the Hon. Mrs V. L. Pandit; Dame Isobel Cripps; Mr Humphry Trevelyan of King's College, Cambridge; Miss Grace Roe (Vice-President, the Suffragette Fellowship); Mr David Carver (General Secretary, the International P.E.N.); Miss Esther Knowles; Miss Irene Harrison; Miss Sybil Morrison; Miss Isabel Seymour; and Mrs Mary Mazzoletti for kind permission to quote copyright letters; to Mr Rafiq Sakaria for quotations from his Anthology *A Study of Nehru*; and to Odham's Press Ltd for allowing me to quote from their publications *Mahatma Gandhi* and *If I Had My Time Again*, and to the *Hindustan Times* for permission to reproduce their cartoon 'Try, Try, Try Again'. I am also grateful to Miss Roe for most kindly checking the chapters on the Suffragette Movement.

In addition to those already mentioned, I am much obliged for useful information to Dr G. P. Gooch, C.H.; Miss Mollie Bell, Information Officer at Transport House; Mr H. F. Rubinstein; Mr William Kean Seymour and Miss Rosalind Wade; Miss Stella Newsome of the Suffragette Fellowship; and to Mr N. N. Gupta, Information Attaché at India House, for the gift of *A Study of Nehru*.

I am also greatly indebted to the Copyright Department of the B.B.C. for allowing me to quote Lord Pethick-Lawrence's broadcasts without restriction or obligation.

Finally, it is difficult sufficiently to thank Mr H. D. Harben for valuable aid in the production of the book; Miss Esther Knowles for checking and correcting the whole manuscript; and my husband, Professor George Catlin, for performing a similar service, and for much valuable criticism and many useful suggestions.

VERA BRITTAIN
November 1962

CONTENTS

FOREWORD		page 7
ACKNOWLEDGMENTS		9

PART I. THE SUFFRAGIST

1.	Son of Fortune	17
2.	Conversion	21
3.	'Sister of the People'	26
4.	A Partnership Begun	30
5.	The Young Editor	35
6.	The Pankhursts in Orbit	42
7.	Revolt Against Submission	47
8.	Dominant Trio	52
9.	The Old Bailey	58
10.	Aftermath	66

PART II. THE SOCIALIST

11.	The Four Years' War	75
12.	Would-be Politician	83
13.	Parliamentary Apprenticeship	90
14.	Junior Minister	96
15.	After the Blizzard	103
16.	Home to Edinburgh	109
17.	The Six Years' War	115
18.	The Day the War Ended	123

PART III. THE STATESMAN

19.	The Indian Story, 1900-1945	127
20.	Traveller to an Appointed Bourne	135
21.	The Cabinet Mission	143
22.	Persons and Problems in Delhi and Simla	152
23.	Ordeal by Frustration	162
24.	The Price of Achievement	169
25.	Rough Road to Independence	178
26.	India's Tryst with Destiny	185
27.	A Partnership Ends	192
28.	The Long Afterglow (1)	199
29.	The Long Afterglow (2)	205
30.	Requiescat	210
APPENDIX 1		215
APPENDIX 2		219
APPENDIX 3		221
INDEX		223

ILLUSTRATIONS

Pethick from the painting by John Barker at Dorking	*Frontispiece*
Pethick and Emmeline as children	*facing page* 32
Pethick as President of the Union at Cambridge	33
Emmeline aged 25	33
Pethick at the time of his marriage	48
Olive Schreiner at De Aar in 1908	49
Emmeline in 1910 at the height of the Suffragette Movement	80
Pethick at the time of the Bow Street Trial, 1912	80
Emmeline as Parliamentary Candidate at Rusholme in 1918	81
Pethick as Labour Candidate at West Leicester in 1923	81
An afternoon in Surrey	96
Tennis Champion	96
Fourways, Gomshall, Surrey	97
Victory at Edinburgh	128
The Labour Cabinet in the garden of 10 Downing Street, 1945	129
Emmeline and Pethick at Fourways, 1945	144
Pethick and Gandhi at Delhi in 1946	144
The Cabinet Mission in Delhi, 1946	145
Line Cartoon 'Try, Try, Try Again'	208
Pethick and Emmeline two years before their Golden Wedding	209
Pethick and Helen Pethick-Lawrence after their marriage in 1957	209

The generosity of Mr H. D. Harben, a close friend for many years of the late Lord Pethick-Lawrence, together with a subvention from the Pethick-Lawrence Memorial Fund, has enabled the published price of this biography to be 25s. The author and publishers gratefully acknowledge this valuable co-operation.

PART I
The Suffragist

CHAPTER 1

Son of Fortune

In 1897 a young man called Frederick William Lawrence came down from Cambridge who seemed to possess every worldly advantage that fate could provide. He had good looks, a brilliant intellect, a strong though not yet co-ordinated sense of social obligation, and sufficient wealth to pursue his chosen purposes in any direction where they seemed likely to take him. Much of this worldly endowment was subsequently to be spent on these impersonal ends.

The Lawrence fortune was founded by his grandfather, William Lawrence, a carpenter, whose family had been established in Cornwall for three generations. In 1809, aged nineteen, William left St Agnes, his native village, with two guineas in his pockets, and with a couple of young friends skilled in the same craft worked his way to Plymouth and thence to London. By 1825 his firm had prospered to the point of issuing a trade card:

"LAWRENCE & CO., Sash Makers,
PITFIELD STREET, Hoxton Square, and at No. 31 BREAD STREET, Cheapside,
Submit their List of Prices for Sashes, etc.
    for Ready Money only."

In 1853 the extension of Cannon Street gave a strong impetus to this prospering business, for Lawrence & Co. had prudently acquired extensive property near the new thoroughfare which they pulled down and rebuilt.

William Lawrence, a Unitarian, was from his youth an advocate of reform who took a leading part in the agitation for the Reform Bill of 1832. Though the Tories were then, as now, dominant in the City, he won the respect of his opponents through the consistent independence in which the granite of his native county seemed to come to life, and in 1849 he became Sheriff of London and Middlesex. Had he lived till 1857 instead of dying two years earlier, he would in the natural order of events have become, like Dick Whittington, Lord Mayor of London. Instead his eldest and second sons, William and James, respectively held that office in 1863 and 1868. For a century this substantial middle-class family hovered on the edge of political significance, but never quite achieved it until Frederick Pethick-Lawrence became Secretary of State for India and for Burma in 1945.

William Lawrence's large family ran to eleven children, of whom Alfred, the fifth child and fourth son, became Frederick's father. A serious-looking, black-haired and black-bearded man who died at forty-nine, he was one of the shortest-lived of a long-lived family. Frederick, who though fairer closely resembled him, was Alfred's youngest child, following a son and three daughters. By 1900, before he was thirty, he had inherited not only his father's fortune but that of his elder brother, who when nine years old had suffered an internal injury from a blow at school which prematurely cut off his life.

Frederick's own school was Eton, which soon discovered his exceptional mathematical gifts. His youngest uncle, Sir Edwin Durning-Lawrence, a strong supporter of Bacon's claim to be the author of Shakespeare's plays, kept a list, which still survives, of the marks obtained by his nephew in the Easter school examination of 1886. Marked 'V. well. Distinction', this list shows that the promising fifteen-year-old had won 193 marks out of a possible 200 in Mathematics.

Sixty-five years later, in an essay included in a symposium entitled *If I Had My Time Again*,[1] Pethick analyzed the implications of this talent. The possession of it, he wrote, did not merely signify that he could do sums more quickly than others; 'it also means that I generally saw things in harder outline than they did, and that I tried to reason from the abstract to the concrete and particular, instead of proceeding in the reverse direction as most other people appear to do'.

At fifteen he had not reached the analytical stage; the quality which impressed his Eton and Cambridge contemporary, Dr G. P. Gooch, was 'the abounding energy which marked his whole career'. Before he left Cambridge his vigour and intelligence had

[1] Odhams Press Ltd. 1951.

made him Captain of the Oppidans (students not on the foundation who board in the town) and Head of the School. Even when he had been a practising Socialist for half a century, Pethick never indulged in the popular hypocrisy of decrying his education. He knew that Eton was not only the largest school in England, but the most famous in the world. 'If I had my time again,' he said unrepentantly in 1951, 'I would go to the same school, university and college, and would read the same subjects' (Mathematics, Natural Science and Economics).

This conclusion is hardly surprising, for Trinity College, Cambridge, was to prove as rewarding as Eton. For him it meant six years of complete happiness, and an academic record of unbroken success. He was Fourth Wrangler in the Mathematical Tripos in 1894, took a First in Natural Science in 1895, won the Smith Prize in Mathematics, and the Adam Smith Prize for his earliest work, *Local Variations in Wages*. A Fellowship at Trinity followed these achievements. The other Fellow of Trinity in the same year as himself was Sir William Morley Fletcher, the physiologist. G. P. Gooch was the third possible choice, but at that time Trinity had never appointed a Fellow in History. Its first Fellow of History was G. M. Trevelyan, two years younger than Dr Gooch. Another contemporary was Bertrand Russell, whose masterfulness even at that date Dr Gooch clearly recalls.

The gifted undergraduate was no one-track-minded scholar. He became President of the Union, the historic debating society which at Cambridge as at Oxford so often proves to be the nursery of future statesmen. He played billiards for Cambridge against Oxford and won, and found further outlets for his physical energy in tennis, football and racquets. College societies also claimed him, and he addressed them on such topics as 'Evolution', 'The Treatment of Animals', 'Wages', and 'Gambling'.

He evidently set some value by these efforts, since his notes on the four subjects appeared among his papers after his death. 'Evolution', delivered to the Cambridge Nonconformist Union in 1892, ends with a surely characteristic comment written in an open boyish hand: 'We look forward to the continued existence of improvement, till every creature which God in His infinite power has created, shall be won over to God by His infinite Love, and as ages upon ages pass away shall draw nearer and nearer to the time of infinite perfection, holiness and love'.

It was not until the rise of the Nazi movement in Germany that Pethick found, to his dismay, that this happy belief in continuous human improvement could not be sustained.

When he left Cambridge, records Dr Gooch, 'he might have succeeded in half a dozen spheres, at the Bar, in the City, in journalism, as Professor of Mathematics or Political Economy no less than as a Cabinet Minister'.[1] At least two conventional paths which guaranteed a triumphant future opened before him. He could become a Cambridge don and live an honourable if sheltered life of scholarly achievement. Or he could join one of the two great established political Parties, stand for Parliament, and adopt a more adventurous but still highly respected career which in due course would lead straight to the Front Bench, the Privy Council, and the Cabinet.

Yet two years after going down from Trinity, Fred Lawrence had joined the struggling Labour Party which could offer its devotees no scintillating prizes, and was humbly working as the Treasurer of a well-known nonconformist Settlement in Canning Town. A dozen more years found him in prison as the unequivocal protagonist of a passionate revolution, the militant suffrage movement. Eventually longevity, reinforced by the persistence and vitality to which it was largely due, took him among the statesmen of his generation, but had he died at sixty instead of living for another thirty years, he would have gone down to history only as a courageous rebel and a political 'also-ran'.

The student of human nature inevitably asks 'Why?' What motive or experience turned this favourite of fortune into the staunch champion of unpopular causes who not only supported his fellow rebels, but was ready to share their fate? The answer seems to lie with three individuals: Professor Alfred Marshall of Cambridge; Percy Alden, the Warden of the Mansfield House University Settlement in Canning Town; and Emmeline Pethick, his wife for 53 years.

[1] *Contemporary Review*, November 1961.

CHAPTER 2

Conversion

Alfred Marshall had an influence on Pethick's generation comparable to that of Professor R. H. Tawney on its successor. Of all the men whom he met at the University, none, wrote Pethick in *Fate Has Been Kind*, made a greater impression upon him. 'He really cared passionately that a knowledge of economics should be applied to bettering the lot of humanity and in particular of the underdog.' It was he who stimulated Frederick Lawrence to enter for the Adam Smith Prize.

Percy Alden, born in 1865, subsequently became Radical M.P. for the Tottenham Division of Middlesex from 1906 to 1918, and Labour M.P. for South Tottenham from 1923 to 1924. At the age of seventy-nine he was killed by one of the last 'doodlebugs' of the Second World War while waiting at a bus stop in Tottenham Court Road. Like Pethick he had a University background, and had been at Balliol College, Oxford, before serving as the Warden of Mansfield House from 1891 to 1901, and becoming a Councillor of the Borough of West Ham in 1892. Pethick met him when Percy Alden visited Cambridge to address the undergraduates.

'He succeeded in rousing my social conscience and persuaded me to come and visit the Settlement. I went more than once.... What I saw about the Settlement I liked. It breathed a real spirit of fraternity and there was no trace of sectarian religionism. Alden and I became close friends and I promised him my active support.'

Pethick had always regarded Cambridge as the gateway to a larger life rather than an end in itself. If ever he had contemplated the possibility of remaining there, he now gave up the idea. But before settling in Canning Town he decided, in the process of finding himself, to make a tour of the world which future commitments might render impossible.

He began with India, where several of his college friends had found posts, and visited Bombay, Madras, Calcutta, Benares, Lucknow, Delhi and Agra. His family, being Unitarians, had already made contact with the Brahmo-Samaj movement, an endeavour to link Christianity and Brahminism with which the Tagore family was identified. In Calcutta he met one of its leading representatives, Mr. Muzoomdar, and was taken to a university club where his hosts garlanded him with flowers. It was the first of many similar tributes, which the experienced Secretary of State was to find less embarrassing half a century later than the conventional young Englishman of 1898.

From India he travelled to Ceylon, Australia and New Zealand, visited China and Japan, crossed the United States from San Francisco, and celebrated New Year's Day 1899 on a homeward-bound Atlantic liner still uncertain where his long preparation for life would eventually lead him.

It led first to Mansfield House, for he had decided to fulfil his promise to Percy Alden. This Settlement, founded from Mansfield College, Oxford, was part of a new movement which in the eighteen-eighties had begun to claim the attention of well-to-do men and women who, like young Frederick Lawrence himself, had previously not thought much about the problems of wealth and poverty, or had shared with him the comfortable belief that people tended to find their own level and the best usually reached the top.

From their sheltered homes, schools and universities, it was difficult to realize imaginatively the appalling living conditions of the poorer sections of society eighty years ago. The total absence of security meant that life for the widowed, the sick, the aged and the unemployed was lived beneath the shadow of a perpetual haunting terror. Poverty and pauperism, scourges in themselves, were regarded as disgraceful; out-relief was looked upon as demoralizing, and a widowed mother with a family of young children often broke down under the strain of not only rearing them single-handed, but working at starvation wages in order to feed them. Such children were usually brought up in dark airless buildings where plants could not flower, and wore the bedraggled garments and tattered shoes which were then the virtual uniform of the poor.

For adults the public house offered 'the quickest way out of London'. Opportunities for entertainment hardly existed; there were no cinemas, radio or television, no motor charabancs, and no access to the country to give colour and variety to the lampless routine. Holidays with pay, like holiday camps and youth hostels, lay in the distant future. Forty years afterwards, when Pethick was Financial Secretary to the Treasury from 1929 to 1931, he was able to initiate a full week's holiday with pay for all manual workers in government service.

'Nothing that I was able to do while I was Financial Secretary gave me so much satisfaction as this action,' he wrote ten years later. His initiative has borne rich fruit today, when holidays with pay for at least two weeks are a normal expectation of both industrial and professional employees.

About fifteen years before Frederick Lawrence arrived at Mansfield House in 1899 to begin his apprenticeship, there had been, in the words of Canon S. A. Barnett, the Warden of Toynbee Hall, 'a stirring in the waters of benevolence which are for the healing of the weak. Men and women felt a new impulse towards doing good, and that impulse took shape in the creation of these Halls and Houses.' Among the concerned men and women were such social reformers as Ben Tillett, John Burns, Bob Smillie, Keir Hardie, Arnold Toynbee, Beatrice Potter (later Mrs Sidney Webb), and Charles Booth, author of *Life and Labour of the People*.

Kindred groups at the Universities had long mistrusted the existing machinery for 'doing good'. To them the new Settlements were a means of sharing themselves with their poorer neighbours, and by 1890 some fourteen of these had been founded. They included Toynbee Hall, Oxford House, Mansfield House, and the Bermondsey Settlement. Those who ran them welcomed the idea of living their own lives among the poor, becoming their friends, and acquiring hard facts rather than sentimental illusions about the actual existence of the submerged and exploited workers. Thus, by the time Frederick Lawrence went to Mansfield House, the old patronizing philanthropy of well-to-do individuals who fancied themselves as benefactors and missionaries had long been out of date.

Percy Alden had hoped that Frederick might write a companion volume to Charles Booth's book, which described only London west of the River Lea. But after he had taken rooms in the Barking Road and for days tramped or cycled through

Canning Town, of which he had characteristically bought a large-scale map, he found himself pressed into so many Mansfield House activities that the book was perforce abandoned. He became the Settlement Treasurer, quickly revised its finances, ran the working men's club, and organized such then novel forms of diversion as billiards and lawn tennis. With typical generosity he presented the billiards table and built the cement tennis court.

From games he turned to At Homes with light refreshments and musical programmes, another innovation. Gradually he introduced into the community the idea of recreation to which thirty years later he was to give political shape. Since he was reading for the Bar[1] he also acted as assistant Poor Man's lawyer, and listened to strange tales of marital tragedy arising from the cruelties of circumscribed lives.

Years afterwards, in a B.B.C. broadcast delivered in 1955, Pethick recalled a visit made to Mansfield House about 1900 by Sir Henry Campbell-Bannerman, then leader of the Liberal Opposition. At this time there was no separate Labour Party, and Sir Henry came to discuss with several Trade Union secretaries the possibility of securing Labour representation in the House of Commons through the medium of the Liberal Party. When they complained that very few of them could secure nomination as Liberal candidates, Campbell-Bannerman told them frankly that the responsibility lay not with him, but with the constituencies which could not be compelled to select Trade Unionists as candidates.

'I am convinced,' Pethick added, 'that this reply given by C.B. played a considerable part in the decision which was subsequently taken by organized Labour to form, in conjunction with the Socialist Societies, the body known as the Labour Representation Committee which after the General Election of 1906 rechristened itself "The Labour Party".'

In his contribution to *University and Social Settlements*, a symposium edited by W. Reason and published in 1898, Percy Alden had written: 'I have often said that if one wealthy man with knowledge and sympathy consented to live in East or South London until the prejudice against him had been overcome, he

---

[1] He was called to the Bar on June 1, 1899, as a member of the Inner Temple.

might . . . do an enormous amount to change the environment and life of the district'.

When Mr Alden persuaded Frederick Lawrence to come to Canning Town, he began a process of reform which was eventually to extend from a district to a nation and thence to a Commonwealth, and to be carried out not only by one well-endowed citizen but by two in co-operation. Another contributor to *University and Social Settlements* chanced to be 'Miss Emmeline Pethick', who brought into her essay on 'Working Girls' Clubs' the significant statement: 'There was a time when I thought of working girls as a class. Now I am more inclined to think of young ladies as a class, and of working girls as individuals.'

Soon after Frederick Lawrence had organized the wedding reception in 1899 for Percy Alden and Dr Margaret Pearse he was summoned to help with some amateur theatricals, to be provided at the Mansfield Hall adjoining the men's club by a group of working girls under the supervision of two 'Sisters' from West Central London. He was to act as host and take charge of the practical arrangements for the party. And it was there that, for the first time, he met Emmeline Pethick and his future.

CHAPTER 3

'Sister of the People'

Emmeline Pethick, born on October 21, 1867, was the second of thirteen children of whom eight survived. Her large family belonged to the agricultural middle classes then emerging from farms to business prosperity. Soon after her birth at Clifton, near Bristol, the family moved to Weston-super-Mare. Though a narrow evangelical outlook dominated her childhood, her father was a natural rebel, who later took pride in her suffragette record. After various experiments with nonconformist denominations, he finally returned to the Established Church.

Among their acquaintances was A. V. Alexander, later Earl Alexander of Hillsborough, a native of Weston who then acted as Honorary Secretary to the Somerset County Branch of the League of Young Liberals. At that time Weston had no Labour Party. Earl Alexander still recalls the prowess of Emmeline's brother Tom at hockey and tennis—later a link with Pethick, who was also a fine tennis player. At sixty he could defeat A. V. Alexander, fifteen years his junior.

No ideas about women's higher education had reached Weston in the 'eighties and 'nineties,[1] and Emmeline knew no girl whose aspirations included college or university. For a brief period she attended a conventional finishing school which she disliked. Coming gradually to deplore the dependent position of women, she found herself stirred by the changing social ideas discovered on a visit to London where she heard Ramsay MacDonald address a meeting of the New Fellowship at the Inns of Court.

[1] When my book *Testament of Youth* was published in 1933, Emmeline, whom I had never met, wrote me a long letter in which she said: 'One thing surprises me—and that is to find that the domestic and social environments in Buxton in 1914 were so exactly similar to conditions in Weston-super-Mare in the 1890 years when I was a girl. *Just the very same.*' After I had replied to her letter she asked me to come and see her at 11 Old Square, where I met Fred. This was the beginning of my friendship with the Pethick-Lawrences.— V.B.

About this time she read two or three novels which greatly influenced her. One was George Eliot's *Adam Bede,* with its picture of the plight of Hetty Sorrell, and another a Besant and Rice story called *Children of Gideon,* in which a young heiress changes places with a penniless factory girl. Through her friend Mabelle Pearse, Emmeline now heard of the West London Mission, founded in 1887 by Hugh Price Hughes and Mark Guy Pearse in the labyrinth of mean streets stretching from Regent Street through Soho and Seven Dials to Lincoln's Inn. With its gin palaces, night cellars and lodging houses, the district offered a sharp challenge to social workers.

Emmeline's vague yearnings towards independence and a useful life began to take shape. A brief but deeply experienced friendship with a young naval officer gave her confidence that she could overcome her shyness and find her own friends. She remembered the group of educated young women whom Mrs Price Hughes had gathered round her at the West London Mission, and wrote volunteering to devote herself to London's working girls. Soon afterwards a telegram offered her a place as 'Sister of the People' in charge of the Working Girls' Club. Emmeline responded immediately, and entered upon a totally new life at Katherine House in Fitzroy Square, the centre of the Mission's Sisterhood. Here she took the place of 'Sister Mary' (Mary Neal), who had left owing to ill-health. (Mary soon returned and eventually, overcoming her tubercular tendency, became a pioneer of Folk Dancing and a Suffragette.)

Emmeline began her work at Cleveland Hall in Cleveland Street, where she won the affection of the high-spirited but frustrated girls by teaching them the active games which had amused her young brothers. Soon she learned the contrast between their values and hers.

'Do you mean you really use a toothbrush?' said one after a talk on hygiene. 'I thought it was only bad women did that.'

At length the revolutionary idea occurred to her and Mary of taking the girls for a week's country holiday. Funds were raised and the holiday was organized. After four years at the Mission the two decided to leave it and, in spite of opposition, began another experiment. They took rooms in a block of artisan dwellings off the Euston Road, and became the nucleus of a small colony of social workers. In 1895 they founded the Esperance

Girls' Club, and two years later the Maison Esperance. This co-operative dressmaking business practised the almost unheard-of innovations of an eight-hour day and a minimum weekly wage of fifteen shillings. Three years later Emmeline and Mary joined two other well-known pioneers, Lily and Marian Montague, the daughters of Lord Swaythling, in founding the Green Lady Hostel at Littlehampton for working girls' holidays.

'It was a wonderful thing at that period to be young among young comrades, for the ninth decade of the last century was a time of expansion and vision,' Emmeline wrote forty years later in *My Part in a Changing World*. But the expansion and vision had not come in time to save many 'second-class citizens' from personal tragedy. Numerous sorrowful episodes still live in Emmeline's pages; she writes of a child who became insane when her mother was sent to the Infirmary and the four children to the Workhouse. In *The Suffragette* Sylvia Pankhurst recalled a story told her by Emmeline of a gentle young teashop waitress who quietly committed suicide, leaving a note with the words: 'I am worn out'.

In that final year of the departing century, Emmeline had no intention other than that of continuing her social service indefinitely. She certainly did not contemplate the interruption to her plans which occurred when Fred Lawrence took over, with typical efficiency, the inadequate arrangements made for the amateur performers at Mansfield Hall. He helped her negotiate a refractory curtain, offered his own coat as substitute for a missing 'property', and finding that supper for the party had been overlooked, improvised a meal and served it himself. Emmeline was greatly impressed by his resourcefulness; the various near-catastrophes had broken the top layer of reserve for them both.

They walked back to the station together, and Fred told Emmeline of a book which he had just completed on the economic backgrounds and wages of men. Perhaps, he suggested, she might enlighten him about the comparable problems of women. When the train left and he raised his hat in a parting salute to the two young women alone in their compartment, Mary Neal remarked casually: 'Emmeline, I feel that you are going to marry that man'.

Emmeline was shocked. In their dedicated lives marriage was not part of the picture and, unlike most young women, they never discussed it. But already the consequences seen by Mary's insight had begun. By the time he reached home, Frederick Lawrence found himself the victim of a totally unexpected emotion—spontaneous love. He contrived opportunities for further meetings and finally, fearing that he might be forestalled, made a special appointment to call at her flat, and there proposed to her. But if, with the customary assurance of attractive early manhood he expected an immediate capitulation, he was disappointed.

The young woman whom he desired had vowed herself to social service. Though she had no prejudice against marriage as such, she had no intention of entering into a conventional Victorian marriage with the wife's ideals and activities subordinated to her husband's interests. Especially she doubted whether such a born rebel as herself could do anything but wreck the career of an embryo politician who then saw himself as a future Liberal-Unionist M.P. Just as Jacob had to serve for Rachel, so Emmeline imposed a period of probation on Frederick Lawrence.

Fortunately his apprenticeship was to be shorter than Jacob's, for he found himself most adversely affected by this initial setback. In *Fate Has Been Kind* he describes frankly the physical and mental consequences of his interrupted suit. No longer sure of his powers, he imposed on himself a period of auto-analysis. Reading early and late he lost his ability to sleep, and his normal resilience gave way to depression.

'The tide of life had gone out,' he recorded. 'It had to come in again before we could resume our courtship.' In this period of unsparing self-criticism, he regretted that he lacked sufficient quiet strength for his spiritual crisis. Suddenly came a conviction, which he believed for the rest of his life to have been a message from the unconscious, that an 'inner calm' was his only salvation. This certainty was to sustain him through much future turmoil.

CHAPTER 4

A Partnership Begun

A few months before Frederick's meeting with Emmeline, the South African War had broken out on October 10, 1899. It had been foreshadowed since 1884 when Britain, in a compromise peace, the Convention of London, made by Mr Gladstone after the Boer victory at Majuda in 1881, had recognized the Transvaal as the South African Republic, but retained control of its foreign policy. Hitherto Frederick had assumed that war was an inevitable outcome of this decision, but Emmeline's different view now raised doubts. Just as he had travelled round the world in order to make up his mind what part in life to play, so now he decided to see South Africa for himself and study the origins of the war.

When he returned he purchased *The Echo*, an evening paper then in the market, and asked Emmeline to serve on a small council which met every week to discuss its policy. At these meetings the fires deliberately kept dormant blazed into love. She knew by then that her work would be as important to him as his own, and he realized that their respective gifts were part of their common possession. In May 1901, when the perpetual miracle of spring had given life to the fields and hedges after the bitterness of winter, 'the equal miracle of human love was manifested to us with its rich pageant of life and joy'. They became engaged at last, and he shared her daily life until their autumn wedding.

They were married in the Town Hall at Canning Town on October 2, 1901, three weeks before Emmeline's thirty-fourth birthday. Percy Alden, Mark Guy Pearse, and the Unitarian minister of Frederick's family chapel performed the ceremony. The guests at this unusual wedding, apart from relatives, came from the people amongst whom they had lived—girls, boys, men and women, and the elderly occupants of the local workhouse. Mr Lloyd George, that notorious pro-Boer, was also invited, and came. This disturbed Emmeline's uncle William Pethick, a former

High Sheriff of Bristol, who attended the wedding but refused to travel with Lloyd George in the special coach chartered for the guests. Frederick's uncle, Sir Edwin Durning-Lawrence, declined to come at all owing to the outlook on the war which his nephew had developed.

These family idiosyncrasies troubled neither the bridegroom nor the bride. 'I was living too vividly in my own experience on that day to remember any incidents not directly concerning myself', Emmeline wrote later. They went off for a honeymoon to the Abinger Hatch Hotel, and soon afterwards Frederick wrote to Emmeline's father asking permission to add their family name to his own. This request greatly pleased Henry Pethick, and thenceforth Fred and Emmeline were known as the Pethick-Lawrences. 'They became,' writes Dr G. P. Gooch, 'as inseparable in thought and deed as Beatrice and Sidney Webb'. He does not speculate whether the Webbs had experienced a comparable emotional prelude to their partnership.

Thus began what the *Daily Herald*, in its account of Emmeline's funeral fifty-three years afterwards, described as 'one of the happiest marriages of the century'. Yet its exacting preface, though an indispensable preliminary, had given no guarantee for its ultimate brilliant success. The differences between their personalities were conspicuous; only in after years did their qualities appear so complementary as to suggest that a benevolent deity had designed their union.

Throughout his political career, Pethick showed evidence of a precise and logical mind, dominated by his respect for law and justice. 'He would always say "What are the facts?"' recalls Earl Alexander of Hillsborough. Pethick himself, in the symposium *If I Had My Time Again*, explains that one consequence of his mathematical endowments was to cause him to take a keener interest in mankind as such than in individuals, whose personal peculiarities, in his opinion, tended 'to cancel one another out in the larger entity. The wrongs of a class or sex or race have appealed to me more cogently than the purely personal troubles of a particular John or Mary.'

While refusing to regret this trait, he admitted that in his youth he had not realized the limitations which it imposed. Even when he reached the House of Commons, he was told that his speeches often failed to attract sympathetic attention because the human element was lacking. With characteristic deliberation he was to devise a remedy for these shortcomings, though the real remedy was supplied by his wife.

If Frederick in his youth appeared to lack humanity, Emmeline possessed it in superabundance. Her autobiography, describing the same world of poverty and endeavour at the same date as Frederick describes it in *Fate Has Been Kind*, brings the men, women and children for whom she worked to life in a series of loving incidents and vignettes. Though Frederick's book does not omit them altogether, it is hers which gives real insight into the lives of underprivileged Londoners in the eighteen-nineties.

Emmeline, four years older than her husband, had always thought herself unattractive in comparison with her better-looking sisters. But while no evidence seems to exist that Frederick in his early and middle years ever loved any woman but Emmeline (with the possible exception of Christabel Pankhurst, who clearly captivated him), she herself had been twice in love before she met him. In her youth the young naval officer who came to Weston had no home and no money, and at the close of his short holiday had to leave 'for the ends of the earth', but from the first time they met he openly appropriated her. They spent the week in each other's company, and ended the 'dreamlike experience' with a last walk together hand in hand.

More profound, if less potentially destructive to marriage, was her intense friendship with Mark Guy Pearse, a well-known Methodist preacher of her father's generation who, like all such minor prophets of that date, eventually gravitated to Darkest London with his wife and family. There he helped to found the West London Mission, and dominated Emmeline's imagination for twenty years. Though she was once precipitated into an admission of love for him, his influence over her did not cease with her marriage to Pethick. Eventually the suffrage movement, which Pearse could not accept, interrupted their relationship until the First War brought militancy to an end.

Sylvia Pankhurst, in her book *The Suffragette*, describes her first meeting with Emmeline in the little room where Sylvia was living in Park Walk, Chelsea. 'I can never forget how much I was attracted by her dark expressive eyes. . . . It was later that I noticed the untrammelled carriage and the fine free lift of the head.' Another former suffragette, Grace Roe, thought her

Pethick and Emmeline as children

(top left) Pethick aged 2½ years
(top right) Emmeline aged 6 years
(below) Emmeline aged 11 years

Pethick as President of the Union at Cambridge, circ. 1894

Emmeline aged 25

beautiful because of the spirit that shone through her face. This colleague, later Christabel Pankhurst's chief organizer, decided to join the Suffragette movement because of the poise and background intelligence shown by Emmeline at an early Albert Hall meeting after a very emotional speech by Sylvia.

A portrait of Emmeline taken in 1908, when she was forty-one, shows a broad nose and full lips in a square face, its shape emphasized by the inelegant hair-dressing style of that date. But the picture does justice to her intense dark eyes, though it cannot show the spiritual dynamism which periodically set them alight. In her old age she was to be physically more impressive (so at least she appeared to one who never saw her in her volcanic middle years), but the earlier fires had inevitably died down.

As a serious young man, Frederick looked beneath these external traits to the profounder qualities which really moved him, and caused him to write in the symposium already quoted: 'If I were lucky enough to find and win her, I would marry the same wife'.

From the Abinger Hatch Hotel the Pethick-Lawrences explored the Surrey countryside with which their name was to be permanently associated. They had decided to have a simple flat in London for their working life and a small country house for weekends. The country home, already discovered, lay within walking distance of Abinger Hatch. It was called 'The Dutch House', later renamed The Mascot, and had been built in The Holmwood three miles from Dorking by Sir Edwin Lutyens for a family which had not liked it.

Its unconventional shape followed the pattern of a three-leaved clover, branching out from a central hall. The front faced a wide common across a country road which did not yet foreshadow the hideous automobile traffic that would impair its beauty. The west windows looked upon a low range of hills adorned with the trees of Redlands Wood. A garden, a small paddock, and a wide green bank where a large white cherry tree blossomed in spring, completed its attractions. The Pethick-Lawrences furnished it as the large cottage that it was, and there enjoyed nearly twenty years of happiness.

Their flat they took in Clement's Inn, facing the new Law Courts and backed by a maze of old streets being cleared to make room for Aldwych and Kingsway. The Inn had recently been rebuilt as offices and flats. Neither of them dreamed that sixty years later it would carry a plaque inscribed with the words: 'Here were the headquarters of the Women's Social and Political Union known as "the Suffragettes" led by Emmeline and Christabel Pankhurst. Here also lived Emmeline Pethick-Lawrence who with her husband played an invaluable part in building up the organization and edited *Votes for Women*.'[1]

After the small Euston Road apartment at 14s 6d a week which had housed her contented executive life, Emmeline could hardly believe in the luxury and loveliness which seemed to have fallen from Heaven. The flat in Clement's Inn appeared perfect except that it faced east, and she loved the sun.

On the first anniversary of their wedding, Pethick took her in a lift to the top of the building and gave her a key which opened the door of a garden flat drenched with sunshine. Two deep couches and four large ottomans stood on a moss-green carpet beneath red canvas-covered walls. The apartment had also a bedroom and bathroom, and a garden door leading to a flat roof adorned with vivid window-boxes.

'This is your very own apartment,' said Pethick. 'No one but you has the key, and when you come here to rest, your staff can say you are out.'

Already he was learning to be not only efficient, but human.

[1] This tablet was unveiled by Dame Sybil Thorndike in October 1960.

CHAPTER 5

The Young Editor

Though Frederick's family had followed the Liberal tradition, like many successful men of business they changed their old Whig loyalties for a conservative policy known to them as Liberal Unionism when the Home Rule issue split the Party in 1885. Fred's elder brother Alfred alone remained faithful to Gladstone; his three uncles supported Joseph Chamberlain.

One of these was his Uncle Edwin, who had been virtually a parent to him after his father's early death, and Sir Edwin Durning-Lawrence was soon to become Liberal Unionist M.P. for the Truro-Helston division of Cornwall. When he suggested that his nephew should also stand for Liberal Unionism at the next election, Frederick welcomed the proposal and the Selection Committee at North Lambeth adopted him as their candidate.

Soon afterwards, his relatively conventional attitude to the Boer War shaken by Emmeline, Frederick left for South Africa in search of the answers to three questions: Was the war important enough to compel him to make up his mind on the issues involved? Had the British a good case? If not, could he remain a Parliamentary candidate supporting the Government?

It seemed clear that for a future M.P., the answer to question One was Yes. In search for the reply to question Two, he interviewed statesmen and editors, ministers of religion, and exiles from the Rand. Among the statesmen was W. P. Schreiner, who did not agree with Chamberlain's policy, but thought it his duty as Prime Minister of Cape Colony to allow British troops to pass through Cape territory. His sister Olive, a vehement opponent of the war, deplored the Prime Minister's decision.

Frederick spent many evenings in discussion with her and her husband Cronwright. Years afterwards he wrote in the *P.E.N. News* that if he had not carried an introduction from his future wife, Olive might well have thought him a 'spy'. As it was, she received him into her small like-minded circle, where they discussed not only the war but her opinions, so far ahead of her time, on religious rationalism, and sex and race equality. On one occasion Fred joined a small party of friends who shared her views on a 35-mile ride round Table Mountain in a wagonette driven by a Malay coachman with a huge straw hat.

Olive was a pro-Boer because she regarded the British intervention in South Africa as that of a powerful bully attacking a little nation. Once during the war she addressed a mass meeting of Boers in which the presence of guns pointed at the assembly carried her to heights of oratory which cast a spell over the whole audience. But she had no regard for either Boer or Briton who ill-treated or exploited the native Africans. Had she and Frederick anticipated that fifty years of Boer fanaticism would produce Dr Verwoerd, their views on the struggle might have undergone some modification. No one, however, foresaw such a development, and Frederick returned to England with his mind made up that the war was unjust.

He relinquished his candidature at Lambeth and joined the Liberals, who then, as Dr. G. P. Gooch has reminded us, 'stood for drastic reform at home and self-determination abroad'. It was the first move to the Left which was ultimately to take Pethick into a Labour Cabinet. Political passions as vehement as any that have ever existed marked the struggle between Joseph Chamberlain and the Colonial Office on the one hand, and on the other the Liberal leaders, inspired by Gladstone, who included Campbell-Bannerman, James Bryce, and John Morley.

Now classified as a 'pro-Boer', Frederick sought further to enlighten himself by reading, and found great inspiration in the works of Joseph Mazzini. He met Emily Hobhouse, whose work for the Boer families interned in British concentration camps had already moved him, and became honorary secretary of the South African Women's and Children's Distress Fund which she had founded. He also accepted an invitation from Manchester College, Oxford, to deliver a weekly Economics lecture for a year as 'Dunkin' professor. In the summer term he used Charles Booth's *Life and Labour of the People* as a text-book, and was agreeably surprised by a crowded lecture-room even in Eights Week.

In 1902 a Cambridge group inspired by C. F. G. Masterman published a symposium entitled *The Heart of the Empire*; its purpose was to transfer the attention of politically conscious persons from distant areas to social problems at home. They invited Frederick to write on housing; other contributors included G. P. Gooch, Noel Buxton, and G. M. Trevelyan, who supplied the title. Frederick's essay foreshadowed the idea of town planning, and with youthful indignation emphasized the contrast between 'the spacious homes of the rich' and 'the wretched tumble-down dwellings . . . in which the poorest of our population seek to find a shelter, if not a home'.

'Do not,' he concluded, 'let the century go by without finding a solution for this problem.'

The volume had an unexpectedly good sale, and the authors subsequently congratulated themselves that it had helped to bring the Liberal victory of 1906.

Before his marriage Frederick had bought *The Echo*, the first halfpenny London evening paper which had been founded by Passmore Edwards in the eighteen-sixties. Its progressive outlook had commended it to Radical readers, but newer publications had overtaken it and it was now in financial difficulties. Frederick, supported by Lloyd George, acquired it in order to propagate social reform at home and oppose imperialism abroad. He financed it mainly from a small fortune left him by his elder brother Alfred, who had died in 1900.

For a time Percy Alden acted as editor, and the contributors included J. L. Hammond, who wrote the leading articles until H. N. Brailsford took them over. Long afterwards Pethick recalled that Brailsford, who cycled from Hampstead, always arrived late and flustered, but, once the subjects of his contributions had been settled, provided first-class material in a minimum of time. When he left for Macedonia in 1903 to distribute relief, McCallum Scott and Ramsay MacDonald produced the editorials. MacDonald also supplied a series of Labour notes. Other contributors were Leonard Courtney, Frederick Harrison, Canon Barnett, Canon Scott Holland and Mark Twain. Towards the end of the experiment Pethick himself took over the function of editor. Under his control the paper denounced the introduction of Chinese contract labour into the Rand by the Transvaal mine-owners which had followed the Peace of Vereeniging.

The Echo now incorporated a Year Book, previously produced by Joseph Edwards of Glasgow, entitled *The Labour Manual*. The 1903 edition appeared under a new title, *The Reformers' Year*

Book, which Pethick kept going until 1908. This publication included pictures and biographies of all the candidates of the Labour Representation Committee and thus helped them to enter Parliament in 1906. Another journalistic innovation was a monthly magazine, *The Labour Record and Review*, which also produced character sketches of Labour personalities and a summary of Left-wing events.

This venture brought the Pethick-Lawrences into closer touch with Keir Hardie, who as early as 1906 advocated Woman Suffrage in a pamphlet, 'The Citizenship of Women', which commented on the absurdity of British women having no legal existence. He became an honoured guest at The Mascot, and in Emmeline's view was 'the greatest person we have ever known'. Alone he represented Independent Labour in Parliament, where his speeches already foreshadowed unemployment maintenance, old age pensions, and a People's Budget. In the country he threw off the scorn of the Press and the mockery of his opponents, and took an uninhibited pleasure in books and literature, children and birds and animals. His majestic head suggested to Emmeline a mountain peak against a sunset sky.

His influence reinforced another scheme then adopted by the Pethick-Lawrences. They pulled down two old cottages near their home, built others to replace them in the village, and transformed the originals into a guest house for London children which welcomed all the juveniles associated with the Esperance Social Guild. One little girl, Esther Knowles, who climbed up to stand on Pethick's head later became for many years one of his two secretaries. He designed a mural sundial for the east wall which looked over the flagged path with its formal design of miniature flower-beds. As the sundial recorded only the early sunshine he gave it an appropriate inscription:

> 'Let others tell of storm and showers
> I tell the sunny morning hours.'

Though this cottage has long passed into other hands, the sundial is still visible to anyone who looks for it where the Horsham - London road begins to descend the hill at Holmwood.

Early in 1905 the Pethick-Lawrences returned from a visit to Egypt, where a view of the Sphinx at sunrise convinced Pethick that this immemorial image represented the sculptor's conception of the 'eternal feminine' though the Arabs spoke of it as 'he'. Examining anew the finances of *The Echo*, Pethick concluded that though he had increased its circulation by sixty per cent and had taken a branch office in Soho which Mr Lloyd George had formally opened, he could no longer meet the continuous deficit. The main purpose for which he bought the paper had ended with the Boer War, and as he did not wish to dispose of it to the Conservative group which alone offered to buy it, *The Echo* quietly ceased publication.

Pethick was not however prepared to penalise his loyal staff, and on the day that they ceased work paid them from his own pocket a salary for several months in advance and also met in full the claims of all the company's trade creditors. The total outlay about equalled his legacy from his dead brother. Since Alfred had a passion for managing newspapers which he was never able to indulge, Pethick felt that his brother's money had been used exactly as he would have wished.

Now that this responsibility was over, Pethick and Emmeline decided to visit South Africa together. They travelled to Cape Town on the same ship as W. P. Schreiner, and in South Africa met many politicians who had been involved in the war. They stayed with John X. Merriman at his fruit farm, and later visited Jan Steyn, the ex-President of the Orange Free State. Mr Steyn told them that when he returned, broken and dispirited, from signing the peace treaty, his six-year-old daughter greeted him with the words: 'So *you* are the man who has signed away our country!'

The Pethick-Lawrences also saw three Generals, Hertzog, Botha and De Wet. They went down a gold-mine in Johannesburg, saw the plan of the future Bulawayo, and went as far north as the Zambesi Falls. The most memorable visit of all had preceded this long journey, when they stayed for ten days at Hanover, then the home of Olive Schreiner. Her house was too small to accommodate them, so they stopped at a local hotel and saw her daily for several hours.

Her prophetic vision and remarkable intuitive judgments made a lasting impression on Pethick. When he inquired, as authors' visitors usually do, how she worked at her writing, she said she was obliged to have unlimited time, with nobody disturbing her. She might have added that these advantages, then even rarer for women than they are today, would have been unattainable without a co-operative husband and freedom from the demands of a young family.

'It is no good my sitting down,' she told him, 'because when my ideas start coming I have to get up and walk.'

After they parted, she corresponded with Pethick at intervals. In March 1909 she wrote him prophetically in the midst of the suffrage campaign: 'In fighting for women we are fighting a battle in which the dawn is near. But in fighting in South Africa for justice to the native we are fighting a battle in which there is first a long dark terrible descent of years, into a depth of oppression and wrong, before the slow ascent towards better things even begins.'

On August 5, 1910, twelve months before the publication of *Woman and Labour*, she sent him another letter. 'It doesn't matter much,' she commented, 'if you don't get the franchise at once; this fight is educating women as nothing else could, and educating the world to know what women can do.'

The Pethick-Lawrences were still in South Africa when the first heralds of that fight reached them in the newspaper account of a disorderly scene at an election meeting in Manchester preceding the General Election of January 1906. The speaker, Sir Edward Grey, had been rudely interrupted by two young girls called Christabel Pankhurst and Annie Kenney. After defying the police they had, of course, been arrested and sent to prison.

South African women who had been working for years to get a vote in the Cape Parliament were much perturbed by this revolutionary behaviour. The cause of woman suffrage, they considered, had been retarded for generations. But Emmeline was not so sure. When she and Frederick hurried back from South Africa for the Election, she felt that she would like to meet these rebellious women and judge the significance of their action for herself.

From her roof-garden in Clement's Inn, they watched the Election results thrown by a lantern-slide on to a high white board in the Strand. Almost incredulous, they saw victory after victory announced for the Party which had taken the unpopular side in the war. Not until 1945 was a similar switch to the Left to be recorded in political history.

Emmeline had been brought up to believe that the Liberal

Party stood for Peace and Reform. She welcomed its triumph though for some years she had transferred her allegiance to the little Party represented in the House by one man, Keir Hardie. Now he would be no longer alone. Though his Party would remain small for years to come, thirty Labour representatives had been elected. When the final results showed that the great Conservative Party had been reduced to 158, with Arthur Balfour himself unseated in Manchester by Winston Churchill standing as a Liberal, the Pethick-Lawrences thought that the millennium had come. No fewer than 379 seats had gone to the triumphant Liberals, and in Pethick's home constituency of Reigate a Liberal had been returned for the first time in history. He himself had spoken in Denbigh District for Clem Edwards, who had opposed the Boer War.

But though the victorious Party stood for Peace and Reform, there was one reform which did not appear on its future programme. During the Election all the Parties had paid lip-service to the cause of women, betrayed by Mr Gladstone at the end of the century but now, it seemed to many hopeful suffragists, ripe for revival.

Yet the King's Speech at the opening of the new Parliament was ominously silent on the subject of women's enfranchisement

CHAPTER 6

The Pankhursts in Orbit

'No idea has done more to retard the progress of the human race than the exaltation of *submission* into a high and noble virtue,' wrote Pethick in a book entitled *Women's Fight for the Vote*, published during the Suffragette movement. That movement newly justified the comment quoted thirty years afterwards by the late Dr Harry Roberts in *Britain in Pictures*: 'It was a distinguished Christian minister who said that "all our liberties are due to men who, when their conscience has compelled them, broke the law of the land" '.

Two major reasons justify civil disobedience: first, the lack of democratic rights; secondly, a degree of public apathy which prevents a campaign from making an impact. Both these disadvantages alike handicapped the suffrage movement and the struggle for Indian independence, until Mrs Pankhurst put the one cause on the map and Mahatma Gandhi established the other. These achievements proved that the sacrificial fervour of great idealistic crusades begins to capture public imagination and attain its ends when it takes an active and 'dangerous' form.

Millicent Fawcett, the constitutional suffrage leader throughout her long widowhood, recognized the compelling power of peril and sacrifice even though she herself never departed from strict legality. In her book on *Women's Suffrage* she quoted Thomas Carlyle: 'It is a calumny on men to say that they are roused to heroic action by ease, hope of pleasure. . . . Difficulty, abnegation, martyrdom, death, are the allurements which act upon the heart of man.'

In 1905, before militant tactics developed, the Press had almost ceased to report woman suffrage meetings or even to publish relevant letters. Between John Stuart Mill's Woman Suffrage Amendment in Parliament in 1866 and the foundation of the Women's Social and Political Union in 1903, enormous petitions had been organized and supported by nearly 1,400 public meetings, which included nine great demonstrations in the largest halls of the chief towns. Yet New Zealand, Australia, Finland, Norway, Iceland, Denmark and the USSR were all to forestall Britain in giving votes to women owing to the long stalemate imposed by Mr Gladstone's hostility to female enfranchisement.

Mill's *Subjection of Women* had stirred new thinking, but had not suggested new political tactics. Throughout the latter half of the nineteenth century women remained second-class citizens, and when the twentieth began the Boer War eclipsed the issue. Newspapers wrote of the suffrage movement as 'dead'; it was too unaggressive and ladylike to challenge their attention. When militant tactics started the Press hurled abusive epithets at the Suffragettes, but for the first time in years seriously discussed the basic issues.

Describing the huge Hyde Park demonstration staged by the WSPU on June 21, 1908, a leading London daily commented that the militant movement had done in less than three years what all the gentle persuasion of a generation had failed to effect. One result of this new upsurge of awareness was an increased membership for the constitutional societies — a result which Mrs Fawcett, more generous than some of her followers, handsomely recognized.

'By adopting novel and startling methods not at the outset associated with physical violence, they succeeded in drawing a far larger amount of public attention to the claims of women to representation than ever had been given to the subject.'

Three years before her death in 1929, Dame Millicent was to propose the health of the Pethick-Lawrences at their Silver Wedding.

In his autobiography Pethick has stated that, owing partly to the apparent indifference of women themselves, he had never been greatly concerned about their enfranchisement—a statement confirmed by Dr G. P. Gooch in *The Contemporary Review* for November 1961. 'Lawrence,' he wrote, 'had always regarded woman suffrage as part of democracy, but it had never gripped his imagination.' In the end it was Emmeline who claimed his inexhaustible energies for the cause, but when they first met, her devotional fervour had long been dedicated to finding remedies for the real grievances of the poor. Pethick, a psychological Socialist though still nominally Conservative, felt that chiefly middle-class women would benefit by a change in the law, and he could not see what useful political contribution they would make.

On the other hand, he did not share the typical anti-feminist prejudices of his day. At this time most ordinary males thought a woman too foolish to vote, but a few, like Mr Gladstone, believed — or said they believed — that she was too noble. Innumerable arguments against the claims of women appeared in articles and speeches. Men and women, it was said, rightly had different spheres and should keep to them. If women obtained the vote they would create dissensions in the home and lose the respect of men. They were emotional and had no judgment; they were deficient in physical force on which governments rested; they would not be content with votes but would want to be Members of Parliament. All this, commented Pethick in *Fate Has Been Kind*, could be summed up in the one word *fear*; fear of what women would do with the vote when they had it.

In the end it was their friend Keir Hardie, now Chairman of the small Parliamentary Labour Party, who introduced the Pethick-Lawrences to the Pankhursts and thus brought them into the Suffragette movement. His acquaintance with the Pankhursts had been lifelong and he greatly admired their courage and audacity.

By now Emmeline Pethick-Lawrence was becoming aware that social reforms planned only by the male half of humanity were unlikely to touch the worst evils imposed on women. Hardie persuaded her that the Pankhursts' demand for the vote arose from their concern for working women in the north, but when Mrs Pankhurst called on Emmeline in February 1906, the founder of the WSPU was disappointed.

'She will not help; she has so many interests,' she told her daughter Sylvia. But after Mrs Pankhurst came Annie Kenney, enthusiastic and trustful, who prevailed on Emmeline to meet Sylvia at Sylvia's lodgings in Park Walk, Chelsea. That evening six women around Sylvia's table ambitiously formed themselves into a Central London Committee of the WSPU. Although by her own admission 'not of a revolutionary temperament', Emmeline left the small house committed to become Treasurer of this wild little group which had no office, no money, no stamps for correspondence, and not even a remote idea of the art of organization.

Thus the three extraordinary women who were to have an ineradicable influence on Pethick's career entered it, as it were, by a back door. Mrs Pankhurst, who had founded the WSPU at 82 Nelson Street, Manchester, on October 10, 1903, was the daughter of a prominent Salford cotton-spinner. Beautiful, dedicated, and utterly without fear, she became one of the world's greatest orators, who was to leave her gifts enshrined in stone beneath the historic shadow of the House of Lords. But it was Christabel, her brilliant daughter, who really captured Pethick, and permanently transformed his imagination.

In 1906, when they met, Pethick was thirty-five and Christabel twenty-six. By taste, temperament and ability, she was ideally qualified to typify 'modern youth' for the new century. Her political *flair* was a match for the subtlest wits, as her cross-examination of Lloyd George eventually proved, and she had a genius for leadership which inspired unlimited daring in others. When she took her LL.B. degree at Manchester University that year, she was bracketed first with one other student.

Christabel's overriding motive was shame that women should acquiesce in the position then accorded them by society; she and Pethick were initially united by their belief that submission was the greatest evil. 'For her,' he recorded, 'the "subjection of women" about which John Stuart Mill wrote had ceased to exist.' They both feared, and continually fought against, the ingrained sense of inferiority which even in the nineteen-sixties prevents women from taking their full part in public life.

Danger and drama were to Christabel the breath of existence. 'How glorious those suffragette days were!' she comments in her posthumously published book *Unshackled*. 'To lose the personal in a great impersonal is to live!'

Mrs Pankhurst's second daughter Sylvia possessed the same incredible courage and inflexible sense of purpose as her mother and sister, but her nature, continually violated, intended her to be an artist, and she did not share their political dynamism. Between 1901 and 1912 she won many prizes and scholarships in art in spite of constant interruption and her absorbing compassion for the poor and humble. The third daughter, Adela, also took part in the suffragette movement, but eventually settled in Australia where she married a Labour M.P., Tom Walsh. She died in Sydney in 1961.

After Emmeline Pethick-Lawrence became Treasurer of the embryo WSPU, the little London group organized a deputation to the Prime Minister, Sir Henry Campbell-Bannerman. Very soon a demand came for Pethick's shrewd judgment. In July 1906 his wife summoned him from their country garden to come to London and help to secure defence for some prisoners. These prisoners, Annie Kenney and two other WSPU members, Mrs Knight and Mrs Sharboro, learning from the deputation to the Prime Minister that Cabinet hostility was the major obstacle, had been arrested in Cavendish Square while persistently ringing the doorbell of Mr Asquith, their notorious opponent.

Pethick wiped the dirty dock clean with his handkerchief and thus symbolically identified himself with the prisoners. Thenceforth the Suffragettes called him 'Godfather', though Roger Fulford, in *Votes for Women*, more romantically dubbed him 'The Prince Consort of Militancy'.

CHAPTER 7

Revolt Against Submission

'From that time,' Pethick recorded in his autobiography, 'the suffragettes surged up into my life.' They needed his business experience and financial knowledge, and soon took possession of his wife and his flat. Christabel, fresh from her university honours and in his opinion 'quite irresistible', arrived to occupy their spare room, and remained for five years. His journalistic flair also went ungrudgingly into the campaign. At least half a dozen of the books and pamphlets have survived which he wrote for it between 1907 and 1912; titles in the London Museum include *Is the English Law Unjust to Women?*, *The Bye-Election Policy of the W.S.P.U.*, *Women's Work and Wages*, *Mr Asquith's 'Pledge'* and *Treatment of the Suffragettes in Prison*.

'He underwent every variation of the sacrifice demanded for the freedom of women—imprisonment—hunger-strike—forcible feeding—bankruptcy—loss of financial substance—expulsion from his Club,' his wife wrote twenty years later. 'All this he went through unflinchingly on account of the faith that was in him. I have always been glad that deep as is the love between us he never took up the women's cause for my sake but as the result of our common outlook.'

The summer campaign of 1906 continued in the form of open-air demonstrations in Hyde Park and other recognized pitches for orators. Here large crowds, attracted by the new militant technique, replaced the small audiences hitherto customary at suffragist gatherings. Occasional meetings, though these were exceptions, became rowdy and hostile; one at Boggart Hole Clough in Manchester so roused Pethick's chivalrous wrath that he vowed to stand by the suffrage movement till victory was won. That day he personally rescued Adela Pankhurst from a vicious attack by a hysterical mob.

Already the WSPU had an inner circle of organizers and voluntary workers, mostly young, highly intelligent, and attractively dressed, who like their Treasurer thought of propaganda and money-raising in totally new terms. A surviving letter from Emmeline, in the London Museum, dated August 20, 1907, conclusively reproves a well-meaning Miss Cullen whose notions of gathering funds were too orthodox.

'Bazaars are all very well when women have never conceived the idea of anything else, but in a movement like ours, when we are exerting all our influence to induce women to take up more strenuous and active forms of work, I think that there are very serious objections to the bazaar idea.'

Her own more revolutionary methods eventually brought the WSPU an income of £200 a week. The bulk of these funds went on rent and printing. Only the organizers and clerical staff received modest salaries; no payment was given for speaking, and none for militant action. The Union's accounts were carefully and efficiently kept by the Treasurer and her staff.[1]

Amid the exuberance that surrounded them, Emmeline and Pethick soon recognized the lack of such utilitarian skills as planning and co-ordination. Offices were the first practical need, and they found that two rooms beneath their flat in Clement's Inn had conveniently been vacated by the Land Registry Office. Gradually room after room in the building was added until the WSPU possessed the largest headquarters of any political organization in London.

Here from September 1906 the Union held Monday 'At Homes' in which its leaders developed the technique of militancy —the outward sign that the 'false and pernicious doctrine' of submission had been wholly abandoned. Here too they explained

[1] After the publication of my book *Lady Into Woman* in 1953, I became strangely involved in a controversy over the administration of WSPU funds. In a chapter called 'The Struggle for Political Equality', I quoted (in order to criticize them) some tendentious strictures on suffragette account-keeping in Ray Strachey's history *The Cause*, which reflected the constitutional movement and was singularly unobjective in its treatment of the militants. In consequence, unknown to me, the first edition had been withdrawn owing to representations made by Emmeline Pethick-Lawrence and Sylvia Pankhurst.

I discovered this to my cost after I had innocently quoted the offending passage from an early review copy of *The Cause* that I chanced to possess. Although my quotation had been used to illustrate Mrs Strachey's prejudice, I found myself the astonished target of Sylvia's indignation. On that occasion Pethick himself nobly came to my rescue, and persuaded Miss Pankhurst to accept an erratum slip in my book, instead of the libel action which she clearly thought I deserved.—V.B.

Pethick at the time of his marriage (October 1901)

Olive Schreiner at De Aar in 1908

their anti-government by-election policy to indignant supporters who thought it immoral to attack the Liberals, until they realized that the power to give or withhold the vote rested with the existing government irrespective of party. A short book, *Women's Fight for the Vote*, published by Pethick in 1911, estimated that the WSPU had been responsible for the defeat of between thirty and forty Government candidates in the General Election of February 1910. Neither Sylvia nor Adela Pankhurst, both ardent Socialists, ever fully accepted this policy, which later brought a parting of the ways.

In October 1906 the movement assumed a new aspect for Pethick when Emmeline herself was arrested for taking part in a demonstration in the Central Lobby of the House of Commons on the day that Parliament opened. The shock that all private individuals feel when public drama breaks into their lives was intensified for him by the discovery that Emmeline was not yet able to 'take' her experience.

After she was removed to Holloway he had promised, carried away by sudden emotion, to give £10 to the WSPU for every day of her imprisonment. 'A pity Fred put it like that', her mother subsequently commented, but by the time this gesture had travelled round the world as a funny story, her breakdown in health had left him beyond caring whether he had become 'famous, notorious, or merely ridiculous'. With her father's help he secured her release from prison, and took her to Italy to recuperate while he shouldered the Treasurer's responsibilities.

Many years later Emmeline explained in her autobiography that the journey to prison in the cramped Black Maria—later described by Lady Constance Lytton as that 'hearse with many coffins'—had brought to the surface a half-realized form of claustrophobia which temporarily destroyed her powers of resistance. Once she recognized this weakness she proved characteristically able to overcome it, and in later imprisonments brilliantly redeemed her humiliating collapse. But though she continued her successful fund-raising, and in 1908, when Mrs Pankhurst, Christabel, and 'General' Flora Drummond were all imprisoned, she was left to conduct the campaign alone with Pethick's unobtrusive help, it was not until February 1909 that she again put her powers of endurance in prison to the test.

She returned from Italy to join in the endeavour to secure the passage of a Suffrage Bill during the Parliamentary session of 1907. The constitutional suffrage societies took part in this effort, and in support of it conducted their celebrated 'Mud March' in bad wintry weather from Hyde Park to a meeting at Exeter Hall off the Strand. Some recognition of the value of militancy occurred at this meeting, when the writers Israel Zangwill, Elizabeth Robins and Evelyn Sharp defended the militants in their speeches.

Roger Fulford's opinion that no bill enfranchising women had the least chance of success unless it was a Government measure could only have been tested if history had moved in a different direction and war had been avoided in 1914. But in February 1907 a Government measure alone seemed likely to be of any value, and for this—in spite of growing public sympathy with the women—the Establishment of that day was quite unready. The King's Speech on February 7th contained no reference to Woman Suffrage, and the subsequent 'Women's Parliament' at Caxton Hall which appointed a deputation to carry the WSPU protest to the House of Commons led to the arrest of fifty-four women, who included Christabel and Sylvia Pankhurst and Mrs Despard. A second similar protest on March 20th brought seventy-two arrests.

As Cannon Row Police Station, where they were taken, had no all-night accommodation for prisoners in such numbers, they had to be released on bail. This led to 'Godfather's' historic function of bailing-out suffragettes. During the six years of his association with the WSPU, Pethick made himself financially responsible for nearly a thousand women, of whom he subsequently recorded that 'not one . . . ever attempted to escheat her bail'. Among them was a determined young girl, Helen Craggs, who half a century later became the second Lady Pethick-Lawrence. In addition to these financial undertakings he used his legal training to instruct many volunteers who had never been inside a police court on the conduct of their defence.

In the autumn of 1907 a difference of opinion within the WSPU gave Pethick more power in the movement, though it was finally to lead to his departure. A question concerning the Union's policy arose among the members. Should it be decided by a free vote of delegates who would elect an executive committee at an annual conference, or be virtually dictated by the movement's founders?

Mrs Pankhurst and Christabel entertained no doubts at all. In *Unshackled* Christabel records that she was 'astonished by the suggestion. The idea of diverting attention from the cause to constitution-making, conference-holding and committee-making, struck me as incongruous'. Mrs Pankhurst, back from a series of meetings in the North, was even more emphatic.

'I shall tear up the constitution!' she exclaimed, and when Mrs Despard, the Secretary of the Union, protested that such a step would outrage democratic principles, Mrs Pankhurst declared herself to be in sole control of the WSPU. When the Pethick-Lawrences and the five paid organizers supported this drastic decision, 'the Split' occurred by which Mrs Despard, Mrs How-Martyn and Theresa Billington (later Mrs Billington-Greig) withdrew, and, in September 1907, founded the Women's Freedom League. This second militant organization was to last for forty-seven years. In 1926 Emmeline Pethick-Lawrence, succeeding Mrs Despard who lived to be ninety-five, was appointed President and held the office for nearly a decade.

The WSPU, now under unified control, became a dynamic spearhead, later to be destroyed less by the War than by spontaneous combustion. Christabel records triumphantly that it was organized and led 'in much the same way as the Salvation Army under General Booth'. The Pethick-Lawrences, loyally devoted to Mrs Pankhurst and Christabel, chose to ignore the implications of this arrangement for themselves. Owing to Mrs Pankhurst's persistent evangelism and her constant absences, they became, with Christabel, an unofficial organizing committee of three, subsequently described by Pethick as 'the Triumvirate'. At this period their sense of dedication had reached its peak.

'We must go into every town and village in the land if possible,' Emmeline had said at the Essex Hall the previous May, 'and preach to the women there the word of freedom and bid them rise up now and work out their own salvation.'

CHAPTER 8

Dominant Trio

Militancy, which officially began on October 13, 1905, when Christabel Pankhurst and Annie Kenney interrupted Sir Edward Grey in Manchester, was now in full operation. 'Deeds, not words' represented its guiding principle. A main task of the three organizers was to make it effective and control its limits, which were not yet a subject of controversy.

From 1907 to 1909 the militant techniques most often used were 'raids' on Parliament and the interruption of Cabinet Ministers. By the first, as Dr Gooch has put it, 'the main conflict was transferred from the hall to the street', and the subsequent police court proceedings meant heavy work for Pethick. The second tactic, which caused women to be officially excluded from large political meetings, involved great ingenuity to enable the interrupter to be present (usually hidden under the platform, concealed in the rafters, or located at an adjacent window). The nerves of leading members of the Government soon became frayed; at a Birmingham meeting addressed by Prime Minister Asquith in September 1909, a *Daily Mail* report described him as 'surrounded by precautions that might have sufficed to protect a Czar'.

The education of sheltered and inexperienced women by this work was comparable to Gandhi's later training of Indian women in his Civil Disobedience campaign. With every militant act the temperature rose, and in Emmeline's words, 'there was a heightening of the values of life for us all'.

A pamphlet published by Victor Duval in 1910 recorded a total of 294 arrests and 163 imprisonments during 1909. In aggregate sentences, members of the WSPU served over eight years in those twelve months, bringing the total since militancy began to nearly twenty-eight years.

Various forms of prison mutiny, especially the hunger strike, represented another type of resistance which started when the suffragettes were denied the status of political prisoners.[1] In *Women's Fight for the Vote*, Pethick wrote of the effect of forcible feeding on its victim: 'She went in a Suffragette; she came out a living flame'.

Miss Wallace Dunlop initiated the hunger strike in 1909 and moved Pethick to a deeply-felt expression of humble appreciation. A more famous victim of forcible feeding was Lady Constance Lytton, who as 'Jane Warton, seamstress', stripped herself of the privileges previously conceded to her rank, and eventually became paralyzed owing to her prison experiences. In her book *Prison and Prisoners* she added much to the revelations which society owed to the Suffragettes of prison archaisms and barbarities.

Her case brought about the resignation of Herbert Gladstone as Home Secretary. His successor in this office was Winston Churchill, who as might be imagined formulated new methods of dealing with the militants. These included some concessions and the occasional use of wholesale release, which his successor Mr McKenna followed by re-arrest when the victim had recovered. In *Votes for Women* Pethick described this procedure (which had to be legalized by a special Act of Parliament) as 'the Cat and Mouse Act'.

Votes for Women had been jointly founded by the Pethick-Lawrences as the official organ of the WSPU in October 1907. It began as a 3d monthly, and after six months sold weekly at 1d. By 1909 it had become a widely-read newspaper with a circulation of nearly 50,000 and a large revenue from advertisements. The Committee which it represented now included four officers, Mrs Pankhurst, Christabel, and the Pethick-Lawrences, and four ordinary members, Mrs Wolstenholme Elmy, Annie Kenney, Mary Neal, and the writer Elizabeth Robins. But Pethick, reinforced by his earlier journalistic experience, took a strong individual line; he used his columns to make readers see problems as they were, divorced from wishful thinking.

---

[1] The London Museum contains a poem by Sylvia Pankhurst, 'Writ on Cold Slate', composed while serving six months in Holloway Gaol, which comments on the refusal of writing materials to prisoners, and concludes as follows:
'Only this age that loudly boasts Reform
hath set its seal of vengeance 'gainst the mind,
decreeing nought in prison shall be writ
save on cold slate, and swiftly washed away.'

This realistic treatment brought the paper many masculine readers. Victor Duval organized the 'Men's Political Union', and a second group described itself as 'The Men's League for Woman Suffrage'. Two distinguished journalists, H. W. Nevinson and H. N. Brailsford, resigned from the Liberal *Daily News* as a protest against the treatment of Suffragettes in prison. They explained their position in a letter to *The Times* which said: 'We cannot denounce torture in Russia and support it in England'. A leaflet entitled 'Prominent Men in Favour of Women's Suffrage', published by the MPU in 1909, gave a long list of names which included Lord Robert Cecil, Lord Lytton, Sidney Webb, Professor Gilbert Murray, Sir Oliver Lodge, J. M. Barrie, John Galsworthy, Thomas Hardy, John Masefield, Sir Hubert Parry, and a number of Bishops and lesser clergy.

In a talk given by Pethick for the BBC in 1960, he recalled George Lansbury's passionate support of the Suffragettes. Lansbury approved of militant tactics which, like Pethick, he considered to be 'fully justified by the trickery of politicians in dealing with the question'; he spoke at Suffragette meetings, and kept their cause alive in the House. Another prominent supporter was Bertrand Russell, who stood as a Woman Suffrage candidate at a Wimbledon by-election in 1909 and polled nearly 4,000 votes. Half a century later he was himself to adopt militant tactics in protest against nuclear weapons, but the militants, according to Roger Fulford, did not support him at Wimbledon because he proclaimed his belief in Liberalism.

An immense expansion of the WSPU occurred from 1907-8. Christabel had been Organizing Political Secretary since 1906, and Pethick, her devoted back-stage henchman, shouldered such routine occupations as answering letters, acting as emergency bookkeeper, and interviewing the ubiquitous police. This work occupied nearly all the working hours of himself, Emmeline and Christabel; 'I had to make an appointment even with my own wife if I wished to discuss anything of moment with her,' he subsequently recorded.

An intensive educational campaign involved thousands of public meetings, which attracted huge audiences; the most important were held three times a year at the Albert Hall, where dramatic collections conducted by Emmeline raised spectacular funds which Pethick recorded on enormous blackboards. During the five years of her Treasurership she raised a total sum of £100,000. The London head office now ran to nineteen rooms with a paid staff of seventy-five, and hundreds of volunteers whose ludicrous shortcomings were swiftly modified by experience which revealed their undeveloped powers. Pethick made himself responsible for all the business involved by this expansion, and was chief organizer of the historic Hyde Park demonstration of June 21, 1908, at which an audience estimated by the newspapers as half a million listened to eighty women speakers from twenty platforms.

In October 1908 the defence at Leeds Assizes of Mrs Baines, a WSPU organizer, gave Pethick his first opportunity to practice as a barrister, while the beginning of unofficial window-breaking in 1909 added to the number of his busy days in the police courts. On October 13th the famous raid 'to rush the House of Commons' when Parliament opened led to the sensational Bow Street trial at which Christabel eloquently examined Lloyd George and Herbert Gladstone, whom she had subpoenaed as witnesses owing to their presence in Parliament Square during the raid. Half a century later, in August 1957, the writer Christopher St John, collecting material for her biography of Dame Ethel Smyth, wrote Pethick to ask what the exact charge had been against Christabel at this trial. With his usual efficiency he replied in two days that 'Mr Muskett, prosecuting, said that the summons charged them with having been guilty of conduct likely to provoke a breach of the peace'.

In February 1909, to Pethick's alarm, Emmeline decided again to face arrest and imprisonment by taking part in another raid on Parliament which followed the exclusion of woman suffrage from the King's Speech. In a subsequent pamphlet, 'Why I Went to Prison', she explained this decision in terms of her personal story; 'I went to prison because the power that has shaped my whole life has led me there step by step'. But undoubtedly the real reason was her determination to erase the memory of the earlier humiliation; her collapse had served only to increase her sense of dedication. In the interval she had overcome her horror of the Black Maria, and familiarity with the prison routine itself now enabled her to serve the two months' sentence with tranquillity.

Pethick took her place and, as Joint Treasurer, acquired for the first time an official status in the WSPU. During her association with the movement she received seven sentences altogether. She left Holloway smiling gaily beneath a wide-brimmed picture hat trimmed with two ebullient ostrich feathers, and a great welcome by six hundred colleagues at the Wharncliffe Rooms celebrated her release.

Eleven pamphlets have survived which she published during those years of probation. One, 'A Call to Women'[1] quoted a letter from Olive Schreiner, who wrote: 'The sense of the wrongs and sufferings of women seems again to have swept all before it in my heart. I would be so glad to think a new world was coming for the women just after us.' Emmeline's own letters to colleagues at this period show a shrewd grasp of the tactics required to elicit further sacrifices from those who had endured punishment already. She encouraged the diffident and inexperienced with warm letters of congratulation signed 'Affectionately yours'; only for Pethick an occasional deeper note of tenderness illumined the working routine that they shared. 'Dearest, I thank you for bringing me the sweetbriar and the lilies that have made my office so fragrant and sweet,' ran a note written in May 1910.[1] 'You have been so busy lately and you are playing so very important and essential a part in the scheme of things.'

During 1910 the Pethick-Lawrences became somewhat less busy owing to a nine months' truce from militancy while a widely supported Bill drawn up by a Conciliation Committee, with Lord Lytton as Chairman and H. N. Brailsford as Honorary Secretary, was debated in Parliament. A Second Reading was carried by 299 votes to 190, but Asquith refused further facilities for discussion, and announced the Dissolution of Parliament for November 28th without mentioning women. A deputation four hundred strong marched to Parliament in protest, and the subsequent six hours' battle with the police became celebrated as 'Black Friday'. Two women died later from the violence they encountered, and the rest decided that the cost of the franchise should henceforth be paid by property rather than by battered female bodies.

At the General Election 400 Members pledged to support votes for women were returned to the new Parliament, and when the Coronation year of George V opened, the suffragist prospects

[1] London Museum.

seemed better than ever before. In *Women's Fight for the Vote* Pethick made a final plea to the 1911 Government to end the conflict 'which has converted honourable and law-abiding women into rebels against authority'.

CHAPTER 9

The Old Bailey

During 1912 Pethick ceased to be merely the loyal henchman or even the Prince Consort; instead he moved to the centre of the stage. As a major actor his performance was outstanding amid the heroic records of the militant movement.

After the second General Election of 1910 the Conciliation Bill, slightly modified, had been reintroduced, and on May 5, 1911 passed its Second Reading by 255 votes to 88. When Mr Lloyd George stated that the Government could not find further time for it that year but would give a whole week in 1912, the WSPU agreed with many misgivings to a second period of truce. Had the Prime Minister kept his word women would have been enfranchised in 1912, and to this change public opinion was more favourable than it would ever be again till the end of the 1914 War.

But on November 7th Mr Asquith virtually killed the Conciliation Bill by announcing that in 1912 he would himself introduce a Manhood Suffrage Bill (for which there was no demand), and the women's cause was relegated to a possible amendment to which the Bill would be theoretically open. As so much national uneasiness followed this cynical departure from the spirit of the earlier agreement, the Prime Minister finally consented to receive a deputation from nine suffrage societies, and repudiated the accusation of bad faith. But the women knew all too well that the road to any serious consideration of the Conciliation Bill would be blocked by the new Reform Bill.

The reply of the WSPU to the dishonest manoeuvring of ministerial tricksters was an Albert Hall mass meeting to which Mrs Pankhurst sent a message from America: 'I share your indignation at the Government's insult to women and am ready to renew the fight'. The speakers proclaimed the end of the truce, and announced a new deputation to Parliament the following day. Emmeline led this protest and was arrested with 218 other women and four men. Their number swamped the limited facilities of Bow Street Police Court, and the prisoners had perforce to be given a near-political status. This time Emmeline was soon released owing to a technical illegality in the charge brought against her.

The period March 1st to 4th saw the beginning of a large-scale campaign of window-breaking; the places attacked included Government windows in Downing Street, the National Liberal Club, and a number of West End stores. According to a story told by herself years afterwards in a BBC programme, 'Scrapbook for 1912', Dame Ethel Smyth, the composer, accompanied Mrs Pankhurst and Mrs Tuke to Downing Street.

This was the first official assault by the militants on private property. The cause lay largely in a speech made a few days earlier at an anti-suffrage meeting in Bristol by a member of the Government, the Rt. Hon. C. E. H. Hobhouse. Mr Hobhouse taunted women with being less militant than men, and scornfully compared their restrained actions with the burning of Nottingham Castle by men during the Reform Bill agitation of 1832. At the subsequent police court proceedings, Mr Hobhouse's words were described as an 'incitement' to militancy.

By one of history's peculiar ironies, Mr Hobhouse's eldest son Stephen was destined to spend two years in prison as a conscientious objector during the First World War.

On March 5, 1912, just after Pethick had completed bailing arrangements for the hordes of window-breakers and was writing their story at Clement's Inn in *Votes For Women*, a police superintendent entered with a warrant for his arrest. Charged with him were Emmeline and Christabel, and also Mrs Pankhurst and Mrs Tuke, the honorary secretary of the Union, who were already in prison. At the Pethick-Lawrences' flat the officer found Emmeline but not Christabel, who unknown to the police had recently changed her residence. These wholesale arrests were intended to break the movement by immobilizing its leaders.

While the Pethick-Lawrences talked with the police officer, their literary colleague Evelyn Sharp chanced to come in, perceived what was happening, undertook to edit the paper in their absence, and disappeared to warn Christabel. That night Christabel crossed to France in disguise and thereafter, while the whole detective force searched for her, directed the movement from Paris. When the Pethick-Lawrences were taken to Bow Street, Emmeline records that her husband said to her with uncharacteristic emotion, 'This is their hour and the power of darkness'. In fact he was filled with exultation—'a kind of fearful joy'—because fate had now summoned him to share the risks and sufferings of his women colleagues.

Bail was refused during the period of the police court hearing; Emmeline was detained in Holloway and Pethick in Brixton while the police searched the vast quantity of letters and papers seized at Clement's Inn. On March 8th 'No. 3408 F. P. Lawrence' wrote to his wife from Brixton Prison: 'When Aeneas was at Carthage and he and his comrades were having a distinctly odd time, one of the party gave vent to the following remark: *"Haec olim meminisse juvabit"*—we shall have pleasure in looking back on this some day! Does not that rather describe our position?'

Meanwhile Christabel, writing in *Votes for Women*, publicized the rash words of Henry Hobhouse as 'the most calculated and wicked incitement to violence that any responsible public man . . . has ever uttered'. At Brixton a visitor was Pethick's Uncle Edwin, who had broken off their relationship during the South African War, but now brought his staunch avuncular disapproval to support Pethick in his predicament.

On March 28th the Pethick-Lawrences were committed for trial and released on bail. Both were able to hear speeches at a mass meeting in the Albert Hall that night by Israel Zangwill, Annie Besant, and Elizabeth Robins, and then Pethick, asking no one's permission, slipped across to Paris semi-disguised *via* Newhaven and Dieppe, and spent a few days discussing Union affairs with Christabel. During this eventful period Rabindranath Tagore visited England, and in a broadcast delivered on January 12, 1961, Pethick recorded the impression then made on him at a private party by the Indian poet: 'I had the strange feeling that he had not walked into the room as everyone else had done, but had floated in like some supernatural being'.

The final days before the trial opened were spent on preparations for defence. The Pethick-Lawrences arranged for Tim Healy, the eminent Irish politician and a distinguished lawyer, to represent Emmeline — who thus waived the right to cross-examine witnesses and address the jury—while Pethick and Mrs Pankhurst conducted their own defence. For the second time

Pethick confronted an Attorney-General, as Sir Rufus Isaacs (later Lord Reading) was appointed to lead the prosecution.

Before the trial began, Pethick wrote Emmeline a letter quoted in her autobiography: 'Beloved, we are very near to a great day, the greatest that we have seen in our lives. To me it seems that an honour such as is conferred only on a few in many centuries is about to be conferred on us. We are to stand where the great and noble have stood before us all down the ages . . . It is supreme joy that you and I will stand there together. It is the complete and perfect expression of that faith to which we by our travail are giving birth.'

The trial opened on May 15th in the Central Criminal Court of the Old Bailey before Lord Coleridge and a jury, and lasted for three weeks. Many years earlier, by an ironic coincidence, the Judge's father had appeared as Counsel with Dr Pankhurst in a famous case (Chorlton v. Lings) which sought to establish that women were entitled as *persons* to vote under the Franchise Act of 1867.

The prosecution's charge was that of Conspiracy 'to damage the property of liege subjects of the King'. They quoted from one of Emmeline's speeches: 'We have only to be militant enough, and twenty-four hours will see us victorious'. The defendants, who pleaded Not Guilty, emphasized the political character of the trial which the prosecution sought to deny, and the incitement to violence offered to women by members of the Government itself. Standing in the dock with Mrs Pankhurst and the Pethick-Lawrences, invisible but formidable spectres, were the Liberal Governments of Mr Gladstone and Mr Asquith, who by their disingenuous manoeuvres in response to a legitimate demand had driven women to civil disobedience.

Among a long series of witnesses appeared Dame Ethel Smyth, summoned from prison, whose 'March of the Women' had become the song of the WSPU. Before the trial, she had written to Pethick of 'the honour and joy it is to me to have put your spirit into music'. A lively duologue between herself and Mrs Pankhurst illuminated the constitutional aspects of the movement.

In his speech Pethick sought to persuade the jury, initially bored and unsympathetic, to add a political rider to their verdict.

'Speaking for myself,' he began, 'I loathe the idea of any

such thing as the deliberate breaking of shop windows. But I know that these women who have taken that course have been driven, by the inexorable logic of facts, to do what they did . . . You are dealing here with people whose life is devoted to an ideal.'

After describing the lives and characters of the defendants, he summarized the story of the suffrage struggle as 'forty years of patience'. He then outlined the history and methods of the WSPU, spoke of their frustration by the Prime Minister and the Government when they tried peaceful methods of approach, summed up the Conciliation Bill, and described its ruin by the proposed new Reform Bill following the events of 'Black Friday'. After calling his witnesses for the defence he appealed to the jury, now fully alive to the drama in which they were involved, to show by their verdict that 'you understand that this is a political fight'. The remainder of his address dealt with the value of the educational work done by the WSPU, the tendentious evidence of the police, the real significance of militancy, and the fundamental relationship between woman suffrage and the welfare of the race.

Contemporary witnesses have testified to the restrained brilliance of this historic speech, which finally introduced a statement on his own position.

'I am a man and I cannot take part in this women's agitation, but I intend to stand by the women who are fighting . . . I think it is a battle waged for the good of the people of this country, waged by one half of the community whose deeds are valuable to the other part of the country and should not be excluded.' Stating that the risk of a sex war had been prevented by the men who had shared in the campaign, he concluded by quoting no less a witness than their arch-enemy Gladstone: 'If no consideration had ever been addressed to the people in this country except to remember to hate violence and love order and exercise patience, the liberties of this country would never have been obtained'.

After stirring speeches by Mrs Pankhurst, who insisted that the only conspiracy, if any, was the Government's, and by Tim Healy who warned the jury that a conviction would not end the movement, a verdict of 'Guilty' concluded the trial. But the jury, absent for an hour, added their memorable rider. 'We unanimously desire to express the hope that taking into consideration the undoubtedly pure motives that underlie the agitation that has led to this trouble you will be pleased to exercise clemency and leniency in dealing with the case'.

Emmeline Pethick-Lawrence, by arrangement, then addressed the Judge, urging him in a speech described as 'a little gem' by her husband to consider the 'inalienable right of the prisoners to political status'. Disregarding this appeal and the jury's recommendation, the Judge, whose own summing-up had been a second speech for the prosecution, passed a sentence of nine months imprisonment in the Second Division and added an unprecedented penalty; the defendants must pay the whole cost of the trial.

Several unforeseen consequences followed this verdict. The Judge's daughters, Phyllis and Audrey Coleridge, applied for membership of the WSPU, while the prisoners received a spectacular ovation from the waiting crowd. Public indignation found vent not only in the Press, but in a letter of protest to the Home Secretary from some members of the jury. When Pethick reached Wormwood Scrubs he found himself, after altercations with the Governor and a 'visiting magistrate', who went out of his way to insult him, transferred to Brixton as a 'one-and-a-half' class prisoner who was allowed to have writing materials and wear his own clothes. Nevertheless he soon concluded that 'the essential fact in the life of a prisoner is that he takes on a sub-human status'.

Meanwhile petitions for political treatment of the prisoners sprang up all over the country; one especially for Pethick came from graduates of Cambridge, Oxford, and London. The Government capitulated, but the prisoners discovered that the concessions given to the three leaders were denied to the eighty-one Suffragettes still in prison for the same demonstration. The solitary prisoner in Brixton learned that his wife and Mrs Pankhurst had adopted a hunger-strike in protest, and at once joined it himself. 'The first day,' he relates, 'I was all hot and bothered about it', but 'the second day I took myself in hand'.

Against a rising barrage of national protest the Home Office ordered forcible feeding. This was never performed on Mrs Pankhurst and only once on Emmeline Pethick-Lawrence, but twice a day for several days Pethick had to endure the rubber tube pushed up his nostrils and into his throat while liquid was poured through it and the warders held him down.

In the House of Commons George Lansbury, undaunted as always, attacked Mr Asquith for a bland comment that the women had only to give an undertaking of future good behaviour in order to be released.

'You know that they cannot!' he exclaimed. 'It is perfectly disgraceful that the Prime Minister of England should make such a statement.' Leaving his seat below the gangway, he walked to the end of the ministerial bench and addressed the Government. 'You call yourselves gentlemen and you forcibly feed women!' Ordered by the Speaker to leave the House, he went with a parting shot.

'I cannot contain myself when men sitting here say the women can walk out when they know very well that they are fighting for a principle. Members would be better employed in doing the same.'

From Holloway Prison 'No. 15581 Emmeline Pethick-Lawrence' wrote to her husband on June 18th: 'What a joy to write to you at last! A fortnight ago I should have written in spite of our agreement. But then it occurred to me that if you accepted my letter, it would mean that no news of the outside world or of your many friends would reach you. As for me—well you knew then and you know now how it is with me. And I knew then and I know now how it is with you — *Well — infinitely well!* For, the purpose to which we were born and for which we were mated is accomplished. The hour is come and we are delivered . . . Indeed my assurance born of knowledge of you, and faith in the universal sustaining Life in which we partake—and then the news of you that I have received from those who have seen you—are the last drop in my cup of content. It will not surprise you when I tell you that these past weeks have been a time of peace. Like the hermits of old, I often feel inclined to exclaim: O *beata solitudo!* O *sola beatitudo!*'

In similar mood, '7294 Lawrence F. W. P.' wrote her from Brixton the following day: 'I have not been in any way anxious about you, and equally you have I am sure not been anxious about me. You know that the one thing, which alone seems worth while to me, is that the human spirit should transcend the whole of the material world; and therefore you do not need to be told that not in the very smallest degree have I been dismayed or discouraged by my environment. Dearest, here in the stillness—that is, to me, essentially the stillness of earth *life*—I am conscious only of the great spiritual tie which binds us together and binds us to the great Power which guides us . . .

'The sun is shining brilliantly, it is a gorgeous, a magnificent day! I am full of radiant life.'

Pethick had written from the prison hospital; in spite of his exultant spirit he gradually became very weak, and like his wife was soon released. As he left he found the warders lined up to see him off, and 'it seemed to me that I heard a cheer'.

He and Emmeline returned on a beautiful evening to Holmwood, fragrant in summer with the wild roses which were Pethick's favourite flower. When the trial started, they had just begun to adorn the hedgerows; now, at the end of his imprisonment, he found the last of them still radiantly alive. It was June 27th, 1912.

CHAPTER 10

Aftermath

One of the strangest events in the chequered history of militant suffrage occurred soon after the Conspiracy trial. Different writers have produced different versions of a puzzling development which after fifty years still defies satisfactory explanation. The most magnanimous accounts have been those of the apparent victims, while the least charitable tend to come from narrators who arrived late on the scene. As all four protagonists are now dead (the last being Pethick himself), the rights and wrongs of the story may never be justly assessed. But some aspects of it can still, perhaps, be newly interpreted.

After recovering from their prison experiences, the Pethick-Lawrences decided to spend a fortnight in Switzerland. Christabel's location was now generally known, and the Pankhursts asked Pethick and Emmeline to meet them in Boulogne. There Mrs Pankhurst announced a new policy of widespread attacks on property by which the Pethick-Lawrences, who had hoped to build a vast educational campaign on the sympathy created by their trial, were deeply disturbed. In Emmeline's words, 'something that resembled a family quarrel' developed for the first time between the four colleagues. But they parted apparent good friends, and as Mrs Pankhurst had decided to remain in Paris for the summer, the Pethick-Lawrences followed their Swiss visit by a journey across Canada to see Emmeline's brother Harold in Vancouver Island.

In Canada they learned that, because the expenses of the trial had deliberately not been paid, bailiffs were now established in their house at Holmwood. Since the Pankhursts had no money, the Old Bailey verdict laid its financial implications squarely on the Pethick-Lawrences.

A surprising letter now reached them from Mrs Pankhurst, suggesting that they should remain in Canada, secure their private property against the British Government, and conduct their educational campaign from across the Atlantic. Their immediate reaction was adverse; they had staked life and health on the fight for human equality, and did not propose to abandon it for material reasons.

The danger foreseen by the Pankhursts was none the less real. In spite of his first-class qualifications, Pethick as a man of substance had never attempted to maintain himself; the days when he might have practised as a barrister or occupied an honourable position as a university don had long gone by. Nor had Emmeline, for all her qualities of leadership, ever earned her living; she overlapped, but was never part of, the post-war generation of young women for whom self-support represented an essential part of the claim to equality.

With the loss of their private fortune the Pethick-Lawrences would face financial catastrophe, and the women's cause would suffer with them. Many suffragettes would not volunteer for deeds of destruction if they knew that Pethick had to meet the bill.

He and Emmeline returned to London to find the WSPU headquarters transferred from Clement's Inn to Kingsway. Next day Mrs Pankhurst invited them to her room to hear a shattering announcement; she had decided to sever her connection with them, and thenceforth conduct the policy of the Union with Christabel's help alone. At first they doubted Christabel's support for this ultimatum, but after she made a secret trip from Paris they had no choice but to be convinced. The four of them drew up the final terms of the separation at a small hotel in Boulogne. The newspaper *Votes for Women* remained in the hands of the Pethick-Lawrences (and in July 1914 was briefly attached to a new organization called the United Suffragists), but the rest of the WSPU went under the Pankhursts' control. After a Press announcement of the new arrangement, Mrs Pankhurst appeared alone at the great Albert Hall meeting on October 17th which had been summoned to welcome the three defendants at the trial. There she incited her bewildered followers to rebellion, and an era of extreme militancy began.

Punch reduced the problem to a simple cartoon in which one girl asked another: 'Are you a Peth or a Pank?' Actually the issue was not simple at all, for it turned upon the efficacy of democratic methods to achieve a purpose in which the opposition sprang from irrational prejudice and time was running short.

It is easy to read back into those years immediately preceding the First World War a subconscious intuition among politically-minded persons that apocalyptic events were impending. But in spite of Agadir, the Balkan Wars and the Kaiser's speeches, there is no evidence that any of the militant leaders—not even Pethick himself—prophetically pictured the coming of Armageddon. For the Pankhursts time always was running out, in terms of the long stalemate that preceded them and their continued frustration by guileful politicians.

Christabel, in Dr Gooch's words 'the initiator of extra-constitutional methods', was not prepared to have doubts cast on their efficiency. For her, passion rather than reason marked the road to victory, and who shall say she was wrong when the *status quo* that she was struggling to overturn was itself based on passion—the passion which lies at the root of prejudice? She did not believe that their movement could afford to wait while the wheels of democratic procedure rumbled slowly on. The walls of Jericho were not vulnerable to argument but only to dynamic action.

But the Pethick-Lawrences, in spite of their silver-spoon origins, were natural democrats who believed that major decisions should be taken only after full consultation. They were brave and gentle rebels in a world where the rebel often displays courage but seldom courtesy, and could not share Christabel's view that consultation hampered resolute action in an urgent historical crisis, analagous to a military campaign, in which the postponement of drastic decisions might lose the battle. In his book *Women's Fight For the Vote*, Pethick had clearly stated his own belief that militant methods must never 'exceed by one iota the absolute necessities of the situation'.

How much militancy was essential to sustain the cause? On the hidden rock now revealed by that question, one of the most famous friendships in history had foundered. Emmeline, if treated more gently, might have been readier than Pethick to agree with Christabel. Nearly three decades later, in *My Part in a Changing World*, she described the spirit of revolt aroused in WSPU members by four years of humiliation, trickery and violence. 'The temper of the movement became one of fierce determination to count no cost and to stake life itself in the struggle.' Her Preface contained a further revealing comment: 'It was a long line of political leaders from Gladstone to Asquith who transformed Mrs Pankhurst from an ardent democrat into the autocrat of the Women's Social and Political Union. And it was the pressure of circumstances that transformed a society that was founded upon desire for the extension of democracy into an enthusiastically supported dictatorship.'

Inevitably Pethick and Emmeline took some time to recover from the painful shock that they had suffered; the Union, so largely their own creation, had appeared to them as their child, while Christabel had been virtually an adopted daughter. Not only had they housed her, but provided her clothes; the becoming picture-hat which she wears in the frontispiece portrait of *Unshackled* was Pethick's gift. But less than a year later his biographical entry in *The Suffrage Annual and Women's Who's Who* for 1913 only stated: 'Was requested by Mrs Pankhurst to sever all connection with the WSPU; consented to do so to prevent a split in the Union'.

With time, the unlimited generosity of them both was able to find expression.

'Men and women of destiny are like that,' Emmeline wrote in her autobiography. 'They are like some irresistible force in nature—a tidal wave, or a river in full flood.' In his own book Pethick added four years later: 'Many men and women who have made history have been cast in a similar mould. They seem to be used by destiny for some purpose whether of beneficent constructive reform or of blind destructive retribution. They cannot be judged by ordinary standards of conduct, and those who run up against them must not complain of the treatment they receive.'

It was perhaps the memory of this experience which caused Pethick to include a fragment of his philosophy in the essay published in 1951, *If I Had My Time Again*: 'There is really no satisfaction to be got out of brooding over things that have gone wrong or dwelling on the horrid things some people have said or done to us. And it is often not so very difficult to entice the mind to contemplate instead the things that have gone right and the generosity and friendship that some other people have shown us.'

Possibly he also remembered that magnanimity had not been

wholly on one side. In 1922, for some reason now forgotten by their colleagues, Emmeline wrote to Christabel, then living in Vancouver, and received this illuminating reply:

4th May, 1922.

'Dearest,

'Your letter filled me with joy. In an instant ten years were gone and they have never been. Our love united us all the time and only the surface of it was moved. Wasn't that the way?

'It was like your generous heart to write. I am so glad you did.

'All that morning we (Grace Roe and I) had been jogging along in motor stages and interurban trains through a lovely bit of Washington State and the thought of you and Godfather and our wonderful years of work together came to me so strongly and remained with me and for a long time I talked to Grace of it for my thought would have expression. Then we arrived at Bellingham and when I entered the Hotel a letter was put into my hand. I knew the writing at once! I can only say again with what joy I read it. Something just slipped into its place and I felt comforted . . .

'Yes! I have had great experiences, inward rather than outward—and I was unhappy. Perhaps there was, as you said, something of a penalty about it, though it seemed difficult at the time to understand the need of price and penalty *after* the event. One is inclined to expect that the price will come before and not after, and then to be taken by surprise and be a bit rebellious at heart—or perhaps only stupid and not see that it is the price which one would so gladly pay—understanding it to *be* such!

'But that is all done with now and I am thankful to have learned many lessons and to have won my way to a real freedom of spirit that I never knew before. I had so very much to learn. I depended too much upon humanity—upon myself and other people. One has to find the bedrock. And these turning points in one's life always and *only* come after a time of inward stress . . .

'I am absorbed in viewing the great world situation and mighty developments of this time. It is the end of the Age! The ends of the ages are certainly come upon us and in our very own day one great period of Eternity ends and another begins . . .

'Dear Godfather give him a big message from me.

'With all my love—your same Christabel.'

In June 1913, penalties of a different kind came home to the Pethick-Lawrences. Since Pethick still refused to pay the cost of the prosecution, the Government put the contents of his house and garden up to auction. Friends rallied to their side, buying up and returning their possessions, but the proceeds did not reach the amount needed and Pethick was threatened with bankruptcy. He decided to face the disagreeable results, which included his compulsory resignation from the Reform Club 'on being adjudicated bankrupt'. According to Emmeline in *My Part in a Changing World*, this august Liberal institution did not restore his membership when £1,000 had been seized from his estate and the bankruptcy annulled.

On the top of this ordeal came civil actions from the shops in which windows had been broken, though one Regent Street store protested that it had been involved unwillingly. Pethick and Emmeline contested these actions, and Mr Justice Darling allowed them to address the jury. Though unable to acquit the defendants of responsibility, the Judge agreed with Emmeline that incitement to rebellion had originally come from Mr Lloyd George and Mr Hobhouse, and described her speech as 'one of the most eloquent I have ever heard'. Exactly twelve years later, on June 22, 1925, Lord Darling, replying to a request made by Pethick for one of his constituents, remarked how much he had 'admired and enjoyed' the address to the jury which 'Mrs Lawrence delivered in a case heard before me'.

Though Pethick continued to edit *Votes For Women*, he did not share the extreme experiences provided by the last two years of militancy. He stood aside from the attempt to burn down the house of Mr Lewis Harcourt in 1912, though Helen Craggs, the undaunted young Suffragette who made it, was long afterwards to become his second wife. He had no part in the dramatic offering of her life by Emily Wilding Davison at the 1913 Derby, or in the 1914 attack on the Rokeby Venus by Mary Richardson.

Earlier, in April 1913, the WSPU headquarters had been raided, and the heads of all its departments arrested. Thenceforth much of the movement's impetus went underground, but Suffragettes still filled the prisons in the first half of 1914. No one could have guessed even then that the vote would come through a cataclysm arising, as all shooting wars arise, from irrational violence which would incidentally enable women to prove by their actions the justice of their claims. Had those claims never been made and publicized, the First World War would not have brought their fulfilment. That is the simple answer to the often-argued question whether votes for women came through the Suffragette movement or the War.

Among the Suffragettes in prison during the summer of 1914 was Grace Roe, campaign organizer for the WSPU, who had been forcibly fed for three weeks before being sentenced, and in 1962 would be responsible for arranging the memorial ceremonies for Pethick and Emmeline at Peaslake and Dorking. Like the other final victims, she could not now fail to perceive the warning shadows which lengthened across the tempestuous scene from the darkening international horizon. One August morning her German wardress at Holloway Prison excitedly shouted 'Long live the Kaiser!', and she knew that the War had begun.

PART II

The Socialist

CHAPTER 11

The Four Years' War

Pethick never became recognized as one of the great architects of British Socialism, though he fought seven elections for Labour, won five, spent eighteen years in the House of Commons and served for sixteen in the House of Lords. Long ago, when a Labour victory at the polls came within the range of possibility, a newspaper article described him as 'the first Chancellor of the Exchequer of a Labour government'. But though, in 1929-31, he filled the office of Financial Secretary to the Treasury, his exceptional gifts as a mathematician never seemed to qualify him for the highest post in this category.

Not until he became Secretary of State for India and for Burma, when nearing seventy-four, did he hold a Cabinet post. Writing on August 4, 1945 to congratulate him on this appointment, Colonel Clifton-Brown, then Speaker of the House of Commons and later Lord Ruffside, commented that he had believed that Pethick would have liked the Treasury, and, if so, was sorry. Pethick's reply, if he made one, has not survived.

Why did he scale the heights so late in life? Probably, among colleagues who included several pushful and noisy men, he was disinclined to be pushful himself. Integrity and self-propulsion are seldom compatible, and integrity was the keynote of his character. Though relatively ambitious, he never appeared ambitious enough to adopt behaviour for which he would have despised himself. He was modestly inconspicuous during the famous 1940 Bournemouth Party Conference, at which leading Socialists submitted themselves, with varying degrees of discretion, as candidates for Churchill's National Government. His deep interest in furthering the welfare of others stopped somewhere short of canvassing his own.

To the end of his life he kept aloof from the Labour Party quarrels which have periodically wrecked its effectiveness and undermined respect for it among ordinary citizens. A Press photograph of the 1945 Labour Cabinet[1] shows him standing behind the Prime Minister wearing his usual serene, detached expression, in striking contrast to the pugnacious Bevin, the arrogant Dalton, and the pugilistic Bevan. In 1946, when more assertive politicians concerned with the Indian scene tended to discuss India's future over his head, he gave no sign of exasperation. Back in 1914 no one would have thought him destined for orthodox political greatness, even in a Party of the Left. He still ranked not merely as a rebel, but as a disreputable rebel recently in Brixton Prison and a bankrupt expelled from his Club. It was, perhaps, with the idea of reinforcement by a respectable professional organization that he joined the Society of Authors in 1914. He has recorded that as a child he possessed no aesthetic sense; his interest in authors and authorship was probably awakened by Olive Schreiner, and later found further fulfilment in membership of the P.E.N.

Among the writers with whom he and Emmeline corresponded during and after the First World War were John Galsworthy, Havelock Ellis, and Miles Malleson, who suffered in 1916 the suppression of a volume of plays which Pethick had sought to purchase. Laurence Housman, a pacifist and Suffragette supporter, received copies from Pethick of letters written to the papers during the war, and continued to write to him periodically until the end of his own long life.

The war did nothing to rehabilitate Pethick politically, since his principles compelled him to work for the then 'suspect' Union of Democratic Control, to fight an election as a 'Peace-by-Negotiation' candidate, and finally to become a conscientious objector. By 1918 he was already forty-six, and might have escaped involvement in the Conscription issue had not a panic-stricken Government raised the call-up age to fifty after the great German offensive of that spring. Thus the adverse circumstances which the poet W. E. Henley called 'the bludgeoning of chance' obliged him to add one more unpopular form of rebellion to the others.

He could never, I think, have truthfully been described as a Christian pacifist, though he belonged to a series of churches with high moral standards, lived as a dedicated Christian, developed a philosophy akin to Buddhism, and was buried as an

[1] See p. 129.

Anglican. Though his contacts with India intensified a natural strain of mysticism which found expression in his 'Cosmic Hymn',[1] his First War pacifism betrays no evidence of a philosophical or theological basis. Like the periodic pacifism of Bertrand Russell, it was rooted in political principles and calculations.

Emmeline, on the contrary, was for years a concerned pacifist, though Pethick's official positions obliged her to limit her utterances during the Second World War. In 1914 she severed her connection with the Suffragette organizations which then took to recruiting, and became a founder of the Women's International League for Peace and Freedom. On Christmas Day 1937 she wrote in the Preface to her autobiography: ' "The Word" becomes flesh at every moral crisis of human history. The next deliverance that humanity awaits is its enfranchisement from the enslavement to war . . . Since I have seen women rise up and in a few years cast off the conventions that had enslaved them for ages, I believe that they will in the future rise up and deliver their children from the terrible convention of war, divorced as it is in this scientific age from reason and commonsense.'

In August 1914 Pethick and Emmeline had been making plans for a world tour, then so agreeably free from passport examinations and stringent customs formalities. The sudden severance of relations with Germany came as a personal shock, for both had many German contacts, and were accustomed to the regular pre-war communications maintained by Socialist parties with their opposite numbers in other countries. The militant suffrage movement, like their international relationships, came to a sudden end, though the WSPU remained in being until the vote was won. The United Suffragists, a new organization to which they had handed over *Votes For Women*, soon became more interested in the war-time expansion of women's activities than in the struggle for the franchise.

The demand for enfranchisement was never abandoned and many of the older suffrage societies did quiet educational work for it all through the War, but from the standpoint of public interest the suffrage movement went underground till 1917. So suddenly had the outbreak of hostilities changed all values and perspectives, that the events of 1913 seemed already to belong to an earlier decade.

[1] See pp. 210-11.

While Emmeline discovered scope for her energies in the Women's Emergency Corps, largely organized by Lena Ashwell and immediately concerned with the care of Belgian refugees, Pethick found his attention claimed by the actual conduct of the War. When Sir Edward Grey first disclosed, on August 3rd, the secret negotiations by which he had pledged armed support for France in the event of a European War, Pethick's reactions were strongly critical. The Foreign Secretary, he felt, had manoeuvred Britain into a position in which she could not desert France and Belgium without a breach of faith.

'The war', he wrote long afterwards, 'seemed to me to have started on the Continent without any sufficient cause and to mark a complete breakdown of statesmanship all round. I strongly resented the clandestine way in which Sir Edward Grey had in effect committed the British people in advance behind their back.'

In October, when Emmeline was already considering what women might do to stop the war, she received a visit from a Hungarian suffragist, Rosika Schwimmer, who was on her way to the United States to stir America's neutral women to take an initiative towards peace by negotiation. At this moment a timely cable reached Emmeline from a group of American women who were promoting a new suffrage campaign, and asked her to speak at a mass meeting in Carnegie Hall. This assignment gave her an opportunity to put forward her idea for reconciliation through neutral leadership, and she sailed at once for New York. Before long she cabled Pethick, unwilling to support the War and at a loss for alternative occupation, to join her in America. Still unconcernedly without a passport, he crossed the Atlantic before the year ended.

Both of them immediately became involved in the events which led to the foundation of the Women's International League for Peace and Freedom. In Chicago they met Jane Addams of Hull House, one of the great personalities of that epoch who was often called 'America's first citizen'. An invitation from another suffrage pioneer, Dr Aletta Jacobs of Holland, now offered an opportunity to rebuild the international suffrage movement which had threatened to disintegrate under the impact of war. Dr Jacobs summoned a peace conference to The Hague at which women from both belligerent and neutral

THE FOUR YEARS' WAR

countries would be present. From the United States over fifty members of the National Women's Peace Party of America, led by Jane Addams, sailed in the Dutch ship *Noordam*, which carried a flag decorated with the word 'Peace' in large white letters, presented by the Mayor of New York. Also on board were Pethick, Emmeline, and Rosika Schwimmer.

At the Kent coast the ship was stopped by order of the British Admiralty, which had closed the North Sea. Eventually she proceeded at her own risk, but 150 would-be British delegates—who included Olive Schreiner, Sylvia Pankhurst and Evelyn Sharp—were obliged to stay behind. The only British women present at the Conference were Emmeline herself, and Kathleen Courtney and Chrystal Macmillan, who had been in Holland since February.

This Congress of 1,500 women passed resolutions very similar to the Fourteen Points later put forward by President Wilson, and envoys appointed by the Conference carried them to fifteen governments. The ostensible sympathy with which they were received marked the total lack of true co-operation. When the delegates, now obliged to furnish themselves with passports which proved to be needed for the rest of their lives, returned to their respective countries, the heavy blanket of wartime silence concealed them from one another for four catastrophic years. Each delegate, including Emmeline herself, went home to work throughout the War for Women's International League principles within her national organization.

After Pethick returned he was invited to become treasurer of the newly-formed Union of Democratic Control, founded by E. D. Morel, Norman Angell, Ramsay MacDonald, Mrs H. M. Swanwick and several left-wing journalists such as H. N. Brailsford, to insist on a foreign policy which entered into no commitments without fully informing the peoples involved. A. V. Alexander, who did not know Pethick until 1923, was then working in an office above the UDC at the corner of Marsham Street, Westminster.

Eventually a section of the Press publicized the UDC as opposed to the soldiers fighting at the front, though some soldiers were among its foremost supporters. Several meetings were broken up, and Pethick himself was once thrown from the platform. As Mr Lloyd George, now Prime Minister, had decided on the course described in the Second World War as 'unconditional surrender', the UDC decided to test public opinion at a series of by-elections, and in the bitter spring of 1917 Pethick went north with Emmeline for five icy weeks to contest South Aberdeen.

His election address, issued from 347 Union Street, Aberdeen, wisely urged that 'steps should be taken to end the war by negotiation instead of continuing it for months, or perhaps years, in the hope of a smashing victory'. Though later in the year Lord Lansdowne published a celebrated letter in the *Daily Telegraph* advocating negotiation with the Germans, Pethick inevitably became a target for unorthodox missiles, such as lumps of coal. Though he made many local friends, he collected only 333 votes.

On his return the Air Ministry, using the new menace of Zeppelin raids as a convenient excuse, requisitioned his flat in Clement's Inn. With Government assistance he and Emmeline moved to the flat in Old Square, Lincoln's Inn, which became their London home for the rest of their lives. Soon afterwards a bomb made a large crater in the road near the building, but he suffered nothing worse than a fall of soot down the chimney. About this time he sought to compensate for the censorious action of the Reform Club by founding the 1917 Club with E. D. Morel and Roden Buxton, but its life was brief and he subsequently joined the Royal Aero and Queen's Clubs.

For a time authorship offered a solace; in April 1918 he published a book entitled *A Levy on Capital*,[1] which urged that when the War ended a graduated capital levy should be imposed large enough to sweep away most of the National Debt. This work caused some public discussion, went through three editions, led to a Fabian Society debate with Bernard Shaw in the Essex Hall, and brought him the friendship of Sydney Arnold, later Lord Arnold of Hale, who became his colleague in the second Labour Government. But the crucial crescendo of battle on the Western Front overshadowed political and social controversy, and Pethick found himself faced with the call-up.

As an advocate of peace-by-negotiation he went before a Dorking tribunal, where a military official disparagingly commented that he did not specially 'want this man'. Pethick was awarded alternative service on the land, and worked for a Sussex

[1] London: George Allen & Unwin Ltd.

Emmeline in 1910 at the height of the Suffragette Movement

Pethick at the time of the Bow Street Trial, 1912

Emmeline as Parliamentary Candidate at Rusholme in 1918

Pethick as Labour Candidate at West Leicester in 1923

farmer at 27s 6d a week for the rest of the war. In April, still impelled by the political ambitions which he could never abandon, he had been adopted as Labour candidate for the Tory constituency of Hastings without disguising his views on the war, but his stand as a conscientious objector brought disaffection among his supporters and he finally withdrew. He finished the war without social respectability, a worthwhile job, a constituency, or any hopeful prospect to sustain him.

Meanwhile a new stir of life was reviving the suffrage movement, for which Pethick had sacrificed so much of his prosperity and prestige. By 1916, politicians were becoming concerned about the revision of the Parliamentary register, which had lapsed during the first two years of the war. It was now too much outdated to be a useful instrument for the first post-war General Election, and a Bill to recreate the registration machinery had to be put through Parliament. Inevitably the young soldiers at the front must be included among qualified voters, and how could the women working with them so bravely and effectively be justly left out?

An all-party panel of M.P.s, with the Speaker as Chairman, considered this problem in January 1917. Their report suggested that votes should be given to all men, and to women over thirty (and women university graduates over thirty-five) who were local government electors or electors' wives. This meant that woman suffrage would soon become a political institution. The suffrage societies welcomed the partial victory, believing, as the event proved, that half a loaf brought the whole loaf in sight.

In March 1917 even Mr Asquith—that 'obstacle so formidable', writes Dr G. P. Gooch in *Under Six Reigns*, 'that a world war was needed to blast it away'—withdrew his opposition, and on June 19, 1917, the Suffrage Clause in the Reform Bill passed the House of Commons by 330 votes to 55. The third reading went inconspicuously through on December 7th, and on February 6th, 1918, woman suffrage became part of English law, but even among those most deeply concerned, rejoicing was soon tempered by anxiety due to the falling Allied bastions on the Western Front. Thus 'with an incongruous irony seldom equalled in the history of revolutions, the spectacular pageant of the woman's movement, vital and colourful with adventure, with initiative, with sacrificial emotion, crept to its quiet unadvertised triumph in the deepest night of wartime depression'.[1]

It was none the less a major revolution, brought to its climax after long years of patient struggle by first the militant movement, and then the war, which speeded the collapse of the antiquated prejudices that women had challenged. Its ultimate success was inevitable whenever it came, for the women's crusade was an integral part of the revolutionary epoch from which it sprang. Like the other revolutions with which it coincided—religious, economic, political, and social—it reshaped the lives of the present generation, and even by the close of his long career, Pethick had not seen its end.

[1] *Testament of Youth*, p. 405.

CHAPTER 12

Would-be Politician

Since Pethick had no constituency when Armistice Day 1918 ushered in what a bereaved and exhausted nation hoped would prove to be the dawn of a better society, he decided to support Emmeline in the first General Election that women were qualified to fight. At this date it was she who ranked as a nationally renowned figure. Later, when their positions were reversed, she supported him with the same self-abnegating loyalty.

Before its final demise, the long-lived 1910 Parliament had hurriedly passed a Bill enabling women to stand for the House of Commons. Although the 'coupon' election took place only four weeks after the defeat of Germany, the candidates included seventeen women of whom none, like Emmeline herself, had been able to do any preparatory work in the pioneering constituencies which adopted them. Among these were Smethwick and North Battersea, which respectively chose Christabel Pankhurst and Mrs Despard, and the Rusholme Division of Manchester, which had invited Emmeline to stand for Labour. Against the background of blockaded Germany with its stricken population and half-starved children of whom many had died in the vast influenza epidemic, she felt compelled to undertake this uphill fight though the only consequence seemed likely to be a forfeited deposit.

The election address of 'The Labour Party's Woman Candidate' began with the trenchant statement 'I hold that Democracy must make the world safe for itself', and went on to advocate the payment of war debts from Britain's accumulated wealth, the repeal of military conscription, the abolition of secret treaties, self-government for Ireland and India, and a league of free peoples. In a country shrilly demanding that its next government should hang the Kaiser and make Germany pay, it was perhaps surprising that she polled nearly three thousand votes and saved her deposit. This remarkable rescue was not due to the new women voters who had excitedly absorbed the current spirit of revenge, but to the soldiers now due for demobilization who found hope in the message of a pacifist candidate.

'The electors', she wrote many years later, 'voted, though they did not know it, for another war.' Symptomatic of the mood at that time was the defeat at West Leicester of Ramsay Mac-Donald, who in 1914 had appeared to have an assured position as leader of his Party. Nobody would then have dreamed that this unpopular opponent of the war, now driven into the political wilderness, would have become Prime Minister and Pethick's Parliamentary leader by 1924.

All the women candidates were defeated except an Irish Republican, Countess Markevicz, who in protest against the Government's Irish policy never took her seat.[1] The women voters had themselves to be educated before they began to understand the purpose of electing women to Parliament. Little impact was made upon the young women, even if they had been suffragists as schoolgirls and were to become adult feminists, for their emotional lives had been massacred by years of ruthless slaughter. In any case they had as yet no votes to lift them out of the numb automatism to which war had reduced them. One of Emmeline's chief concerns in the next decade was the campaign for votes for these younger women.

The 1918 Election was the only one in which any of the better-known Suffragettes attempted to enter Parliament. One militant leader, asked long afterwards why those who had fought for the vote did not seek to implement their victory, replied quite simply that they were all too tired. Hunger strikes, tension, persistent work, and physical onslaughts had left many Suffragettes with impaired health and diminished energy. They felt that the next stage of the journey to equality must be carried on by other women with fresh vitality who had not been through the battle.

Already it was clear that women's entry into the House of Commons would not be secured in proportionate numbers for many years, even when men and women had equal voting rights.

---

[1] Apart from Countess Markevicz, who polled 7,835 votes in Dublin (St Patrick's), the highest figures of votes for women went to Christabel Pankhurst (Smethwick, Women's Party), 8,614; Mary Macarthur (Stourbridge, Labour), 7,537; and Mrs Despard (N. Battersea, Labour), 5,634.

A more immediate result of the suffrage struggle was the Sex Disqualification (Removal) Act of December 1919, which admitted women to many hitherto closed professions such as the law, and allowed the older universities to give them degrees. An early and successful campaign for degrees for women at Oxford enlisted a number of girl students who had been too young for the suffrage movement.

Seven months before the Sex Disqualification (Removal) Act was passed, the Treaty of Versailles, in spite of the clauses creating a League of Nations, had destroyed the hope of a better international society which had risen for a moment above the dark horizon. Pethick rightly saw in this Treaty the seeds of a new conflict, though he did not expect it to come in his lifetime. Three years after this Second War which he had foreseen broke out, he wrote in the Preface to *Fate Has Been Kind* that in 1918 the 'revolutionary elements' which dethroned the Kaiser should have been supported in their endeavours to create a viable Republic. He recorded that he had opposed the continuance of the hunger blockade after the Armistice, the terms which placed large numbers of Germans outside the German frontier, the fantastic figures fixed for the indemnity, and the clause compelling the German Government to accept the sole responsibility for the War.

'I further opposed,' he added, 'the way the Treaty was administered. I thought it a blunder to refuse such concessions to the leaders of the German Republic as would have made them partners in the preservation of the peace of Europe. I remain of opinion that these mistakes constituted some of the major factors which have enabled Nazism to dominate the German mind.'

Unable to influence the treaty-makers of 1919, he became treasurer of a 'Fight the Famine Council', founded by Mrs Charles Roden Buxton and her sister Eglantine Jebb, which did not raise relief funds but concentrated on propaganda for lifting the blockade and rebuilding Europe's economy. That spring Emmeline attended the second Congress of the Women's International League at Zurich, where Jane Addams presided. When the terms of the Treaty, published before the Congress ended, seemed to mock their deliberations, each woman present spontaneously dedicated herself to the promotion of world peace.

In the autumn Pethick visited the United States with a party of left-wing politicians, and was in America when the Senate took its decision to stay out of the League of Nations and thus withdrew from Europe at a time when American influence might have changed the direction of history. He visited Jane Addams in Chicago, became acquainted with Sidney Hillman, the secretary of the American clothing trades union, and met two famous Justices of the Supreme Court, Louis Brandeis and Oliver Wendell Holmes. From this visit have survived letters which he exchanged with Senator Robert La Follette, for whose magazine *La Follette's* he contributed a summary of Europe's financial problems, and with Alice Stone Blackwell, who wrote him from Boston in November that she was 'impressed afresh with the great debt that women owe you'.

The following year he gave evidence before a Parliamentary Select Committee on his proposals for a capital levy, and followed his article for Senator La Follette with a short book commissioned by the Oxford University Press on *Why Prices Rise and Fall*. A pamphlet called 'Unemployment' followed in 1921, and two years later another, 'The Capital Levy', explained how the Labour Party would settle the War Debt by levying a special tax on wealth, starting with fortunes of £5,000.

The year 1920 was also emphasized for him by the death of Olive Schreiner, who had left South Africa in December 1913 to spend her last sad years in England. Pethick, always conscious of his debt to her prophetic vision and her books, visited her frequently and was in constant correspondence with her during that final period. In *Olive Schreiner: Her Friends and Times*, Mrs D. L. Hobman has left a moving account of the difficulties which Olive, mentally and physically ill, encountered in wartime London as a pacifist with a German name. She was obliged to move from lodging to lodging until she found refuge with a tolerant landlady at a house in Porchester Place.

There she remained until she returned, mysteriously and briefly, to South Africa only two months after the arrival in London of her husband, whom she had not seen for six years. They parted with regret, and Olive died suddenly at Wynberg, Cape Province, before the year ended. Pethick's last visits were paid to her in Porchester Place. Towards the end of his own life, as a member of the House of Lords, he arranged with the London County Council for a plaque to be fixed on the house, a small three-storey dwelling where the ground floor was then a fruit shop.

In the autumn of 1920 Pethick and Emmeline decided to simplify their lives by selling their property at Holmwood, where *The Mascot* now faced a motor thoroughfare. They bought a field half way between Shere and Peaslake, which Pethick later included in his title, and there put up a labour-saving cottage, which he designed, with windows commanding the North Downs on the one side and the Leith Hill range on the other. This small house with its five acres of garden and copse became their country home to the end of Emmeline's life. They were equally happy in their new London flat, where the walled garden of Lincoln's Inn provided not only tranquillity, but a morning walk for Pethick until his last weeks in hospital.

In 1921 his persistent search for a hopeful constituency appeared to be rewarded when he was adopted as Labour candidate for South Islington. But the breach between Asquith and Lloyd George during the war had inflicted a lethal blow on the Liberal Party, while the pacifist wartime record of such candidates as Pethick impaired Labour's chances with a still belligerent public. When the contest at South Islington took place in the General Election of 1922, the Conservative was at the top of the poll and Pethick at the bottom.

He did not seek re-adoption, for this dormitory constituency had proved a disappointment. It did not provide the outlet required by his overpowering energy, for it had no halls large enough for public meetings, and most of its male residents were out all day. They returned in the evenings to the upper floors of converted mansions, where visits were not easily made or letters and leaflets delivered.

Apart from general propaganda work for the Labour Party, much of his dynamism now went into the games, especially tennis and billiards, at which he had always excelled. Until he was over seventy he played lunch-hour tennis on the public courts at Lincoln's Inn Fields, where owing to his skill and vigour the admiring spectators named him 'Mr Kruschen' after the well-known 'Keep Fit' advertisement. But games alone, however useful as a temporary cathartic, cannot save an intelligent aspiring human being from mental and spiritual frustration.

During those four years of painful endeavour to enter political life, Pethick, now over fifty, clearly suffered more than he had ever done even in prison. The bitter blow of repeated electoral defeat threatened to overwhelm him, but in the search for reconciliation with himself he had recently found comfort in some Oriental books on the purpose of existence. When, therefore, a telegram invited him to speak at a big London demonstration celebrating the improved opportunities which the 1922 Election had created for the Labour Party as a whole, he characteristically put his personal catastrophe behind him and joined in rejoicing for the successes of others.

A visit to Hungary and Czechoslovakia, where he talked with Foreign Minister Benés, provided a welcome break from national politics; like other sensitive and observant persons, Pethick always found solace in foreign travel which so effectively provides a total change of scenes and experiences. But when he returned, the quest for a constituency had to begin with renewed energy, for Stanley Baldwin, now Prime Minister after Bonar Law's resignation, had made it clear that he intended to go to the country. During the scramble for seats Pethick's name went before several selection committees, but he met with no success until he learned by chance that Alderman Alfred Hill, J.P., the boot and shoe operative who was the Labour M.P. for West Leicester — Ramsay MacDonald's old constituency — was not seeking re-election.

He went straight to Leicester and offered to take the place of the retiring Member. After a long discussion, at which he was not present, the selectors' choice narrowly fell on him, and he faced what appeared to be a better opportunity for political achievement than he had secured up to date. But the next morning he had an unwelcome surprise. He had known the identity of the Conservative candidate, who was already in the field. Now the Liberal candidate was announced, and he learned that his second opponent was to be Winston Churchill, who had probably been drawn to Leicester by Press rumours of Labour dissensions.

Such a rival made full demands upon Pethick's energy and wits, but the status of the contest brought him massive support. Local workers, including many newly enfranchised women voters, inundated his committee rooms, and national speakers offered themselves from all over the country. Special pains went into his Election address, displaying a new photograph on the outside which showed a still handsome man with penetrating blue eyes and an almost bald head. This picture bore a striking resemblance to the contemporary actor, Yul Brynner. He treated the West Leicester electors with respect for their intelligence, and his address explained in detail his views on the state of British trade, the need for a capital levy to redeem the War Debt, the reduction of taxation, the increase of pensions, and the absolute equality of men and women before the law.

To make Pethick's name better known in comparison with Churchill's, a leading Leicester citizen, Mr Harry Peach, wrote some verses with a popular refrain to the tune of 'Tramp, Tramp, Tramp', and Emmeline, whose oratorical powers were now at Pethick's disposal, taught it to groups of local children who roared the refrain into the ears of the opposing candidates:

'Vote, vote, vote for Pethick-Lawrence!
Work, work, work and do your best!
If all workers we enrol, he is sure to head the poll,
And we'll have a Labour man for Leicester West!'

So infectious was this song that it spread to several other constituencies, where it was heard during the next two or three elections.

When the poll was declared on December 6th, Pethick headed it with 13,634 votes to Churchill's 9,236 and the Conservative's 7,696. After this sensational result—one of the first to be announced—Churchill, philosophical as always, congratulated Pethick and generously observed: 'Well, anyhow it's a victory for Free Trade!'

Among the many letters that Pethick received, his favourite came from Lady Parmoor, formerly Marian Ellis, whose husband was a future Lord President of the Council and the father of Sir Stafford Cripps. Coming from a staunch Quaker family, she wrote without dissimulation: 'It was plucky to fight W. Churchill and I am so glad he is out of Parliament'.

Quite apart from any temporary consequences which it had for Churchill, this election was to prove the watershed of Pethick's career. Life, from the standpoint that he most valued, literally began for him at fifty-two, and until he reached the verge of ninety, never brought him any total diminution of rewarding experience.

CHAPTER 13

Parliamentary Apprenticeship

For the rest of his days, in one House or the other, Parliament became the centre of Pethick's existence. 'Truly', he wrote in 1942, 'fate has been kind to me in providing this enlargement of my individual life.' It was to be kinder still, for even then, when he had reached seventy, the main enlargement lay ahead.

Humbly he felt it a great privilege to have become part of Britain's political tradition, and eagerly welcomed each modest indication of his new status. To be chosen to play tennis or billiards for the House, to meet overseas politicians at Parliamentary luncheons, to be invited to an ex-prisoners' dinner for Members of Parliament, brought delight which he hardly knew how to express.

When the new House met in January 1924, he found himself in the midst of political drama. Though the election had left the Conservatives still the largest Party, the Labour Members, now 191, and the Liberals, numbering 158, could jointly outvote them. Mr Asquith, as the Liberal leader, had three possible courses before him. He could, by his backing, keep the Conservatives in power; he could become Prime Minister himself with Conservative support; or he could give Labour its first chance to govern. Believing that a Labour Government would soon become inevitable he chose the last possibility, and when Mr Clynes, in the debate on the Address, moved an Amendment that 'your Majesty's present advisers have not the confidence of the House', Asquith rose to support it.

Pethick had never admired that immovable road-block on the path to woman suffrage, but over thirty years later he recorded in a broadcast his respect for the decision and the masterly choice of words in which Asquith announced it: 'I have been in turn, during these weeks, cajoled, wheedled, almost caressed, taunted, threatened, brow-beaten, and all but blackmailed, to step in as "the saviour of society" '.

Liberals and Labour, voting together, carried the Amendment, and Ramsay MacDonald formed the first Labour Government. More than once, in his autobiography, Pethick applauded MacDonald's qualities as a leader up to 1931; on the whole he thought his judgment sound, his command of words exceptional, and his self-confidence adequate without being excessive.

During the next few months, Pethick characteristically made a thorough study of the House and its ways. Conscientiously he mastered its procedure, realized that more than mere sincerity was needed for an effective speech though conviction was essential, learned the demands on M.P.s by different types of debate, and recognized that a Member's influence within his own party was more important than his individual vote. With Emmeline's help he made his maiden speech on pensions for widowed mothers, and two months later, deciding to specialize on finance and economics in which Parliamentary experts were rare, moved an Amendment to a speech by Walter Guinness, the previous Financial Secretary to the Treasury, who condemned Labour's proposal for a Capital Levy.

When friends occasionally took him to task for the impersonal quality of his speeches he began by resisting this criticism, but at length wisely recognized that his preoccupation with the larger issues of politics tended to impair his service to his local party.

For the rest of his House of Commons career, he therefore set aside certain hours each week when he was available in his constituency to anyone who needed advice. At first he found these seemingly trivial interviews tedious, but soon came to enjoy his ability to solve the personal problems of ordinary men and women. He was well rewarded by this attention to the needs of his constituents; when many Labour M.P.s lost their seats in the notorious Zinovieff Letter Election of 1924, he scraped home again at Leicester West by the narrow majority of 737 votes.

In May 1925, at its sponsor's request, he gave his support to the 'Street Bill' for the Repeal of the Solicitation Laws introduced under the Ten Minutes Rule on behalf of the Association of Moral and Social Hygiene by Lady Astor, the unexpected first woman M.P. to take her seat in the House of Commons. Later that year he went with Emmeline to Prohibition-dominated America, where the annual conference of the Interparliamentary

Union met first in Washington and later in Ottawa. The frank exchange of views that occurred at these conferences between the representatives of different countries, especially the French and Germans, fascinated him by its contrast with the amiable informality of the House of Commons. He attended subsequent sessions in 1927 in Paris and in 1928 at Berlin, where the conference met in the Reichstag. Here Emmeline also had spoken at a peace demonstration four years earlier.

During 1926 the collision between the colliery owners and the miners, a long-range consequence of the restoration of the Gold Standard in May 1925, brought about the General Strike. In this struggle the villain of the piece from Labour's standpoint was Winston Churchill, now Chancellor of the Exchequer, who edited the Government sheet which replaced the daily press. At this time, Pethick records, a form of minor but continuous warfare existed between Churchill and the Labour Members. They found his skilful provocations so exasperating that on one occasion Pethick and a group of other back-benchers organized a 'strike' of their own which involved their ostentatious inattention during his Parliamentary speeches. Since no great orator can survive being conspicuously ignored, this manoeuvre caused him to modify his tactics.

Outside Parliament, Emmeline's own work was outstanding this year both for women and for peace. Soon after the General Strike she attended a great suffrage demonstration in Paris, where women were still voteless, and at home became president of the Women's Freedom League—an office which she was to hold for nine years. As president she was responsible for promoting the Women's Peace Crusade throughout England in the summer of that year.

In October Pethick and Emmeline celebrated their silver wedding by organizing four separate parties for their friends and colleagues in Westminster, Leicester and Canning Town. They followed these functions by a three months' 'silver honeymoon' in India just before the meeting of the Simon Commission.[1] After their return Pethick entertained Pandit Motilal Nehru, the father of the future Indian Prime Minister and of Mrs Pandit, during his visit to Europe in the winter of 1927-8. Like everyone

[1] Pethick's visit to India and its significance is more fully described in Chapter 20.

who met Motilal Nehru, Pethick never forgot the keenly intellectual face and magnificent head which caused a man of average stature to appear large and tall. Three years later Motilal died from an illness precipitated by the hardships of the Civil Disobedience campaign.

A notable acquaintance of 1927 was Mrs Cecil Chesterton, to whom Pethick wrote in December for information about the scheme for Cecil Houses with which she followed her book *In Darkest London*. This inquiry brought him an acquaintance which lasted for thirty years, and led to the chairmanship of Cecil Houses during the experiment that he called 'its most splendid project'—the Old Ladies Club in Wedlake Street. The following spring the Labour Party sent him to South Wales to investigate the distress in the coalfields. In May he was again absorbed in finance, which led him to attack relentlessly a Government bill to restore the control of the issue of paper money to the Bank of England. He regarded this move as a dangerous and reactionary usurpation of Parliament's prerogative.

For him the most memorable event of 1928 was the enfranchisement of women between twenty-one and thirty. Emmeline had been working for this consummation since the end of the war through a small representative committee at the Minerva Club, and it was in reply to a question put by Pethick in the House that Mr Baldwin, as Prime Minister, announced that his Government would introduce this final Franchise Bill. When he proclaimed his intention more widely to a mass meeting at the Queen's Hall on March 8th, he dropped one of the famous 'bricks' of history with the comment: 'I would rather trust a woman's instinct than a man's reason'.

On June 14th, three weeks after the Equal Franchise Bill had passed the House of Commons, Mrs Pankhurst died with Christabel beside her, and was buried on the very day that the Bill received its final reading in the House of Lords. 'Man', says the proverb, 'is immortal till his work is done.' She had lived just long enough to see the final triumph of the movement to which she had given her maturity, her health, and in the last resort her name.

Just after her death Emmeline wrote to Christabel: 'My thoughts have been very much with you since Thursday morning, when I heard that the great leader of the first decades of this century had been called to rest. Your dear Mother was a very wonderful personality, for she combined courage, dignity and charm to the highest degree. And her life has influenced the destiny of the peoples of the world, and there will be no end to the direct and indirect fruits of her labours. Looking back I can see that the Heavenly Powers used even our errors for ultimate good, and though I regret the break that came in our comradeship, I believe the work which we had to do together was accomplished, and that there is in reality nothing to regret, but that all has worked and is working together for good.

'I should like to see you again if you have any time before you leave London. We both feel a warm affection for you and interest in your happiness and in your sorrows.'

At the end of 1928 Mrs Ray Strachey published *The Cause, A Short History of the Women's Movement in Great Britain*, which told the story of the struggle for woman suffrage from the constitutionalist standpoint. She was less than fair in her treatment of the militants, and one page cast unfounded aspersions on the account-keeping of the WSPU.[1] Eventually her book was temporarily withdrawn for the correction of the offending page after a long correspondence between Emmeline, supported by Sylvia Pankhurst, on the one side, and Mrs Strachey on the other. In spite of the polite restraint shown by this correspondence, in which Pethick occasionally joined with a wise avoidance of bitterness, it illustrated the strange but undoubted fact that advocates of a great cause who differ regarding the way in which it should be pursued became more mutually antagonistic than any of them ever feel towards the uncommitted majority who do not support their crusade at all.

Apart from Sylvia Pankhurst's *The Suffragette Movement* (1931), an enlarged version of her earlier book *The Suffragette* published in 1911, *The Cause* was the last assessment of the suffrage movement as such to appear until Roger Fulford published *Votes For Women* in 1957, and also failed to satisfy the militants. More authoritative were the large sections on the Suffragette struggle in the autobiographies of Emmeline and Pethick, respectively published in 1938 and 1943. The conclusions

[1] See note on p. 48 concerning the repercussions of this controversy on the present writer.

of both were more encouraging than those reached in 1924 by Christabel, whose book, *Pressing Problems of the Closing Age*, contained in a chapter on 'Votes For Women' an estimate characteristic of her work at that period: 'Who would exchange the grandest of our old illusions concerning what the votes of women could do, for the assurance of what the Lord Jesus Christ will do in time and eternity?'[1]

Also looking forward into time, if not eternity, the Pethick-Lawrences knew that their work had not been in vain. Admitting that her hopes for peace were still unrealized, Emmeline commented that 'the same cannot be said of the suffrage issue, which has brought results beyond all expectation . . . Not only women but the entire human family have reaped the fruits of women's emancipation.'

Five years later, completing a substantial analysis of the suffrage campaign and its results, Pethick added that he felt 'no shadow of doubt' about the changed status of women. Let those who questioned the value of the women's revolution, he concluded, look at the bored expressions shown in the portraits of nineteenth century middle-class women, and the haggard faces of their working-class contemporaries.

'Then let them go out into the streets and look at the upstanding women of today of all ages and of all classes. They cannot fail to note the contrast.'

[1] Her posthumous book *Unshackled*, edited by Pethick and published in 1959, suggests that the perspective of time had brought a different and more positive assessment of the struggle for the vote.

CHAPTER 14

Junior Minister

When Pethick again won West Leicester at the General Election of 1929 with a triumphant majority of 4,327 votes over his two opponents combined, a friend whispered to him: 'You have now got a safe seat for life'. Two years later, as though to emphasize the vast uncertainties of politics, the economic crisis of 1931 wiped the Labour Government off the map and Pethick with it.

But in May 1929 no misgivings darkened for Labour the halcyon experience of being for the first time the largest party in Parliament, with 287 seats. It was true that without the support of the little Liberal Party, now only fifty-nine in number, Labour could not defeat its opponents since the Conservatives were 260 strong, but this did not at present trouble the new Labour Ministers. Among them was now Pethick himself.

Soon after the Election, on Sunday, June 16th, he and Emmeline spent the weekend at their country cottage, where they usually 'did' for themselves. Pethick, who enjoyed cooking, had just started to prepare a succulent piece of salmon for lunch when the telephone bell rang. Philip Snowden, the new Chancellor, was on the line. 'Mac has asked me to choose my own Financial Secretary', he said. 'I told him I wanted you and he has agreed. So you can go to the Treasury as soon as you like.'

For the moment Pethick's habitual equanimity was lost in excited anticipation. Two hours later he remembered the salmon. It had been boiled to rags.

In his spacious office overlooking the Horse Guards Parade he soon became familiar with the Treasury routine, and often faced a conflict involving ideal long-term financial issues and immediate practical needs. The tug of war between them, he soon realized, had to take place within his own head. Philip Snowden set him two special and difficult tasks; one was to investigate and find means of stopping leakages in the collection of direct taxes, and the other to construct an equitable scheme for the taxation

An afternoon in Surrey

Tennis Champion

of land values. His first decision as a Minister concerned a freehold worth £37,000, which another Ministry wanted to purchase. He finally supported his own officials in rejecting this extravagance as unjustified. His relations with these officials was always happy and he unfeignedly enjoyed his work.

A pleasant small success came to him early in his Treasury career. In Opposition he had advocated that all Government employees should be given at least a week's annual holiday with pay; now he was able to persuade his colleagues that this reform, which affected about 100,000 workers, was reasonable and just. When it came into force he was delighted, though his satisfaction was too soon overshadowed by the financial crisis in America which had followed the Wall Street crash of October 24, 1929.

Early in 1930 Emmeline left England for a visit to South Africa, where a letter from General Smuts invited her to lunch and recalled an evening spent at the House of Commons with Pethick the previous December. She visited him and his wife at their home in Irene, and also met General Hertzog in the Prime Minister's residence, Groote Schoor, built by Cecil Rhodes. While she was in the country the white women of South Africa obtained the vote, and she took part in some of their meetings.

This six months' absence was the longest separation that Pethick and Emmeline experienced during their married life, though the three months demanded by the Cabinet Mission to India in 1946 were to be far more arduous and emotionally exacting. In May, on the twenty-ninth anniversary of their engagement, he sent her a poem describing the flowers in their garden which had bloomed during her absence. It ended with a stanza in which he saluted the wild rose, his favourite flower, with anticipations of her return.

> 'But to the wild, wild rose, the rose of June,
> Mine own full song of ecstacy I'll sing:
> "Thy heavenly colours draw from sun and moon,
> From love's sweet breath thy honeyed fragrance bring,
> Weave texture from th'ethereal air at noon,
> Transcend in loveliness all flowers of Spring,
> For my dear love comes home to me in June".'

On March 6th, while Emmeline was in South Africa, Mr Baldwin unveiled Mrs Pankhurst's statue, the work of A. G. Walker, A.R.A., in Victoria Tower Gardens, Westminster, before a distinguished if somewhat variegated assembly. One conspicuous figure, Dr Ethel Smyth, in the cerise and grey robes of a Doctor of Music, conducted the police band in 'The March of the Women', which she had composed to words by Cicely Hamilton, who was also present. Through the crowd too came Sylvia Pankhurst, carrying her two-year-old son, Richard Marsden Pethick Pankhurst, whose name commemorated the generous friendship which Pethick and Emmeline had always shown her.

Pethick was there and spoke briefly, adding his tribute to those of Mr Baldwin, Flora Drummond, and Lady Rhondda. There were people, he said, who took the facile view that success was always assured by persistent effort and victory only a question of time, but many brave souls who had fought for great causes had gone down to unhonoured graves, their names forgotten and their crusade defeated. This ceremony fulfilled a dual purpose; it did homage to an individual who had faced unflinchingly the weapons of ridicule and physical force, and it chronicled in bronze the triumph of an ideal.

Emmeline later underlined his words in her autobiography.

'I never pass that graceful bronze figure . . . so characteristic of the dignified and yet appealing attitude of Mrs Pankhurst, without a thrill of mingled emotion. . . . I sometimes think that she will live in memory not so much as a great reformer (as, of course, she was), but rather as a great *woman*—worker of magic—creator and destroyer—the Woman whom men all down the ages have dreaded and loved."

The controversial Budget of 1930 brought Pethick back from nostalgic Suffragette recollections to the hard facts of contemporary finance. This Budget, making large changes in taxation which put heavier burdens on the well-to-do, was debated clause by clause till the end of July. Twice the Government survived by only two votes, and at one sitting Pethick remained on the Treasury Bench from the usual 11 o'clock hour of adjournment until 12.30 the following day. Throughout the debate Churchill used every device known to Parliament to hamper its passage into law. When Pethick had to make the final reply at the end of the Third Reading, he trenchantly criticized his former opponent's obstructionism and won the private sympathy of many Conservatives.

The Reparations Clauses of the Versailles Treaty, the restoration by Britain of the Gold Standard in 1925, and the American economic crisis of October 1929, were now having their grim international consequences in widespread unemployment and industrial depression. After the former Liberal leader Sir Donald Maclean had demanded an inquiry into the growth of public indebtedness, the Government set up a Committee under Sir George May which later acquired a sinister reputation owing to its share in the overthrow of Labour and the establishment of the Conservative-dominated National Government which abandoned Free Trade.

Pethick found that he could work amicably with Philip Snowden, a downright but embittered man who suffered constant pain through his lameness. From the beginning he invited Pethick to discuss with him any matter of special interest, and conceded his right to deal directly with Treasury officials whenever he possessed special knowledge.

In the spring of 1931 Snowden was absent from the House for some months owing to the after-effects of a serious operation, and Pethick had to carry a heavy burden of work. For the first time, but by no means the last, he found himself in collaboration with Sir Stafford Cripps, now Solicitor-General, to whom he looked for advice on the details of Snowden's scheme for the taxation of land values. At this period Montagu Norman, the Governor of the Bank of England, called on Pethick at his office and gave him some useful help during the Chancellor's illness, though he did not convert him to his own financial values. He reminded the Financial Secretary that he had been in a junior form at Eton when Pethick was Captain of the Oppidans.

Philip Snowden recovered sufficiently to present the 1931 Budget, which almost coincided with the failure of the Credit Anstalt Bank in Vienna on May 11th. Unemployment, which Pethick diagnosed as the consequence of a fall of prices, was now world-wide; Britain had three million unemployed, Germany six million, and the United States seven million. Against this discouraging background the House debated the Finance Bill, and again the Government benefited from the brilliant support of Sir Stafford Cripps. His able arguments did not reduce the hostility of the Opposition, and Pethick felt later convinced that from this time onwards they determined to destroy the Labour Government. But though the Bank of England had to borrow

£50 million from France and America that August owing to the 'freezing' of British assets in German banks, the Government adjourned for the summer recess without any expectation of immediate political catastrophe.

In Southern France European holidaymakers found that the bleak weather matched the news, and Winifred Holtby, briefly visiting Monte Carlo while rumours of political debâcle began in England, saw Sir Oswald Mosley still playing roulette in the new Casino, and sent an exuberant satirical poem called 'Crisis' to *Time and Tide*:

> 'Is not Roulette
> As important to those who play it
> As Politics?
> And almost as expensive?
> And what the Hell is Reality, anyway,
> Especially in a wet August?'

By the end of that saturating month, Pethick was facing reality in top-level terms. The May Report on national expenditure, published early in August, had drawn an alarming picture of unbalanced budgets with the intention of compelling Parliament to confront uncomfortable economic facts. It thus gave a disastrous but misleading impression, emphasized by sensational headlines both at home and abroad, that the British Budget showed a deficit of £120 million. The French and Americans refused to lend any more money to the Bank of England so long as the British Budget remained, in their view, unbalanced, and, in Pethick's words, 'the Prime Minister was confronted with an ultimatum which he reported to the Cabinet'. This indicated that if the British Government was unable or unwilling to follow the advice of the international bankers, the Bank of England would be unable to meet its liabilities and Britain would have to go off the Gold Standard.

Pethick hurried back to his office to find a request from Victor Gollancz Ltd for a 25,000-word book on the Gold crisis, to be done in three weeks. Energetically he set to work, but before he finished his diagnosis the Gold Standard had been abandoned and he was obliged to rewrite the final chapters. This book, in its clarity, brevity, and masterly grasp of essentials, showed that Pethick would have made a first-class Professor of Economics had not his outlook embraced a wider panorama. It explained, like a subsequent letter which he published in *The Spectator*, that the supposed threat of national bankruptcy was an illusion due to financial ignorance; the country was still basically solvent and the Government could borrow much more money from its own citizens.

Several pencilled drafts have survived of urgent letters, inspired by the suggested cuts in Government expenditure and especially in unemployment pay, which Pethick sent to the responsible Ministers at this period. To Philip Snowden he wrote that sustained thought on the economy scheme had convinced him that it did not penetrate to the root of the trouble.

'A promise to balance the Budget in the future is all very well, but has after all only a psychological effect on our credit, whereas a direct weapon is at hand for dealing with the exchanges if we are prepared to use it. I hold that we should mobilize foreign securities owned by British subjects. I also fail to see why we should not obtain from the Banks and big Houses a voluntary conversion of all their holdings of five per cent War Loan to four per cent as the price of any economies we make at the expense of the workers.'

A note to the Prime Minister maintained that 'the crisis in so far as it is of home origin is not solely—not even mainly—due to Budget policy. The City and the Bank must bear a large share of the responsibility. It will therefore materially influence acceptance of the scheme as a whole if in addition to equality of sacrifice in balancing the Budget it includes taking such other steps as will guarantee that the immediate crisis is in fact met and not merely postponed for a few weeks.' A second note suggested, as he had proposed to the Chancellor, the mobilization of foreign British-owned securities, and offered to wait on the Prime Minister the following day for a further elucidation of financial problems. In conclusion he added: 'You know I also feel most strongly that the lowest paid Civil Servants are being very badly treated'.

When the suggested summons to Downing Street came after the Cabinet had sat for three days and nights in almost continuous session, its consequences for Pethick were quite unexpected. Far from attending for a personal interview, he found himself one of several junior Ministers who simultaneously heard the Prime Minister explain that instead of the anticipated cuts in their salaries, they would now receive no salaries at all. They were, in fact, summarily dismissed. MacDonald announced that he was forming a National Government with Conservative and Liberal colleagues; whatever equalities of sacrifice were involved, he clearly did not propose to be one of the contributors.

As the disconcerted Ministers filed out of his room, MacDonald detained Pethick and suggested that he might like to stay with the new Government. Without hesitation, Pethick declined.

'I had already decided to resign even if the whole Cabinet had agreed to the "cuts" programme,' he wrote later. 'I was certainly not going to support it when they had rejected it.'

CHAPTER 15

After the Blizzard

When the House of Commons was called together on September 8th, the Prime Minister sat opposite most of his former colleagues, now his political opponents. In great perturbation the Parliamentary Labour Party had met, and elected Arthur Henderson as their leader. MacDonald had been their hero; why had he joined their public enemies? Why had he insisted that the salaries of all public servants and even unemployment benefits must be cut in order to keep the pound on the Gold Standard, when his friends in the new Opposition regarded the catastrophe as essentially a banking crisis which had been exploited in order to defeat the Labour Government?

Pethick had no doubt of the answer to this conundrum; he believed that MacDonald and Snowden had been genuinely convinced by the case put up to them by the Bank and the City because they had never troubled to consult the financial experts on their own side. On September 8th, MacDonald's speech to the House emphasized the disasters which would follow the abandonment of the Gold Standard, and on September 14th the new Government introduced an Economy Bill which enforced the threatened cuts. Soon afterwards it had to face an Atlantic Fleet mutiny of the seamen whose wages had been reduced.

In spite of these drastic measures the Gold Standard, which the National Government had been elected to defend, could not be maintained, and on September 21st the Government asked the House for its abrogation in a Bill to be hurried through in one day. Learning that the drain of gold had continued at such a rate that the Bank of England must be relieved of all further obligation to pay it, the Members obliged and passed the Bill. In a broadcast a quarter of a century later, Pethick, never a devotee of the Gold Standard, recorded that no runaway inflation had resulted.

With his usual tolerance he maintained a friendly relationship with MacDonald until his former leader's tragic and solitary end. In April 1956 his broadcast concluded: 'Whatever the verdict of history on his action in 1931, the startling success of the Scottish lad who by his ability won his way to become the first Labour Prime Minister will remain embedded in the annals of British democracy'. Later in 1931, at the end of the abortive Round Table Conference on India, MacDonald privately conveyed to Pethick and Emmeline his regret that he had been prevented from advancing further towards India's independence.

Towards the end of September, when the cuts had been enacted and the Budget balanced, the Prime Minister, now the virtual prisoner of the Conservative Party, found himself under pressure to hold a General Election in order to obtain a 'doctors' mandate' from the country. Although no national necessity existed and the House had over two years of its term to run, he dissolved Parliament on October 7th and fixed polling day for the 27th.

In the midst of the Election Pethick found time to write to *The Spectator* and refute its statement that Britain was 'on the very edge of bankruptcy'. The country's assets, he insisted, vastly exceeded its liabilities. 'You certainly would not call a rich man "on the very edge of bankruptcy" because, in a year when, in common with all his neighbours, he was suffering unprecedented calamities, he did not conform to the strict practice of living within his income.'

The Spectator, in a laconic footnote, merely referred 'Mr Lawrence' to a statement by Philip Snowden, with whose economics he had already publicly parted company. 'If Mr Snowden had consulted him more', Lord Attlee remarked drily in an *Observer* article after Pethick died, 'the debâcle of 1931 might have been avoided.'

As so often during General Elections, a baseless 'scare' arose to influence the bewildered voters; irresponsible rumour, uncontradicted by the Chancellor, suggested that the seceding members of the Labour Cabinet would have drawn upon the Post Office savings of the people to meet unemployment payments. This, Pethick recorded later, was an 'outrageous half-truth'. The moneys needed weekly to reinforce the unemployment fund had always temporarily to be found from increasing balances elsewhere, but the notion that the workers' deposits were thereby insecure was a total mirage.

'Behind all such loans,' he added, 'are the whole resources of the nation, and default is unthinkable.' But the scare had achieved the purpose doubtless intended by Labour's opponents. Of the 288 Labour Members elected in 1929, only fifty-two were returned.

Already out of office, Pethick was now out of Parliament; at West Leicester he went down to massive defeat with all but half a dozen of the former Labour Ministers. To the astonishment of himself and his single Liberal opponent, who had undertaken the contest only for the experience, he found that the unknown Mr Pickering had polled 26,826 votes to his own 12,923. The political prospects which had looked so bright only two years earlier were now quenched in gloom. But he refused, as always, to be dismayed. To an old friend and suffrage organizer, Isabel Seymour, who had sent him a letter of sympathy, he replied on October 28th in courageous words.

'I don't think I am sad but intensely interested to see what is going to turn up next. I have a conviction that the Great Dramatist has an exciting next Act and very likely I shall have a part in it.'

He was right, but he had to wait another fourteen years for the total fulfilment of his prophecy.

The defeat of the Labour Government had far-reaching effects not only at home but abroad; for the time being its policy of racial equality and the advancement of submerged peoples had suffered a setback. In order to investigate these consequences for himself, Pethick spent much of the next four years in widespread travel and contacts with foreign peoples. Following his journey to India in 1926, he was invited to serve in November 1931 on the second Round Table Conference,[1] and in 1932 made one of a small party chosen by the New Fabian Research Bureau to undertake a tour in Soviet Russia.

Between 1932 and 1934, he and Emmeline twice visited Majorca and travelled through Spain, so soon to be devastated by civil war.

In the winter of 1933-4 they spent several weeks in Egypt, went on to Palestine and returned in 1935, and in that year also made a long visit to Turkey, where Emmeline was a delegate to the International Suffrage Congress in Istanbul. Amid the

[1] See Chapter 20.

changes wrought by Ataturk, Pethick was especially impressed by the revolution in the status of Turkish women. Ten years earlier they had still been in purdah, but now they went about the streets in European clothes, took part in conferences, and entered Parliament. The Pethick-Lawrences returned home with a feeling of pride in their own contribution to this now almost world-wide revolution.

An expedition to Russia was still adventurous in 1932, and the New Fabian Research Bureau mapped out the work of each traveller in advance. The whole group numbered twelve and, in addition to Pethick, included Hugh Dalton, Margaret Cole, Rudolph Messel, and Gilbert and Naomi Mitchison. The financial system of the USSR was allocated to Pethick as his subject, and like his companions he spent some months in preparing himself before starting out.

In Russia he visited Leningrad, where he shared a room at the Oktober Hotel with Hugh Dalton; Moscow; Nijni Novgorod (now Gorki); Stalingrad; Rostov-on-Don; and Kiev. A luncheon with the British Minister revealed to him that most of the Diplomatic Corps lived in splendid isolation. Thirty years later an eye-witness[1] in the Indian Embassy at Moscow showed that the dubious status of foreign diplomats in Russia had made little advance by 1948.

Pethick's search for financial information brought him personal interviews with Grinko, the Finance Commissar; Arkus, the Vice-President of Gosbank (the Russian equivalent of the Bank of England); Smilga, the acting head of the Planning schemes; and Ossinsky, chief of the Statistical Department. In Leningrad the principal finance officer, Roslyakov, explained to him the financial system of the city and province which were under his control. On his return Pethick contributed the chapter on finance to *Twelve Studies in Soviet Russia*, published in 1933 by Gollancz for the New Fabian Research Bureau.

He also compiled a private typescript on his impressions for circulation to interested friends. One recipient was another recent traveller to Russia, Mrs Mary Stocks, to whom he confessed that his strenuous tour had cost him twelve pounds in weight. She replied cheerfully that if some members of her own party had shed twelve pounds, they would have been delighted.

[1] Nayantara Sahgal: *From Fear Set Free*. Gollancz, 1962.

In his memorandum he wrote that, though he had been warned that he would be shown only what the Government wanted him to see, and was indeed handicapped by dependence on Intourist owing to his ignorance of the language and to the confusing variations in prices, he found that whenever he knew his objectives clearly, facilities were given him. He added that it would have been useless to seek enlightenment on the censorship, the secret police, and the summary justice meted out to political offenders, though practices repugnant to British standards could be studied in unofficial ways. But he warned the inquirer that 'he must not think such practices are peculiar to Communists. He will find their counterpart in most countries east of Vienna.'

Like the rest of the party he had little contact with the peasant population, but could not imagine, he wrote, 'that the stoutest champion of the Soviet Government would claim that the peasants have been handled with faultless wisdom'. At the top he found none of the inefficiency often reported as characteristic; the financiers whom he interviewed impressed him as exceptionally able specialists. Hence he saw no likelihood of the Communist rule being overthrown either from within or from without; the Nazi invasion of Russia still lay nine years ahead. He concluded: 'If I may hazard a prophecy I would say that the present régime will continue and will carry Russia a long way on the path of industrialization. How far it will embody the full principles of Communism or conform to the ideals envisaged in 1917 is another story.'

From his contacts with Soviet financiers Pethick returned to his usual concentration on the economics of the West. In August 1932 he wrote to Arthur Henderson, whose health had been undermined by his onerous work in Geneva, to express his misgivings about the current trade negotiations in Ottawa. Though Pethick was no longer a prospective Parliamentary candidate, his official leader arranged for him to address the forthcoming Labour Party Conference in Leicester. Before going he joined the new Socialist League out of respect for Sir Stafford Cripps, and sent him a long financial memorandum on the strength of which they dined together at Leicester's Grand Hotel.

A letter of November 1st expressed his disagreement with Sir Stafford's belief that a Socialist State must nationalize the Joint

Stock Banks; 'I wish', he added, 'you would seriously reopen your mind on this issue'. The following day Sir Stafford replied with a good-humoured rebuke: he hoped he would always keep an open mind, capable of being convinced in these matters, but Pethick must have an open mind too. Their correspondence and meetings continued at intervals, and eventually bore rich fruit in their historic association on the Cabinet Mission to India.

Pethick never lost sight of the younger politicians whose future lay in one and sometimes in both Houses of Parliament. A note from Dr Edith Summerskill thanked him on November 14, 1932 for material on his Russian visit, and laid the foundations of a valued friendship which endured for the rest of his life. A pencilled note on the top of her letter instructed his secretaries: 'Put her on the special list'. Two years later he was congratulating her on a near-success in a Putney by-election, and soon afterwards she became his colleague in the House of Commons.

International events now diverted his mind even from finance; regarding the departure of the United States from the Gold Standard in the winter of 1932-3 he wrote in *Fate Has Been Kind*: 'This catastrophic event was naturally of supreme interest to me', and noted that American unemployed then numbered twelve millions. Hitler's accession to power in the spring of 1933 eventually caused him to revise his nineteenth-century philosophy of continuous progress, and the physical cruelties reported from the Reich led him to gather together an all-party group of well-known men and women which called itself the Dimitroff Committee. It did not last long, but helped to secure the release of one or two outstanding Nazi victims, including Dimitroff himself. Partly owing to its intervention, Dimitroff was able to leave Germany and live in Russia.

Pethick dealt with these gathering clouds over Europe in the numerous addresses which he gave for the Labour Party during his absence from Parliament. His humble readiness to talk to any audience, however small, remained characteristic of him to the last; several letters to and from Laurence Housman in 1934 concerned an engagement to open a Labour Party bazaar in the Somerset village of Street where Laurence lived. By the time he went there, Pethick was no longer a free-lance; his selection for a new constituency had given him once more the status of a prospective Parliamentary candidate.

CHAPTER 16

Home to Edinburgh

Soon after his defeat at West Leicester, Pethick had been concerned to find a means of returning to Parliament. In the autumn of 1933, Transport House directed him to the headquarters of the East Edinburgh Labour Party.

By present-day standards, with their emphasis on youth rather than experience, he might have been thought too old at sixty-two to attract a new constituency. But his record as a Socialist ex-Minister stood high; in 1931 he had staunchly demanded equality of sacrifice. Without waiting to see what his colleagues were going to do, he had given up his own ministerial office rather than endorse economies at the workers' expense. Scottish Socialists were well able to appreciate the cost of convictions sustained in the face of heavy financial loss, and he went back to London already sure of selection by the Edinburgh committee.

In the General Election of November 14, 1935, the Government stayed in power with another large majority, but 154 Labour Members got back to the House and Pethick was one of them. Owing to the enthusiasm of the local party and the help of Emmeline and a former Suffragette, Joan Cruichshank, he won the seat with a majority of 1,112 votes. Shortly afterwards he was elected to the Labour Party Executive, and thenceforward hardly ever missed its meetings.

It was as M.P. for East Edinburgh that he took part in the tense international crises of the nineteen-thirties. Long before the Election the heralds of these crises had begun to create a rift in the Labour Party between its pacifist members and the supporters of collective security. Like many others who had hoped to ride both horses at once, Pethick found that Japan's invasion of Manchuria, Hitler's totalitarian rule in Germany, and Mussolini's antics in Italy with Abyssinia as their destined victim, compelled him to make a choice.

With great reluctance he came down on the side of collective security, though when war was imminent he actively supported provisions to safeguard the position of conscientious objectors. When the League of Nations Union organized the Peace Ballot in the summer of 1934, he answered 'Yes' to the questions involving support for the League of Nations, though some of his friends, such as George Lansbury, voted otherwise. In after years this Ballot came to be rated, strangely enough, as a pacifist effort, and was even attributed to the Peace Pledge Union. Actually the vote showed overwhelming support for collective security, and had no connection with pacifism whatsoever. On September 11, 1935 the Government, which had characteristically wavered in its support of the League, felt able owing to the result of the Peace Ballot to make a positive pronouncement endorsing the Covenant.

In December 1935, when Pethick was back in the House, Parliament debated the infamous 'deal' between Sir Samuel Hoare and the French Minister Pierre Laval to partition Abyssinia for Mussolini's benefit which produced one of David Low's most famous cartoons of Stanley Baldwin, 'You know you can trust me'. Pethick was among those Members who indignantly criticized this camouflage 'agreement'. A week later he wrote to Laurence Housman: 'We are in a horrible dilemma. The Government's actions have landed us in a mess from which there is practically no honourable escape.'

Sir Samuel Hoare resigned and his place was taken by Anthony Eden, himself to resign in 1938 when Neville Chamberlain, as Prime Minister, proposed a new 'deal' with Mussolini. During the Abyssinian War, which Mussolini eventually won in May 1936, Pethick asked himself in deep perturbation why even a reactionary Conservative Government should have behaved as it did. He concluded that its complacent acquiescence in the nefarious manoeuvres of current dictators sprang from a lack of belief in League principles. Had he thought further he might have added that the main principle behind the League was that of enlightened expediency, which stops a long way short of spiritual demands upon courage and self-sacrifice.

By now Pethick was widely recognized as the Opposition's financial spokesman. In that capacity he supported Ellen Wilkinson who in April 1936 introduced a motion in favour of giving the same scales of pay to women as to men in the 'common' classes of the Civil Service where their work is interchangeable. The Government was narrowly defeated on this motion, but the Prime Minister caused the decision to be reversed on a vote of confidence.

In January 1936 the death of George V had led to Pethick's appointment to the Select Committee on the Civil List which advised Parliament regarding financial provision for the new reign. After the abdication of Edward VIII and the accession of George VI he served again on this Committee, and at the King's coronation became a member of the Privy Council. In the summer of 1937, he visited Paris with a group of M.P.s who went as guests of the French Chamber. By that time the Spanish Civil War, so soon to be recognized as the curtain-raiser to a greater tragedy, was spreading an anxiety across Western Europe which the non-intervention policy of Neville Chamberlain, who had replaced Mr Baldwin after the Coronation, did nothing to alleviate. Pethick returned from Paris greatly troubled by the sympathy he had found there for Hitler and Mussolini.

The following summer he was to receive the sad reminder of an older and better Germany when a letter came from Mrs Anton Lang reporting the death of her husband, who had played the part of Christ in the Passion Play of 1910 when Pethick sent the leading militants to Oberammergau during the Suffragette Truce.

On April 27, 1938, six weeks after Hitler invaded Austria, he spoke in the House of Commons during the Budget debate and put a question to the Government: 'Where are you going? Where are you leading your country and your countrymen at the present time; where are you leading Europe and the world? . . . To us it seems that you are asking sacrifices not for the things for which unity could be obtained, but for the triumph of aggression, for the suppression of democracy, for the planting of the swastika in Central Europe and in the Pyrenees.'

At this hardly auspicious moment of history, Emmeline's book *My Part in a Changing World* appeared. Though few books published during that time of tension encountered good fortune, she received a number of appreciative letters and criticisms, of which her favourite was written by Mary Stocks for the *Manchester Guardian*. In May 1938 Pethick sent to his old friend Judge Krause of South Africa a comment on both current politics and the book. 'The world seems to be in a terrible mess and one does not know what any day may bring forth. We who have lived through the exciting times of the last sixty years can only hand on the torch of liberal ideas, to the best of our ability undimmed, to the succeeding generation. . . . My wife has had a great success with her book, with fifty or sixty good reviews to her credit.'

That autumn the world's 'Slough of Despond' became deeper through the Munich crisis. Late in the evening of September 12, 1938, Pethick wrote Emmeline a long letter profoundly analyzing the meaning of the Cross which came close to the Christian pacifist interpretation that she endorsed:

'My thoughts have wandered further and deeper even than this tremendous drama. As you know, I see Hitler as an incarnation of Karma—inevitable, ruthless, and in a sense God-sent and God-directed. Yet he is man and those who carry out his will are men and in their brutal bestial acts he and they are committing deadly sin and calling forth an inescapable karma in their turn.

'Here is in fact the dilemma which confronted the Greek poets when they described the tragedy of Orestes. The gods decree retribution (or in Indian philosophy, karma arises). As retribution (or karma) takes material shape, its agent is human act, in a sense God-directed, yet that act is sin and attracts retribution in its turn. The question arises "Is this the working out of some drama ordained by the gods to test some law of life?" If so the son of man (by that I mean mankind in its entirety) would seem in spite of his divine lineage to be in very truth for ever on the Cross.

'But the great religions supply a different answer. Hinduism has the doctrine of what I think they call "Ahimsa" (roughly harmlessness), Christ said "overcome evil with good", Buddha spoke of enlightenment, which covered nearly the same idea.

'Christ himself died on the Cross in justification of his faith. Buddha went through untold trials before enlightenment came. In Wagner's "Ring" Brunhilda's final sacrifice embodies the same essential conception.

'What I understand to be the real meaning of the much misunderstood doctrine of the Christian atonement is that only by the acceptance of the whole basis of Christ's life and death and the spiritual reception of it into one's own personality can the sequence of sin and incarnated retribution (which is again sin) be broken. And forgiveness of sins is not a breach in the law of karma but the substitution of a sublimated karma for a human revenge, and at the same time a recognition of Buddha's truth that the heart of things is not evil, that the wheel of cause and effect can be etherealized in a Self which is selfless.

'Until man grasps this truth with all his being the son of man is indeed upon the Cross.

'We in our human compassion long passionately that in our day and in our generation the tale of suffering may be ended. We desire in particular that war may cease now and forever, and that in order that this may be so the lesson may have been or may be even now learnt before another frightful tragedy overtakes us.

'It is well indeed that we strive for this, for it is part of the great law that only by such striving on our part and others will enlightenment come to us and to all.

'But *"über unserer kraft"* and above and beyond our powers of prophecy are the workings of the law itself and the days when it will be fulfilled. I think Christ (whose assurance always fills me with astonishment) said something to the effect that "of this day knoweth no man not even the Son but only the Father".

'It may be that the wheel has to go round again and the tyre rise and fall—how often? We cannot tell. But in faith, which sometimes falters but is sustained by the reading of the scroll of the past, we see in front of us the ennoblement of life, with sin and evil and death swallowed up in victory.'

To sustain this faith in man's final conquest of evil required all Pethick's courage and optimism when in March 1939 the Spanish War ended in victory for Franco's forces and, almost simultaneously, German troops occupied Prague. Those who knew most shared his perturbation; among them was Sir Stafford Cripps, who in January 1939 had vainly tried to persuade the Labour Party to adopt a Memorandum designed to prevent the capture of the British Youth Movement by the reactionary influences sweeping the world. Within a few weeks Neville Chamberlain's guarantee to support Poland in the event of unprovoked aggression had clearly put war on the horizon.

In mid-August Emmeline had planned to open an International House for the World Women's Party in Geneva, and Pethick arranged to accompany her. After consulting Arthur

H

Greenwood, temporary leader of the Opposition owing to Attlee's absence through illness, they decided to risk the chance of being caught by the oncoming war. The risk was real, for the Nazi-Soviet Pact was signed on the day after their return.

As he attended the brilliant ceremony in Geneva, Pethick knew that he and Emmeline were sharing their last picture of the inter-war Europe which had done so much to rebuild itself since 1918, but had failed to redeem the costly tragedy of Versailles. Long ago he had foreseen the consequences of that titanic error, and the bill had now to be paid.

CHAPTER 17

The Six Years' War

When the Second World War began on September 3, 1939, Pethick felt reluctantly obliged, as he had long foreseen, to support it. Of the First War he had written in the Preface to his autobiography: 'I favoured appeasement, but it was appeasement of the right people at the right time'. In the Second he accepted the current view of the Left that such tyrants as Hitler and Mussolini were outside the range of reconciliation. 'An attempt to appease such men was in my opinion merely throwing our comrades to the wolves, in the fatuous belief that it would save our own skins.'

In March 1940 a letter to Isabel Seymour embodied this attitude. 'Personally I don't see any facile solution of the problem how to stop Hitler without forceful resistance, and with very great heart-searching I found myself compelled to support the war . . . Hitler is a kind of embodied Karma . . . demonstrating on a gigantic scale that brute violence fails in the long run. . . . If he were not to fail all my experience of life and all my interpretation of history as I know and understand it is a delusion and a lie.'

He states in his autobiography that on the afternoon of September 3rd, after the House had carried through a number of emergency measures, he telephoned his wife at Peaslake and 'found her reactions identical with my own'. Only eighteen months earlier Emmeline had written in *My Part in a Changing World*: 'When confronted with injustice and cruelty my instinct is a militant one, I want to challenge evil and fight it with all the powers of mind and body, and yet I recognize the truth that the power of love is alone strong enough to solve all problems and remove all oppressions'.

But in 1941 she was to write to Sybil Morrison of The Peace Pledge Union, who had asked her for a contribution to *Peace News*, the pacifist weekly newspaper: 'Alas! an article from me just now, if I wrote quite honestly, would not be acceptable. Since this terrible business of war fell upon us, I have been driven to re-examine the foundations of our faith . . . I am appalled by this war as I should be appalled by the Day of Judgment. But we cannot stay its execution by crying "Peace"; only by organized repentance and deep searchings of heart.'

By October Pethick and Isabel Seymour were discussing the unnecessary darkness of blacked-out railway carriages, about which he put a question to the Minister of Transport, and in March they were exchanging views on the character of modern conscientious objectors, whom he described as 'a great mixture. Some are deep spiritual souls. Some are the kind of people who are never happy unless they are suffering for their fellows. Some are mere shirkers. But whoever they are they are never improved by being shouted at and asked silly questions.'

When pacifism seemed to Pethick to spring from genuine conviction, his response was patient and tolerant. In February 1941 a writer friend sent him a copy of her new book which approached the suffering caused by the war from a Christian pacifist standpoint. In acknowledging the gift he wrote: 'I never read anything of yours without wanting to have a long talk with you about it. . . . Your reaction to the evils of the day is considerably different from my own. I think we both feel very passionately and deeply about them, but in your case they are more in the foreground of your mind. This is partly a matter of temperament and partly a matter of function. It is your business as a writer to make people feel through your own feeling and power of expression. It is my business as a politician to help to remedy the evils, and I find that to allow my entrails to be lacerated by the distress of others is to weaken and not to augment my power to help.'

Not wholly uncritically she replied: 'I think that one of a writer's chief functions is to make people feel things so acutely as to demand their remedy, but I quite agree that the politician who remedies them must be less passionate or he will not achieve a balanced result. All the same, I feel that you must have felt passionately about woman suffrage to be ready to pay all that it cost you.'

Before this exchange of opinions, England had lived through the period of 'phoney war' in which Pethick's Edinburgh constituents were the first civilians to come under fire. To help them with the social problems arising from the war he set up for them a private Advice Bureau which was already functioning when Norway, Denmark, Holland, Belgium and France were invaded with catastrophic speed. Before the end of May the picturesque statesman whom he defeated at Leicester had become Pethick's political leader. To begin with, he noted in *Fate Has Been Kind*, the cheers for Churchill in the House of Commons came chiefly from the Labour benches.

In the last week of May, Pethick went unobtrusively to the Labour Party Conference at Bournemouth, where under an incongruously cloudless sky Labour's leading personalities were awaiting their political fate beneath gaily-striped sun umbrellas, and Hugh Dalton paced like a caged panther between the lounges of the Highcliffe Hotel until he received his own summons to join the National Government. Thenceforward party strife was suspended for five years, but for the conduct of Parliamentary business a number of Members sat on the Opposition benches.

On his way to Bournemouth Pethick had realized that the technical leader of this 'Opposition' would become the spokesman for the non-official Members of the House of Commons, and before the conference ended he put forward the name of his friend Lees-Smith as the right man for this position. After Lees-Smith was chosen, Pethick became his unofficial deputy and in that capacity put forward some active measures, such as the removal of the Household Means Test and important alterations in the Purchase Tax and War Damage Bill.

He was also appointed Chairman of the Public Accounts Committee, which gave him the obligation of examining the permanent heads of all the Ministries regarding their administration of their offices. When Lees-Smith succumbed to influenza in November 1941, Pethick became the virtual Leader of the Opposition until Arthur Greenwood left the Cabinet and resumed his old post. The party then created the office of vice-chairman and summoned Pethick to fill it.

When the Battle of Britain began in the summer of 1940, it caused the Pethick-Lawrences, like many other Londoners, to change their mode of living. An early 'Molotov breadbasket' brought down a few incendiary bombs on their Surrey garden, and Pethick helped the gardener to put them out. In December

1940 he described to Isabel Seymour another visitation on their London home. 'Lincoln's Inn and neighbourhood got it pretty warmly while special attention was being paid to Central London. 11 and 12 Old Square had no direct hits, but nearly all the windows on the North side were blown in. I slept in a shelter in the Inn some of the bad nights.'

From that date until 1945 he divided his time between London and Peaslake, where he spent weekends, and almost ceased to use his flat in Lincoln's Inn though throughout the war his secretaries took care of it and continued to carry papers to his private office in No. 12. On the days when the House was sitting he slept at the home of friends in Guildford, whence the train journey was easier, and made full use of his office in the House of Commons. After the Chamber was destroyed in May 1941, he worked mainly at Church House, where the Members sat secretly. His secretaries, Esther Knowles and Gladys Groom, visited him regularly; though one lived at Harrow and the other at Highbury, they hardly missed a day in reaching his office in spite of the bombing of railway junctions. This sometimes meant two-hour journeys each way through continuous raids.

Although his habitual equanimity usually appeared unshaken, Pethick's wartime life in the House of Commons was not without its painful incidents. In his biography of Aneurin Bevan, Michael Foot describes two episodes which suggest that a comprehensible antipathy existed between Pethick and Bevan, for which Bevan cannot perhaps be held exclusively responsible. The adjective 'harmless' applied to Pethick by Foot was not always apt. In spite of his gentleness, Pethick was capable of making scathing remarks in a quiet voice calculated to infuriate the flamboyant type of politician.

The first of these episodes, in November 1940, centred round the Bill to abolish the Household Means Test which Pethick had initiated. In spite of a promise to the contrary by the Prime Minister, this was found when brought before the House and examined still to contain elements of the old family test. Though a decision had been made at the party meeting to support the measure without qualification, several Labour Members, including Bevan, put down an Amendment to the Second Reading of the Bill, and stated that they would vote for their own Amendment but not against the Bill as a whole.

Pethick, the front-bench Labour Party spokesman, attacked the Members who had signed the Amendment, and accused them with biting severity of posing as champions of the oppressed while they played politics and tried to sabotage an agreed solution. 'They have allowed themselves', he said, 'to be made tools by others less ingenuous than themselves.' The reference was clearly to Bevan, who thereupon furiously described Pethick's speech as 'hysterical and splenetic'. After nineteen Labour Members had voted for the Amendment the argument was transferred to the Committee Room, where it continued for three hours. Eventually the rebels emerged unscathed, but Bevan's hostility to Pethick was not thereby diminished.

Four years later, a debate in which Anthony Eden was explaining why the British Government could not approve the appointment of Count Sforza as Italian Foreign Secretary brought an acid interruption from Pethick to a speech by Bevan. Aneurin had intervened to protest that the Italian Government did not contain any member 'of any of the parties in Italy who share our views', whereupon Pethick commented coldly: 'Share *your* views, you mean'. Bevan made no attempt to disguise his rage, and created turmoil with the violent comment: 'That is just the answer I might have expected from the crusted old Tory who still remains a member of this party'.[1]

Politicians on the extreme Left have a natural reluctance to credit those nearer the Centre with successful revolutionary achievements. Clearly Bevan regarded, or said he regarded, the unrepentant Etonian as an Establishment figure—an illusion to which Pethick's orthodox and prematurely venerable appearance contributed. Yet few people actually did more to undermine the Establishment in two of the fortresses where it was most strongly entrenched — the denial of equal rights to women, and the refusal of independence to India.

Now mentally far from these agitations, Emmeline, who at seventy-three was increasingly handicapped by deafness, made her home at Fourways throughout the war; in November 1940 she wrote to an old friend, Mary Mazzoletti, that 'there seemed no work for me to do in London'. Her letter expressed a sadness that was to deepen in the next fourteen years as old age, complicated

---

[1] For a fuller account of these incidents, see Michael Foot, *Aneurin Bevan*, Vol. I, pp. 327-9 and 494-5.

by a serious accident, set her increasingly apart from the active life that she had loved. Some solace came from occasional articles in magazines, but apart from her autobiography she was not a writer; the platform and the hustings were her natural element. She was not alone for Mary Neal, whose Littlehampton home was constantly threatened by bombs, came to live with her at Fourways, and Pethick brought her comfort during the 'bucolic weekends' in which he did the shopping, helped with the cooking, bottled fruit, made gooseberry jam, and undertook many other domestic duties which he described as 'good for the body and satisfying to the soul'.

During a visit to Fourways, at the time when only five-inch baths were officially permitted, his cousin George Fox took a photograph of him helping to fill the pond, which had sunk very low, with water from the roof. Beneath the picture he wrote, more prophetically than he knew, 'He that is faithful over little shall be made faithful over much'.

Emmeline's chief solace came always from him; on May 12, 1942 (probably the anniversary of his first proposal to her) she wrote a loving letter to her 'mate and friend and comrade for forty-one years' recalling that first 12th of May. 'The scene is very clearly before me in memory—Regent Park and the chestnut tree in new leaf and all the world in spring as it is today. And now before the day comes with its many distractions I turn back the pages and review the story of our life together—part of the part which never dies, but comes to new life as the seasons in their life cycles go round.'

Though Pethick was now as busy and potentially as harassed as he had ever been, he never failed to respond to the appeals for assistance of many kinds which numerous acquaintances addressed to him, or forgot letters of sympathy or congratulation. Just before the war broke out he had given his vote to help the barrister, Helena Normanton, in her endeavour to obtain a Bar Council election. In 1940 he sent congratulations to Professor G. M. Trevelyan on his appointment as Master of Trinity, his own old College, and the following year to the Speaker, Colonel Clifton-Brown, on his conduct of the Chair. A letter to Leonard Woolf in 1941 followed the death of his wife Virginia; a year later he was sympathizing with Decima Moore-Guggisberg on the winding-up of her Overseas Leave Club after the German occupation of Paris, and reassuring the Association of Moral and Social Hygiene, which had feared the establishment of official brothels. Several letters to the actress Lena Ashwell followed a report which she sent him of the unequal treatment of officers and men on troop ships; he referred this problem to Arthur Henderson Jnr. at the War Office, and also corresponded with him on war-time finance.

One young woman, who ultimately succeeded in entering public life, so persistently wrote to him and sent him her articles in the quest for the kind of war work she wanted, that his patience (though never his courtesy) became exhausted.

'Dear Miss X', he wrote in 1940, 'I am afraid I am not in touch with any work opening that would be suitable for you, but I should say that anyone with your drive ought not to be long in finding a task suitable for your energy at the present time.'

Another letter acknowledging another article in 1943 reminded his one-track-minded correspondent that he himself had just published a book (his autobiography). This long, revealing and often lively self-portrait, written at Fourways and sometimes at Guildford in the intervals of official work, suffered from its war-time format which unfairly gave to all long books an impression of overcrowding. It brought him many favourable reviews and appreciative letters; amongst those he valued most were a friendly word of commendation from Professor G. M. Trevelyan, and a loving message from Emmeline: 'I am specially moved by the dedication of the book to me. It is a great honour and above all a great happiness to be told that I have been a constant inspiration to you.'

One book which deeply interested him at this time was Aldous Huxley's *Grey Eminence*; it moved him to write the author a long letter, and in another to commend it to Isabel Seymour. At the same time he sent her a fragment of his own philosophy; 'I . . . regard it as an impertinence not merely to express but even to think any criticism of another person's choice of spiritual approach. I think you are absolutely right that there are two basic yearnings of the human heart. The first is the urge for individual freedom. The second is the need for comfort and consolation which is only satisfied through union with other beings, human, subhuman and superhuman.'

In February 1944 the Speaker invited him to attend a Conference on Electoral Reform, and in 1945, when expressing his regret that Pethick owing to his peerage would be leaving the House of Commons, wrote warmly of the part he had played at this conference in maintaining an atmosphere of give-and-take. By 1944 Pethick's mind was increasingly concentrated on the coming peace terms, whatever they might be. In February he proposed that a member of the War Cabinet should make a statement to the German people; at the suggestion of Anthony Eden, who felt that a Cabinet pronouncement would be undesirable, he incorporated his ideas in a speech made during a debate on the war situation. In September and December he spoke again in the House on the post-war treatment of Germany.

After the war in Europe had ended and the General Election of July 1945 took him home to East Edinburgh where he had again been selected as Labour candidate, he explained quite simply to the electors his war-time choices and his vision of Britain's future.

'I supported the Labour Party in its decision to join the Coalition Government in 1940 because if the war against Nazi tyranny had been lost everything was lost. But now that this danger is over and plans for the new world are taking shape it is right that the people should decide what those plans should be. The issue is of supreme importance. You have to choose whether we shall go back to the old world in which humiliating class distinctions prevailed or enter into a new world in which the needs of the ordinary man and woman come first.'

All over the country, ordinary men and women listened to the expression of similar views by Labour candidates. On July 12th their votes recorded their own views, but they had to wait two weeks for their decision to be announced so that the young troops and women war workers scattered across the world could record their opinions too. Over city and village, town and countryside, during the latter part of July brooded one basic question; the question to which the answer, so long postponed, would determine Britain's political future.

CHAPTER 18

The Day the War Ended

On July 26, 1945, the evening newspapers appeared with banner headlines: 'Socialists In. Britain Swings to the Left and the Tory Government goes out in a landslide.' More than 200 seats had been won, and Labour had a majority of 199 over all its opponents. By the end of the month Clement Attlee was established as Prime Minister, and Pethick knew that he had been re-elected for East Edinburgh with the large majority of 6,529 votes.

He was glad to be returned for his old constituency but within a few days he learned that he was not to remain there, for the new Prime Minister had asked him to go to the House of Lords as Secretary of State for India and for Burma, with a seat in the Cabinet. Like Sir Stafford Cripps he had been one of the few Parliamentary candidates who had referred to India in his Election address.

'India', he had written, 'must attain, at the earliest possible date, full self-government in friendly association with Britain and the Dominions.'

Now he had become the chosen instrument for implementing this policy. His selection for the India Office was less incongruous than the Speaker had supposed, for he had experienced a long series of contacts with India[1] which, with the single exception of Sir Stafford's, were unique among the members of the new Cabinet. India was the largest and most intransigent problem on the immediate horizon, and the right choice of a Secretary of State was more important than the series of long-range financial problems which had awaited the end of the war.

After much tribulation, the programme which Pethick had been appointed to carry out would lead to two great nations becoming the first non-white members of the British Commonwealth. The path to that future was at present uncertain for Japan still held out, but on August 6th the atomic bomb, falling

[1] See Part III.

on Hiroshima, inaugurated the nuclear age in which the survival of man himself would become problematic. Like others in whose hands great destinies have been placed, Pethick waited on events beyond his control, and endeavoured to acclimatize himself to his new status and coming responsibilities.

As Secretary of State he had been provided with a car and two detectives; one or the other was expected to escort him through the streets wherever he went. On the night of August 14th he had dismissed his car and been seen safely into his Lincoln's Inn flat about 10 p.m.

At 10.15 his telephone bell rang. Would he come at once to Downing Street for an urgent Cabinet meeting? He had now no car and no detective and the streets were still dimly lit, but he groped his way to the Strand and found a late bus going down Whitehall. Downing Street was deserted, but he and his colleagues arrived one by one and were admitted to No. 10.

When they had assembled in the Cabinet room, they learned that the Japanese had offered complete surrender provided only that they might be allowed to retain their Emperor; otherwise, they pointed out, there was no person whom the troops would obey when told to lay down their arms. The question before the British Cabinet was whether this offer was consistent with the 'unconditional surrender' that the Allies, in the mood of wartime intolerance which was already passing, had laid down as essential for the conclusion of hostilities.

'We decided that it was,' Pethick recorded long afterwards.[1] 'The BBC were told to stand by. Attlee in a broadcast at midnight told the people of Britain and of the world that the great war was at an end. I came out into the darkness of Downing Street. Not a soul was there except two policemen. I walked home in the silence.'

[1] In a BBC broadcast entitled 'I Remember' (recorded April 27, 1956).

The Memoirs of Harry S. Truman, Vol. I, *Year of Decisions* (Hodder & Stoughton, 1955), record that the historic announcement was made simultaneously in the four Allied capitals, Washington, London, Moscow and Chungking, at 7 p.m. Washington time.

PART III

The Statesman

CHAPTER 19

The Indian Story, 1900–1945

The General Election of 1945, which for the first time gave Labour a clear majority over all other parties, had a similar significance for India to that of the General Election of 1906 for the South African Republics. But its consequences were to represent a far more positive contribution to history owing to the fortunate chance that a really great statesman, Jawaharlal Nehru, was at the helm in India when independence came.

Fifty years before Pethick became Secretary of State, even the most sanguine prophet could not have foreseen the initiative taken by the Attlee Government. British strategy was largely dictated by the ownership of India, with its huge population of nearly 300 millions under direct British rule and 600 princely states showing a great variety of dimensions and cultures. Some latent evidences of nationalist sentiment emerged after the Mutiny of 1857, but these had no real substance before the first decade of the twentieth century. The Indian National Congress, founded in Bombay in 1885, boasted a modest total of ninety members who were mostly lawyers, journalists and teachers. A link between them was provided by the new network of railways, completed by 1900, which contributed to the nascent sense of unity.

Significant intellectual contacts with the West began after Madame Blavatsky had founded the Western-inspired Theosophical Society in 1875, further interpreted by Annie Besant from her headquarters at Adjar, Madras. In 1893 Vivekananda, a disciple of Ramkrishna Paramhansa, attended the World Congress of Religions at Chicago and thus gave Hinduism a new meaning for the Western world. Indian nationalism developed a link with English liberalism from 1880 to 1884 during Gladstone's Premiership, which saw the beginning of Indian urban and rural self-government.

Between 1885 and 1906, British politics were in the hands of

Conservative administrations which tended to regard nationalist sentiments in imperial territories as a form of sedition. Under their auspices Lord Curzon became Viceroy of India for seven years from 1898. Curzon, though vain, arrogant and ambitious, was also immensely industrious; his consciousness of the responsibilities of trusteeship, combined with his reverence for India's past, gave her the framework of a modern state, and an Archeological Society which preserved innumerable treasures for posterity. But by his partition, for administrative convenience, of the huge province of Bengal he challenged Bengal nationalism, and for the first time a political movement began. Its terrorist form caused Acts to be passed under which revolutionary leaders could be imprisoned. The Congress party was then divided between the moderate Gopal Krishna Gokhale, a spiritual ancestor of Gandhi, and the extremist Bal Gangadhur Tilak, imprisoned from 1908 to 1914, whose programme achieved fulfilment only in 1947.

The British Liberal victory of 1906 coincided with the rising power of both Germany and Japan, whose victory over Russia in 1904-5 had kindled Indian imagination and started a mental revolution which provided the fuel for Asian nationalism. Other events which brought new concepts of freedom and self-government to long-insulated India were the Young Turk Revolution of 1908-9, the Persian nationalist movement of 1910, and the Chinese Revolution of 1911.

Britain's new Secretary of State for India was John Morley, a cautious literary Radical whose policy of mixed experiment and repression took shape in the Morley-Minto reforms. Lord Minto, the new Viceroy, an urbane unostentatious Scot, began through the Morley-Minto Act of 1909 to bring outstanding Indians into the administration. He also created six constituencies for Muslim landowners, who had pleaded under-representation when the new Muslim League was founded in 1906. From the outset the spectre of communalism had appeared at political feasts, and the image of Pakistan now rose above the horizon.

A new and liberal Viceroy, Lord Hardinge, who succeeded Lord Minto in 1911, had the task of implementing the Morley-Minto reforms. One chief contribution made by him to history was his support of Gandhi's non-violent movement in South Africa, a protest against the penalties imposed by the Union

Victory at Edinburgh

[By courtesy of The Times]

Front row (left to right): Lord Addison, Lord Jowitt, Sir Stafford Cripps, Greenwood, Bevin, Attlee, Morrison, Dalton, Alexander, Chuter Ede and Ellen Wilkinson.
Back row (left to right): Bevan, Isaacs, Lord Stansgate, Hall, Lord Pethick-Lawrence, Lawson, Westwood, Shinwell, E. J. Williams and Tom Williams.

Government on the Indian colony which had developed from the indentured labour brought in to sustain the Natal sugar industry. To the alarm of London, which dared not recall him, Lord Hardinge referred openly to the Indian resistance against 'invidious and unjust laws', and thereby brought a unanimous India to the support of Britain in the First World War.

This conflict undermined Europe's prestige in the East by revealing the political divisions of the West, but India proved so loyal that at one time only 15,000 British troops were left in Indian garrisons. Indian soldiers fought beside the Allies in Iraq, Macedonia, and German East Africa; they garrisoned the Suez Canal, and reacted with nothing worse than grieved resentment when five million Indians died in the 1919 influenza epidemic (a larger number than all the European deaths in action). India was rewarded by her official presence at the Peace Conference, and by subsequent membership of the League of Nations. The Muslims, from whom the Westernized figure of Mohammed Ali Jinnah was already emerging, shared with the Hindus a sense of release from the supposed moral superiority of Europe, but the dismemberment of the Turkish Empire severely strained their allegiance.

In 1916 came a new Viceroy, Lord Chelmsford, and the following year a new Secretary of State, Edwin Montagu, succeeded Austen Chamberlain. In 1918 they issued a Report which was liberal in contemporary terms, providing for franchise extension and popular representation, and proved to be a starting-point for British moves towards Indian self-government during the next thirty years. Its effect was unfortunately mitigated by a Committee presided over by Judge Rowlatt, which proposed to control 'subversive' behaviour by giving judges power to try political cases without juries.

At this juncture Gandhi, still under fifty, returned from South Africa, and launched a protest campaign against the Rowlatt Acts. It was the beginning of civil disobedience in which India's women, many already rooted from their homes by the needs of the war, fulfilled women's historic function of keeping pace with other underdogs, and entered Gandhi's movement. The speed of their political education was soon comparable with that of Britain's Suffragettes in the previous decade.

In 1919, after serious outbreaks of violence in the Punjab,

I

came the Jallianwallah Bagh massacre at Amritsar, comparable in its moral effects with the Sharpeville shooting in South Africa forty years later, which played into Gandhi's hands. While Tagore with outraged dignity renounced his British knighthood, Gandhi declared that 'co-operation in any shape or form with this satanic Government is sinful'.

The 'satanic Government' sent a new Viceroy, Lord Reading, to India in 1921, and Gandhi called off civil disobedience for the time being, but shortly afterwards he was sentenced to six years' imprisonment for incitement. When he was released two years later his movement had collapsed, but it had psychologically transformed the outlook of his followers, who now saw themselves as the equals of their rulers. In 1923 Pandit Motilal Nehru, leader of the Allahabad bar and father of Jawaharlal, had formed the Swaraj (self-government) Parliamentary Party within Congress, whence the Muslims, afraid of Hindu domination after the abolition of the Caliphate, seceded in 1924.

The Montagu-Chelmsford Report had provided for a survey of the Indian position in a few years' time, and in 1926, on the advice of the new Viceroy, Lord Irwin (later Halifax), Stanley Baldwin, now Prime Minister, decided that the moment had come. The outcome was the appointment, in November 1927, of an all-British Commission under Sir John Simon, of which a relatively obscure Labour M.P. in his forties, C. R. Attlee, was a member—'on the grounds, I think, that I had a virgin mind on the subject', he wrote years afterwards.

The well-meaning and sincere Lord Irwin—who soon learned his lesson—had made the mistake of putting no Indian on the Simon Commission; intended as a gesture of goodwill, it was greeted with black flags and hostile demonstrations all over India. The young Nehru, just entering high politics, inspired Congress to pass a resolution declaring 'the goal of the Indian people to be complete national independence'. His father more discreetly sponsored an agreed Constitution drawn up at an all-parties conference by himself and the Liberal lawyer Sapru.

Meanwhile the Simon Commission, visiting all parts of India, drew up its own Report recommending the separation of Burma from India and a general quickening of the pace of advance. Nevertheless, for the next twenty years, the British habit of deliberately moving 'from precedent to precedent' was to be a source of exasperation to the quicksilver impatience of sensitive Indians demanding swift action. The sympathetic Labour member of the Simon Commission has however explained in his *Empire Into Commonwealth* (1961) that Britain could not then have conceded full Dominion status, owing to growing communal tension and the existing obligation of the Government of India to protect the Indian princes who were already facing demands from their subjects for more democratic constitutions.

In May 1929 the second Labour Government, though dependent on fifty-nine Liberal M.P.s, took office in Britain. After consulting the new Government, Lord Irwin—a deeply religious man who had been impressed by Gandhi's moral approach to politics—proposed a Round Table Conference, demanded by Congress since the emergence of the Swarajist movement, between the British Government and representatives of India after the publication of the Simon Report.

The autumn of 1930 saw the first meeting of this Conference, which was followed in February and March 1931 by talks between Gandhi and the Viceroy. These resulted in the Gandhi-Irwin truce which caused Congress to set aside its intransigent Left wing, and to appoint Gandhi as its sole delegate to the next meeting of the Conference. He travelled to London in November and, firmly repudiating the luxury accommodation offered at a West End hotel, stayed at Kingsley Hall, Bow, a pacifist East End settlement where he occupied a modest room opening on the roof.

Between the first and second meeting of the Conference another political change had inconveniently occurred in Britain, where Ramsay MacDonald and his supporters had broken the Labour Government during the August economic crisis. Though the new National Government did not discount the work of its predecessor, a different tone dominated the discussions, and the second Conference on which both Attlee and Pethick[1] served broke up in December without any significant achievement. Gandhi returned to India to renew the civil disobedience campaign and within three weeks was back in prison, where 34,000 of his disciples followed him in April.

The next milestone on the road to independence was the Government of India Act of 1935, introduced as the result of

[1] See Chapter 20.

recommendations from a Joint Select Committee of Lords and Commons set up by the National Government after the Round Table Conferences had failed. (Only forty-six delegates attended the third session.) By an unprecedented piece of Parliamentary procedure the Joint Select Committee sat together with representative Indians who were thus able to discuss and influence the precise terms of the Bill.

This measure, reports Lord Attlee, 'was piloted through the House of Commons with great skill by Sir Samuel Hoare against violent and obstructive opposition by Sir Winston Churchill and a handful of Conservatives'. Lord Halifax later recorded his belief that, but for this die-hard resistance, a solution to the Indian problem might have been found before the Second World War. Nicholas Mansergh[1] sees this opposition as closely related to the new problems of imperial strategy created by Europe's growing dictatorships.

The Government of India Act established full Provincial autonomy with responsible Ministers, subject to limited 'reserve powers' vested in Provincial Governors. It separated Burma from India, and provided for the setting up of a Federal Government if and when a sufficient number of Indian States agreed to adhere to the proposed Indian Union. While this Act could have led to full self-government in the Provinces and a very large degree of Indian control in the Federation, it was at that time expected that complete Dominion status on the Statute of Westminster model would not be achieved for some years. In 1939 Lord Linlithgow, the Viceroy who had presented the new Constitution, still found it astonishing 'that there should be any general impression that public opinion at home, or His Majesty's Government, seriously contemplate evacuation (of India) in any measurable period of time'.[2]

Actually the period was now measurable in years, not decades, though the triumphant Congress Ministries made the mistake of refusing coalition with the Muslims. They thus failed at a crucial moment to take the step which alone might have reduced communal antagonism. Instead, the Muslim conviction that self-government meant subjection to the Hindus was strikingly

[1] Survey of British Commonwealth Affairs, Royal Institute of International Affairs, 1958.
[2] Mansergh, op. cit.

confirmed. Faced with the alternative of submission to Congress and the pursuit of a communal policy, Jinnah not surprisingly chose the second course and rallied his fellow Muslims with the cry of 'Islam in danger'.

When the Second World War broke out, India was brought in without the leading Indians being consulted — 'unwisely, I think', comments Lord Attlee, for India was now conscious of herself as an independent entity, and resented this basic implication of dependent status. Indian opinion had been hostile to the aggressive European dictatorships, and had the choice been left to her, India would voluntarily have opposed them. As it was, she suffered from the painful frustrations of a divided mind throughout the war, in which her troops again fought along with the Allies while her politicians stood aside and their leaders went to prison. After the catastrophe at Pearl Harbour had brought the war to India's doorstep and the Japanese occupation of Burma cut off five per cent of her rice supplies, Indians heroically defended their frontiers while the wartime British National Government endeavoured to postpone the looming political issues until the war was over.

It made one attempt at a radical solution. In 1942 it sent Sir Stafford Cripps to India with an offer to set up a Constituent Assembly immediately after the war with the object of creating an Indian Union, having Dominion status, subject to the right of Provinces to opt out of it. Nehru, a friend of Cripps, and the influential Rajagopalachari were prepared for acceptance, but Gandhi rejected the proposal on the ground that it represented 'a blank cheque on a failing bank'. Under the slogan 'quit India'[1] (the Japanese would be resisted but the British must quit India first) he organized a new mass civil disobedience movement, and Nehru, confronted with an all but intolerable choice, found a further period of imprisonment at least an escape from personal tension.

---

[1] The Resolution adopted by the Congress Working Committee at Wardha on July 14, 1942 began as follows: 'The events happening from day to day and the experience that the people of India are passing through confirm the opinion of Congressmen that British rule in India must end immediately, not merely because foreign domination even at its best is an evil in itself and a continuing injury to the subject people, but because India in bondage can play no effective part in defending herself and in affecting the fortunes of the war that is desolating humanity . . . '.

In 1943 Lord Wavell became Viceroy, and at first won great popularity through his masterful relief measures in the Bengal famine partly caused by the loss of Burma. A series of talks between Gandhi and Jinnah in September 1944 emphasized mainly their differences, and contributed nothing towards solving the political dilemma. In June 1945, after the war in Europe had ended, the Conservative (Caretaker) Government made a final endeavour to arrange for a transfer of power on its own terms by calling a conference at Simla. In the belief that it had at least a year of office, its purpose was to find an Indian Government with which to finish the Japanese war, but the speech on June 14th by the Secretary of State (Mr Leo Amery) pulled out the usual stops of admonition, complacency and postponement, and made a final solution seem as far away as ever.

Within eight weeks two apocalyptic events had brought the unexpected end for him and his colleagues. In the last week of July came the spectacular victory of the Labour Party, long pledged to Indian self-government, and on August 14th the surrender of Japan, which removed the need for large military forces to be kept in India. The British Raj, its two centuries of domination nearly over, now faced the new rôle of a well-intentioned but embarrassed umpire between contending Indian forces.

As the leader of the team of umpires, Pethick now entered upon the most historic function which his life of rich experience had held in store.

CHAPTER 20

Traveller to an Appointed Bourne

At the turn of the century, when Pethick visited India as an ex-undergraduate concerned to discover what his part in life should be, it is improbable that he expected his destiny ever to take the form of maximum responsibility for the future of this vast undeveloped land. India was a diverting experience, a colourful episode on the Grand Tour, a source of adventurous posts for his less academic school and college contemporaries. How could it hold any serious prospects for a Fourth Wrangler and Fellow of Trinity?

Yet his attitude to India even in youth was never conventional. In the symposium *If I Had My Time Again*, he recorded his gratitude to his liberal-minded parents who never taught him the 'terrible doctrines' current in his childhood. 'I was never asked', he wrote, 'to regard devout Buddhists and Hindus as "heathen" and, as such, foredoomed to eternal damnation.' Rather was he conscious even then that Christians, Hindus and Muslims worshipped the same God under different names. His Unitarian family had been closely associated with the Brahmo-Samaj movement in Bengal, and its founder, Keshab Chandra Sen, visited his parents in the year of his birth and was photographed with his sisters.

It was therefore natural that, on his first visit to India in 1897, the headquarters of the movement should have been one of Pethick's earliest objectives. But though he travelled widely, he admits in *Fate Has Been Kind* that 'my knowledge was nearly all secondhand and my impressions were mostly superficial'.

A dozen years later his conspicuous rôle in the suffrage movement brought him into contact with Mahatma Gandhi, who came from his own non-violent resistance campaign in South Africa to study the tactics of militant suffrage. Gandhi was the guest of Emmeline and himself at lunch in their London flat (a frugal meal, Pethick recalled, of raisins and milk). 'We found that we had much in common', he related in a broadcast on Gandhi in September 1954, 'not least in his doctrine that a willingness to endure suffering was a surer way to win political reform than to inflict it on others.'

The distant future was to hold many unforeseen vicissitudes which would involve them both, but Pethick put on record that 'even when I was most in disagreement with him I never doubted his sincerity and single-mindedness, and I am confident that he never doubted mine'.

In his obituary article on Pethick in the *Hindu Weekly Review* for September 25, 1961, Mr B. Shiva Rao stated that his continuous interest in India really began with a request to him from Annie Besant at the end of the First World War to write a weekly London letter for her Madras daily paper *New India*. Through mutual friends in the Labour Party, such as George Lansbury, she had heard of him as a man of deep convictions willing to make sacrifices for his principles.

Pethick's autobiography contains no mention of this assignment nor, more strangely, does he ever refer to Mrs Besant herself. As he published this book in 1943, two years before his appointment as Secretary of State, his contacts with India may well not have dominated his memories of his early life. His letters for *New India* appear to have continued until 1923, when he had to give them up owing to his election for West Leicester, but all through the nineteen-twenties he supported Mrs Besant's pro-India group both within and outside the Labour Party.

His first significant contacts with India itself came during the silver honeymoon visit in the winter of 1926-7. On his journey Pethick sent home a series of 'Encyclical Letters' which add life to the short summary of the trip in *Fate Has Been Kind*. Fortified with introductions from Sir Howard d'Egville, the secretary of the Empire Parliamentary Association, they sailed in the P. & O. liner *Ranchi* in mid-October, and found among their shipmates Sir Charu Ghose, a Judge of the Calcutta High Court; Sir T. Vijagaragavacharga of Delhi, India's representative in Canada; Sleem, a famous lawn tennis player; and a number of officials and traders.

Emmeline wrote home warmly of the Indian civil servants on board: 'They are comparable to a crowd of schoolmasters who are proud of their school and deeply interested in the boys'. She had not yet discarded the typical outlook of a liberal ruling class towards the inhabitants of a dependent territory, and had still to equate the reactions of a subject nation with those of the subject sex for which she had fought.

In Bombay the Pethick-Lawrences stayed with Shelton Bunting, whose father, Sir Percy Bunting, had edited the *Contemporary Review*. From his verandah overlooking the city, Pethick observed its enormous growth since his first visit thirty years earlier, and noticed especially the scores of gaunt concrete blocks of workers' tenements which stood wastefully empty because the workers neither liked nor could afford them. At a tea with Mrs Sarojini Naidu they met some of the most politically-minded residents of Bombay, including several Swarajists who explained the significance of Gandhi's crusade for the restoration of home industries. Soon they had to realize the unanimity of the demand for self-government.

They went on to Madras, where Pethick's college friend A. Y. G. Campbell, who had been Assistant Collector at an upcountry station, Nellore, in 1897, was now Secretary to the Madras Government. From their suite of five rooms in his so-called 'bungalow' at Gambiers Gardens, they looked across a park of noble trees towards the Adjar river. Like all new visitors to India, they were delighted by the rich colours and luxuriant vegetation of Madras. Bombay, until they looked into its slums and alleys, had suggested a fine Californian city, but this was the real India.

Their arrival coincided with the elections of the local Legislative Council, for which seventy per cent of Hindus had voted, including a large number of women. 'Everybody', Emmeline recorded with triumph, 'apparently agrees that the women of this country are developing with astonishing rapidity.' The result of the election was a substantial Congress victory, and Pethick's host told him that the Congress Party was now asking for a new type of conference between British and Indians. Pethick wrote home:

'They do not want a commission appointed in 1929 by Britain to consider what modifications of the Constitution she will be graciously pleased to grant to India, but a round table conference of Indians and British to arrange the details of the changeover to complete "Dominion status".'

In his letter he also mentioned the outcast 'untouchables who are so terribly oppressed'. Even then he recognized the 'Mohammedan' fear of subordination to the Hindus, 'which they would resent, and perhaps resist even by violence'. He would have been astonished to learn how far he himself was one day to become the target of this resentment.

At that time, he recorded, skilled men working in the cotton mills of Madras earned less than one rupee for a nine-hour day, whereas bare subsistence for a man with a wife and three children cost 11s a week, and some workers said that 24s was needed for a real living wage. Many of them, he observed, ate their food squatting on the floor amid the machines.

His friend Campbell arranged interviews for him with the Governor and the local representatives of the three political parties; he also visited factories, addressed trade union meetings, and investigated rural life. In a Madras village called Usilempatti he found an experiment in progress for weaning the tribe of Kullahs from *dacoity* (robbery) by the simple expedient of providing them with water, and thus enabling them to earn their own living from the irrigated fields. So far, he commented, it appeared to be successful, 'showing once more that the roots of crime are ignorance and poverty'. Before leaving for Calcutta he visited Mysore and its progressive ruler and there saw the second largest dam in the world, constructed entirely by Indian labourers working under Indian engineers.

In Calcutta he went over a jute mill, talked with Swarajist politicians who were directors of the newspaper *Forward*, and lunched with a group of Bengal Council members. Back there for the New Year, with its races and polo tournaments, he and Emmeline made the short journey to Bolpur for a day with Rabindranath Tagore at his home Uttarayan in Santiniketan ('the abode of peace'). There they saw the international school and university founded forty years earlier by his father Devendranath (known as the Maharsi or 'great saint') on this red rolling plain dotted with palms and pampas grass.

At night Pethick gave a talk to the students while Emmeline wrote an enthusiastic description of the poet for her friends in England.

'He is a very beautiful and lovely person, his aristocratic face and his abundant silky white hair combed back from the forehead, and his young eyes and delicate sensitive hands, all these make a most worshipful presence.' Over thirty years afterwards Pethick recalled their dinner table conversation in a BBC broadcast for the Tagore centenary:

'We talked of all sorts of subjects. He expressed himself strongly in support of the movements in India for self-government and regretted that so many of her young men were in detention or prison under the British rule. He wished to see a more liberal attitude adopted. We spoke too of the natural beauties of India and of her noble monuments. My wife expressed her deep admiration of the Taj Mahal, and Tagore intervened by saying that he had written a poem about it, but that it was in Bengali and had never been translated into English. "Do translate a sentence or two for me", pleaded my wife. So Tagore said to her: "I say to Shah Jehan—you knew that grief however poignant is mortal; so you had the conception of imprinting in marble a teardrop on the cheek of eternity".'

Before finally leaving India, Pethick returned to Calcutta for a talk with the Viceroy, Lord Irwin. He put before him what he had heard from Indians of their desire for self-government, and also mentioned the continued detention of unconvicted prisoners especially in Bengal, where nearly 300 detainees included the chief executive officer, Subhas Chandra Bose. They should either, he urged, be released or brought to trial. He received an impression of sympathy, later confirmed by the Viceroy's actions.

Between the first and second visit to Calcutta he and Emmeline spent a weekend at Ghoom, near Darjeeling, where he climbed three miles with a guide to the top of Tiger Hill. This hill stood 1,000 feet higher than their tiny hotel, itself 8,000 feet above sea level. At sunrise he saw the full panorama of mountains in the huge Kanchenjunga range, and recognized the summit of Everest caught by the rising sun. Another mountainous journey took them from Peshawar over the Khyber Pass, where travelling on one of the bi-weekly caravan days they met four continuous miles of loaded camels. They drove to Landikotal at the top of the pass and looked across the Afghan landscape to the distant mountain peaks beyond Kabul. Peshawar was then surrounded by barbed wire and illuminated at night, as it was liable to be looted by marauding tribes driven by hunger. Their raids ceased whenever there was enough work to bring them food and water.

After a 200-mile journey Pethick lectured at Lahore, where he learned something of the politics of this Muslim-dominated region with which his future contacts were to be much less casual. They went on to Delhi, whence Pethick revisited Agra to renew the enchantment brought him by the Taj Mahal in his youth. 'My view has not changed that of all human achievements in architecture it is without a peer', he wrote in his letter to England.

A stop at Lucknow took them to the home of a former Suffragette, Joan (Duval) Cruichshank, who had seen a newspaper announcement, 'Labour M.P. Touring India'. She and her husband gave a garden party for them to which non-co-operators came in Gandhi caps, and mingled with gorgeously attired Talugdar landlords. They pressed Pethick for a political speech, but he sagely declined. 'Never discuss politics on your travels; wrong reports get about.'

Politics however entered fully into his last two circular letters, written in the *Kaiser-i-Hind* on their journey home. Three men seemed to Pethick to stand far above the many personalities he had met—the poet Tagore, 'a superb figure'; Sir Jagardis Bose, the great plant biologist of Calcutta; and Mahatma Gandhi, whom he visited at Gauhati. Gandhi, he wrote, forcibly recalled to him the image of John the Baptist. After the 1931 Round Table Conference and the 1946 Cabinet Mission, his impression of this 'quiet unassuming man' became perhaps less biblical.

The other letter written on shipboard contained a lucid analysis of Indian problems as he then saw them, with the Hindus passionately desirous of self-determination and the Muslims afraid of subjection to them after the withdrawal of British overlordship. Of the British rulers themselves he wrote that their main fault was not that of the cunning 'divide and rule' policy so widely attributed to them by Indians. Their chief disadvantages were their exclusiveness, which kept Indians at arm's length; their alleged intolerance of the climate, which caused the Government to move to the hills for months on end; their inability as aliens to rectify social abuses, such as child marriage, arising from Indian customs; and their failure to provide more education, higher wages, and better housing.

The housing above all else appalled him, especially in the cities which he could compare with his long-past experience of

London's Victorian slums. He described the dark unventilated tenements, 'huddled together on what are little better than insanitary dustheaps', which were responsible for the terrible infant mortality figures for Bombay (over 500 per 1,000 for the whole city, including the better quarters).[1] The poverty of the workers he also saw as one of the blackest marks against the Government; the income of a rural worker was then as low as £5 a year, and that of 'coolies' in urban areas no more than £15. These underpaid and undernourished toilers put in nine or ten hours daily of unrelieved work; it was hardly surprising that an Indian's output was only one-third of that of a European.

Three main difficulties in reaching self-government he diagnosed as, first, the Army (which he thought would take twenty years to Indianize); secondly, the Indian princes and the complications of their constitutional position; and thirdly, the Hindu-Muslim rivalry, involving the cumbersome system of separate minority representation. Yet to his own question, 'Should India get self-government?' (which he then called 'Home Rule'),[2] he replied with an emphatic 'Yes'. It might be a worse Government than the present, but it would be their own.

Independence, he believed, should neither be immediate, 'nor be doled out bit by bit at the pleasure of the British Parliament'. The demands of the Indian nationalists should be agreed in principle, and British and Indians should then sit down together to map out the stages of self-government, which he thought would take twenty-five years to accomplish. (This, though a fair prediction, proved to be a five years' over-estimate.) The first stage, he thought, should consist of advances in provincial self-government, which might seem less inadequate to contemporary Indian opinion if they were part of a wider scheme.

Above all, the British Government should abandon its 'tone of superiority', and join with Indians on a basis of equality to discuss not 'whether', but 'how and when'. In the interests of fairness, he recorded that his fellow-countrymen deserved high commendation for the roads, railways and ports that they had

[1] According to the 1960 United Nations Demographic Year Book, pp. 512-21, the 1950 infant mortality figure for all India was 185·0 per 1,000 live births. The 1959 figure for England and Wales was 22·2 per 1,000.

[2] The name came from Annie Besant's Home Rule League founded in September 1916.

given to India, and for their general administration of justice. When they faced the problem of understanding another people whom they habitually thought of as 'subject', their achievements were less conspicuous.

These conclusions, reinforced by their Indian experiences, made the Pethick-Lawrences happy to welcome the many Indian visitors who called on them during the next few years. When Pandit Motilal Nehru dined with them at the House of Commons, Members were discussing the revision of the Prayer Book. Pandit Nehru admitted that he often found British behaviour in India beyond comprehension, but so too were the values of a country which entrusted decisions involving religious principles to its elected political representatives.

By the time that Pethick was invited by Wedgwood Benn, Secretary of State for India from 1929 to 1931, to serve in the autumn of 1931 at the second session of the Round Table Conference which was dealing with federal structure, he felt well able to play a constructive part, and helped the Secretary of State to embody a spirit of agreement rather than dictation in some of the official memoranda.

Unhappily the change of Government before the Conference actually met brought back much of the usual unillumined political obstinacy, and the Conference broke up without an agreed decision. But it had enabled Pethick to make a third personal contact with Mahatma Gandhi when he eventually attended, and to re-encounter such distinguished Indian delegates as the Pandit Malaviya, Mrs Naidu, Sir Tej Sapru, Dr Ambedkar, and the Aga Khan. In his autobiography he has described the colourful picture to which the Indian princes in their splendid costumes contributed.

From that time onwards, as *The Times* noted in its obituary article on Pethick, 'he gained increasing respect for the breadth of knowledge and sympathy he displayed in the debates on India'.

CHAPTER 21

The Cabinet Mission

Pethick's appointment as Secretary of State for India and for Burma brought him both surprise and pleasure, though he remained perpetually conscious of overwhelming responsibility for the 400 million people whose fate now rested so largely in his hands.

After his emphatic re-endorsement by East Edinburgh, he had expected that political office (if it came at all, for he was already seventy-three) would mean a return to his former fiscal preoccupations. It had never occurred to him that his lifelong interest in India and the many contacts that it had brought him could have top-level significance for his Party. Now he recognized his travels, reading, and correspondence as a continuous journey towards an appointed bourne for which destiny had steadily prepared him. The measure of the confidence he inspired, wrote Mr B. Shiva Rao in the *Hindu Weekly Review* after his death, was shown by the Prime Minister's choice of him for the India Office rather than 'the brilliant but unpredictable Cripps'.

The announcement of his Cabinet position brought a friendly letter to Emmeline from Mrs Pandit, then in New York. She expressed her satisfaction that Pethick should be in charge of India's immediate fortunes, and wrote of the hope in many Indian hearts that a more enlightened and reasonable policy would now prevail. Emmeline replied with a warm reference to the bonds which attached both her and Pethick to India, beginning with the numerous Indian students who had attended their suffrage meetings. Among Pethick's own numerous letters of congratulation, the one from the Master of Trinity, Dr G. M. Trevelyan, probably pleased him most.

The peerage conferred on Pethick added prestige to his appointment in an Oriental country where pomp and circumstance retained their traditional value. In his own country, except that his political life was transferred from one Chamber

143

to another, his new rank made no difference to his customary routine. Though he was obliged to spend 100 guineas on the purchase of a peer's levee suit and five on the velvet cap of state with its imitation ermine and gold-embroidered tassel, he usually housed this embarrassing fancy dress at a court tailor's in Chancery Lane, and still rose very early at Fourways to put on the breakfast porridge.

On December 10, 1945, an *Evening News* photographer caught him immersed in these domestic activities, and published a picture which showed him standing in line with a shopping basket. The caption ran: 'The man with a muffler in the village fish queue is His Majesty's Secretary of State for India, Lord Pethick-Lawrence. The village is Shere, in Surrey . . . He not only likes doing the family shopping, which he regards as a happy weekend relaxation from his work in the world of politics, but often prepares the meals as well. He is a first-class cook.'

Very soon now the summons was coming to an assignment which would make even more drastic demands on him than his trial at the Old Bailey, over thirty years ago. That trial had been followed by a period of imprisonment; he was shortly to discover that this experience, though it had sometimes helped him in Parliamentary elections, would never be so valuable as he was to find it when he took the Cabinet Mission to India. There he had to deal with many individuals who had been put in prison by the British Government; it was naturally a reassurance to them to learn that the Secretary of State himself had once suffered the same fate.

When the Labour victory was announced in India, the nationalists were jubilant. The President of Congress, Maulana Azad, at once sent a warm telegram of congratulation to Mr Attlee and the people of Britain; the results of the Election, he said, 'demonstrate their abandonment of the old ideas and acceptance of a new world'. Though political India hoped soon to see the end of the India Office, Pethick's appointment was none the less welcome. In late August the Viceroy, Lord Wavell, had long discussions with him when he came to England to consult the new Government.

In September came the Viceroy's announcement that a constituent assembly would be summoned in India as soon as pos-

The Cabinet Mission in Delhi, 1946

Second row, fourth from left: Mr E. W. Lumby, India Office. Sixth from left onwards: Mr F. B. Mottishead, Private Secretary to Lord Alexander; Col. Fraser; Sir William Croft, Deputy Under Secretary of State, India Office; Lord Alexander; Lord Pethick-Lawrence; Sir Stafford Cripps; Mr Frank Turnbull, Private Secretary to Lord Pethick-Lawrence; Mr A. H. Joyce, Information Officer, India Office; Mr Woodrow Wyatt.
Third row, second from right: Major Short, Indian Army.

Pethick and Gandhi in Delhi in 1946

Pethick and Emmeline at Fourways in 1945
A Painting by John Baker

THE CABINET MISSION

sible after elections had been held, since there had been none since 1937. Although the existing political alignments could not be ascertained without them, this plan was not well received by the Indian leaders, who now described Labour's programme as 'vague and inadequate and unsatisfactory'; traditional suspicions, based on habitual delays and disappointments, found difficulty in crediting the good faith of even a Labour Cabinet. Congress therefore reaffirmed its 'quit India' resolution, and the Muslim League was hardly less critical. In his long essay on Gandhi,[1] Pethick has explained that the majority of Congress members, like Gandhi himself, found it difficult to understand the real change of outlook that had occurred in Britain.

By 1945 the British people were tired, to the point of nausea, of the values imposed on them during the past six years in the name of victory; bombing, blockade, unconditional surrender, and the detention of leading Indians were all part of the wartime paraphernalia that they wanted to throw away. But most of the Congress leaders had only recently been released from prison, and their contacts, in any case, were not with the British in Britain but with the British Raj in India, which had so consistently made certain that ' "jam tomorrow" never materialized for Indians as "jam today" '. Few of them shared Mrs Pandit's personal contacts with responsible Left-wing Britons.

'In face of our determination to emancipate India from British rule', writes Pethick, 'we were confronted with political deadlock. Gandhi had lost faith in British intentions about Indian freedom, Jinnah had lost faith in fair treatment for Muslims at the hands of a Hindu majority.'

So urgent was the need to replace this feeling of frustration and bitterness with hope and confidence, and to acquaint India with the change of attitude towards her in Britain, that the Cabinet decided to send out a Parliamentary delegation representing all parties to confer with the Indian leaders.

On December 4th a speech by Pethick in the House of Lords also suggested that the Viceroy's announcement had been imperfectly understood; the discussions for setting up a constitution-making body after the elections were not another expedient for causing delay. His Majesty's Government, he insisted, regarded

[1] *Mahatma Gandhi*, by H. S. L. Polak, H. N. Brailsford, Lord Pethick-Lawrence. Foreword by Sarojini Naidu. Odhams Press (1949).

K

the establishment of an instrument by which Indians could decide their own future as a matter of great urgency.

The elections to India's central legislative Assembly,[1] held in December 1945, showed an overwhelming success for Congress in the general constituencies, while every Muslim constituency was won by the Muslim League. Between them these two parties held eighty-seven seats out of 102, and virtually eliminated such political minorities as the Independents and the Sikhs. Inevitably this result heightened the problems arising from communal tension, which the election campaign had exacerbated; in their speeches the Congress members had advocated a united India, while the Muslim League had demanded the creation of Pakistan.

At the New Year Pethick broadcast to India, prophesying that 1946 would be a crucial year in her age-long history. He therefore felt, he said, that he would like to speak personally to the Indian people, and assure them that the British Government and people earnestly desired to see India rise quickly to the full and free status of an equal partner in the British Commonwealth.

'The problem now is a practical one,' he stated. 'It is to work out a rational and acceptable plan of action. It must be a plan under which authority can be transferred to Indian control under a form of government which will be willingly accepted by the broad mass of India's people.' He pleaded for the help of influential Indians, since it was only through moderation and compromise that great political problems could be solved. 'If we all bend our minds and wills to this high endeavour, we can do something in 1946 for the greatness of India, for the future peace and prosperity of Asia and the world.'

Four days later the Parliamentary delegation reached India; it was led by Professor Robert Richards, who had been Labour Under-Secretary for India in 1924. Eight members of the House of Commons and two from the House of Lords formed the delegation; they came as individuals with the purpose of making contacts. These contacts included talks with both Nehru and Jinnah, who announced that he would take no part in an interim government without a prior declaration accepting the principle

[1] For administrative reasons the elections for the provincial legislatures could not be held until the spring of 1946.

of Pakistan.[1] The delegation travelled widely all over India but had little effect on the prevailing attitude of suspicion, which was rooted not least in the heart of Gandhi. 'More talk and enquiry and no action' was the judgment passed on it by Congress.

On January 28, 1946, the Viceroy addressed the newly-elected Legislative Council, and emphasized the determination of the British Government to bring into being an Indian constitution-making body as soon as possible. 'The ship has reached the shore', commented the Congress leader Sardar Patel. 'The freedom of India is near at hand'. But Jinnah remarked that if the British had only one such body in mind, the Muslims would revolt throughout India.

Two weeks later the Prime Minister told the House of Commons that the British Government had decided to send a special mission of Cabinet Ministers to India to seek agreement with the Indian leaders in framing a constitution. On February 19th the forthcoming departure of the Mission was formally announced. Its members were to be the Secretary of State, who would lead it; Sir Stafford Cripps, the President of the Board of Trade, who had been responsible for the mission of 1942; and Mr A. V. (later Earl) Alexander, the First Lord of the Admiralty, who knew Ceylon though he had not previously visited India.

Long afterwards, in a letter to Irene Harrison, Agatha's sister, Lord Alexander described himself as the 'ballast' of the good ship 'Commission'. His cheerful, friendly disposition enabled him to get on well with both Hindus and Muslims; he was especially successful with the would-be Pakistanis, whom he perhaps found easier to understand than the more complex and temperamental Hindus. Both Liaquat Ali Khan and Jinnah—whom he has described as 'a tedious but conscientious man'—became his close friends.

'The decision of His Majesty's Government to send three Cabinet Ministers to confer with Indian political leaders was an unprecedented step', writes Mr V. P. Menon, one of the chief authorities on the transfer of power in India. 'But the situation

[1] Percival Spear (*India*, 1961) explains the term 'Pakistan' as a name invented by the Muslim visionary Rahmat Ali in 1933. P stood for Punjab, A for Afghans (Pathans), K for Kashmir, S for Sind, while 'stan' means 'country' in Persian. 'Pak' in Persian-Urdu is also the term for 'pure', so that the whole word means 'Land of the Pure'.

in India was equally unprecedented; a complete deadlock had been reached which, if peace and progress were to be maintained, had to be broken.'

In Delhi the Viceroy, who was to be associated with the work of the Mission, remarked apprehensively that it would have to stay until a satisfactory solution had been reached; 'it would create the worst possible impression if a high-grade mission were to leave without having achieved results'. The Indians themselves received the announcement with enthusiasm tempered by caution; there was a genuine expectation that the Mission and the Indian leaders together would find an answer to India's problems. Azad, the helpful and co-operative President of Congress, thought the decision wise; Gandhi appealed to his fellow-countrymen not to suspect the Mission's *bona fides* (knowing that inevitably they would), and Jinnah reiterated his demand for the division of the country into Hindustan and Pakistan.

On March 15th, Mr Attlee sought to reassure the Indians by intervening in a debate initiated by Mr R. A. Butler just before the Mission departed. Though high tension existed in the present critical relations between Britain and India, he said, his colleagues would be going to India in a positive mood. They would be looking to the future rather than the past, for the temper of 1946 was not that of 1920, 1930, or even 1942. Their intention was to help India to attain freedom as speedily and completely as possible.

'What form of government is to replace the present régime is for India to decide, but our desire is to help her to set up forthwith the machinery for making that decision . . . India herself must choose what will be her future constitution . . . I hope that the Indian people may elect to remain within the British Commonwealth . . . Asia has been ravaged by war. Here we have the one great country that has been seeking to apply the principles of democracy. I have always hoped myself that political India might be the light of Asia.'

While Pethick was packing at Fourways for his journey, Emmeline in another room wrote him a long letter. Although they spent the greater part of their lives together they were steady correspondents, and he tried to write to her each day when he was in town and she was in the country.

The series[1] which covers the period of the Cabinet Mission is

[1] Some of her earlier letters are clearly missing. His appear to be complete.

probably the only written record of Pethick's real feelings, which he so discreetly suppressed in his public statements and appearances. There is pathos, even tragedy, in the gradual disappointment of his dedicated hopes, and the final transformation of his glowing certainty of achievement under the impact of frustration. Happily he lived long enough to realize that, in the perspective of history, his sad but pardonable sense of failure had been an illusion.

Emmeline's own letters reflect the lifelong discipline which enabled her, though now seventy-eight and hampered by deafness, to lose her own anxieties in her sense of Pethick's public obligations. He was himself seventy-four and compelled to spend a long period in an unhealthy tropical country where the cooler weather was already over, and he had many air journeys to make when the experimental technique of air travel was far from reassuring. But never once did she add to his burdens by communicating any of the apprehensions which she can hardly have failed to experience.

'For many days,' she wrote on March 18th, 'I have had no thought, no life (except on the surface) apart from you and your great mission. I have not put what I feel into words because the high adventure on which you are starting out is too important to allow any place for personal consideration but you will know how my love and my thought and my prayer will be with you every hour of the day. That is what is expressed in the little charm or keepsake I have given to bear you company. I have very deep roots in you as you have in me. We share our deepest attitude to life and being. To some extent at any rate, like the Buddhas in Tibet, we have found our being *outside* the wheel of Birth and Death . . . If not only we two but all those involved in the great enterprise of reconciliation can live, even if only for a few minutes every day, in this consciousness the 'miracle' may happen. I have always felt that the marvellous outpouring of what we call The Holy Spirit at Pentecost was due (in part at any rate) to the sudden consciousness of oneness generated by the vigil together, and to the realization of what St Paul in his great chapter in Corinthians calls 'charity' — understanding Fellowship—oneness—so that all spoke in language understood of every tribe and nation'.

Referring to a letter in the Press signed by the Archbishop of

Canterbury and others wishing the Mission Godspeed, she continued: 'I believe it will impress many Indian leaders, whether they admit it or not. At any rate you and your colleagues are going with the ardent goodwill of the whole of the country. This realization will bear you up as on eagles' wings . . . All the time until next Sunday, one part of me will be flying, flying —or sharing your experience in Tunis and elsewhere.'

On March 20th, Pethick and Sir Stafford Cripps left for India; A. V. Alexander was to meet them in Karachi. They travelled by the pleasant slow planes of those first post-war days, in which the countryside below was agreeably visible at their flying height of 7,000 feet. Until India had been reached their itinerary was not to be made public, but Pethick's first two letters to Emmeline described the snow-capped French mountains, the colourful urban stretch of Marseilles, and their landing at Tunis where they stayed in a villa ten miles from the city. Though the temperature was only moderately warm, he observed with delight a great bougainvillea in flower in the courtyard. Throughout the weeks in India which stretched so much further than anyone had intended, its vivid plants and trees furnished one of his main consolations.

From Baghdad, where he and Sir Stafford stayed with the British Ambassador on the banks of the Tigris and met the Iraqui Cabinet, he wrote on March 23rd: 'I have enjoyed every moment of my time so far . . . I have great faith in my colleagues to reach a real solution of our problems, and your prayers and good wishes and those of our friends and the nation as a whole are a great support'.

They came down that evening at Karachi—only eighteen months later to become the capital of Pakistan—and Pethick made a short statement to a group of pressmen. 'As my colleagues and I set foot on the soil of India, we bring to the people of this country on behalf of the British Government and of the British people a message of cordial friendship and goodwill. We are convinced that India is on the threshold of a great future . . . I am confident we shall face our task together in faith and with determination to succeed.'

Sir Stafford Cripps, replying to 'a barrage of questions', added that it was not true that a draft treaty of alliance between Britain and India had already been discussed. 'We have come with an open mind. We are here to investigate and enquire.'

Next day they arrived in New Delhi, where their welcome, if still tentative, was assured. They had enjoyed, reported Pethick, a perfect journey and found the weather surprisingly cool, 'like a delightful June day in England'. The Viceroy met him and took him to his official residence. 'His bereavement' (the recent loss of his son) 'has visibly affected him. He looks haggard and weary.'

Characteristically Pethick added: 'It is an entirely novel experience for me to be a "great" personage and to be received everywhere with the state befitting my position. But it doesn't embarrass me any more than it would to peel potatoes with a cottager's wife.'

CHAPTER 22

Persons and Problems in Delhi and Simla

The Mission began its work on March 25th with a conference of 250 pressmen. Answering at least fifty questions, Pethick sought especially to reassure the Muslims. 'While the Congress Party are representative of larger numbers, it would not be right to regard the Muslim League as merely a minority political party. They are in fact majority representatives of the great Muslim community.'

To Emmeline he wrote that he would be moving next day to a private house given for the Mission's use in Willingdon Crescent. 'Though everyone has been more than kind I shall not be sorry to shake off the excessive formality and ceremony.' In the Viceregal residence, larger than Buckingham Palace, there were as many red-liveried servants as diners. But he described with appreciation the glory of stocks, roses and red bougainvillea cared for by 250 gardeners.

The first three weeks went on conferences with the Viceroy and interviews with Party leaders and other outstanding persons. These inevitably included Gandhi, who travelled especially from west India and remained in touch with the Mission throughout the negotiations. Early visitors were Agatha Harrison, the Quaker friend of India, and Sarojini Naidu, 'still full of energy and fun at sixty-seven'. Apart from the leaders of the main parties, the Mission had also to see the representatives of the Princes, the Untouchables (now more tactfully described as 'Scheduled Castes'), the Sikhs, and the Indian Christians. In his obituary article on Pethick, B. Shiva Rao recalled that among others to be interviewed was Sir Tej Sapru, then a very sick man. Pethick decided to spare him the journey to their office; instead the three Cabinet Ministers called on him at his home.

Though Pethick found his preliminary talk with Gandhi 'delightful', the Mahatma remarked at his formal interview that if he were not an irrepressible optimist he would despair of any solution; he had spent eighteen days in fruitless discussions with Jinnah, and was completely opposed to the two-nation theory on which Jinnah's claim for Pakistan was founded. Long afterwards, in an article in the *Asian Review* for January 19, 1954, Pethick wrote that it was not easy to conduct negotiations with Gandhi owing to 'the subtlety of his mind which made it impossible to assess at their true value the precise meaning of his words'. But he concluded his published essay on Gandhi with the saying of Christ which represents the finest tribute that one human being can pay to another: 'Greater love hath no man than this, that a man lay down his life for his friends'.

'We have to build bridges over two gaps', Pethick wrote to Emmeline. '(1) The Hindu-Muslim dispute over Pakistan; (2) the time-gap between now and the full realization of independence. The real test is to come. I remain an optimist.'

On April 5th, after successive days of interviewing from 10 a.m. to 5 p.m. in a temperature now up to 101 degrees, he wrote reassuringly: 'I have never felt better in my life'. They were making good progress with the interviews but that was different from making political progress. 'How to abate the mutual suspicion between Congress and Muslims—that is the question.'

A happy description sent two days later referred to 'light, heat, colour, experience, endeavour, endless patience, and my family motto *per ardua stabilis*. My body . . . has played the game magnificently. My spirit has not flagged. Your noble words written before I left . . . have come to me from time to time. Your love token bearing witness to our relationship to the central life is with me. It is of course much too early to begin to think of the time when I shall be coming back. There are many rivers still to cross, many adventures still to undertake, many problems still to face. But these are all part of the great enterprise on which I have set out and which God willing I have to carry through to a successful conclusion.'

Much of the Press, he reported, had been friendly, though some papers were less amiable; he described one in particular as 'Albert's arsenic' because its opprobrious and unfair strictures so infuriated the good First Lord of the Admiralty. Cartoons were plentiful; 'one of me as a cook is perhaps the best'. He added later: 'We shall very soon have to be thinking in earnest of our method of tackling the main problem or problems'.

One main problem was unquestionably the cold, determined, rigid Mr Jinnah, immaculate in his Savile Row suit, whom they had interviewed for the second time on April 16th when he had declared that 'the unity of India' was a myth. Previously he had told Sir Stafford Cripps that the Muslims had a different conception of life from the Hindus and there was no solution but the division of India.

On April 10th Jinnah had called a Convention at which 400 of his Muslim League supporters passed a resolution demanding an independent State of Pakistan. The dilemma facing the Mission, explains V. P. Menon, 'was to devise some constitutional arrangement which would secure the essence of the Muslim League demand and at the same time be acceptable to the Congress. This was no easy task.' Already Gandhi and Nehru had informed Sir Stafford that an all-India Union on a 'three tier basis[1] would not be acceptable'.

Early on the morning of April 14th, Pethick broke away for a few hours for an air journey to Agra to show A. V. Alexander the Taj Mahal. This time they saw the dazzling white of the marble suffused by burning sunlight: 'its outstanding beauty', wrote Pethick, 'is undimmed by repetition'. They were back in their house by 11.30 a.m., and as usual his early rising gave him the triumphant sense of capturing time that most people lost. 'What a wonderful morning! So much to have seen and done before many people are fully awake.'

Later that day he found time to send Emmeline a vivid analysis of his companions and himself.

'All my colleagues are delightful and interesting and so different. Cripps the brilliant rapier-witted improviser with strong Left tendencies, vegetarian, teetotaller; Alexander the Britisher, who wants cheddar cheese and English food, and is so proud of the British Navy; the Viceroy, the soldier, sparing of speech, suspicious of new-fangled ideas and I imagine of all foreign ways of thought and action, straightforward, blunt, but with his own sense of humour. And P.-L., what of him? Well, not so resourceful as Cripps, not so downright as the V., not so British as Alexander. Perhaps more judicial than any of them. Weighs up the pros and cons.'

A colleague on their staff recalls that Pethick was the only

[1] See Appendix 2, line 1, ff.

member of the Mission who was never ill; he avoided evening functions so as to be fit during the day. Though Cripps went round seeing everybody, Pethick was the one who applied judgment to situations. In another letter he himself commented on the activities of his energetic second-in-command: 'Sir Stafford Cripps is like the dove that Noah sent out from the Ark. He is constantly going out making contacts but up till now finding no solid ground.'

Pethick's letter of April 14th concluded by saying that 'perhaps more than any of the others I have convinced the Indians of our sincerity'. This, he had explained earlier, was largely due to his readiness to come to India at the age of seventy-four. He added: 'But sincerity alone won't solve the communal problem, and when we get back from Kashmir we have got to face it in earnest'. He had confessed to her the previous day that 'what I would love most is to spend Easter with my darling at Fourways. But since that is out of the question a few days' recess in Kashmir has its charms.'

At Srinagar they were to review the position disclosed by the main interviews, which showed that the Congress leaders were not prepared to see India divided into two separate states, but recognized that the central government must be federal and that the provincial units must have a large measure of autonomy. The Muslim League, on the other hand, stood for a separate sovereign state of Pakistan. They demanded the prior recognition of this principle, and consequently the establishment of two separate constitution-making bodies. This diversity of objectives was the main dilemma for the Cabinet Mission to resolve.

Before leaving for Kashmir, Pethick sent Emmeline an Easter letter: 'I see a still hotter and still more difficult task in the time ahead. Sir Stafford Cripps says he feels assured that somehow the hour is striking when India is to attain her new freedom. I have commended myself to God for Him to fit my little piece of Himself into His great plan as He thinks best.'

Two days later he was writing of their flight over huge snowy peaks at a height of 15,000 feet, followed by a descent into the sunny vale of Kashmir 5,000 feet above sea level. As there were no pressure cabins in the Dakotas of that date, they all had to suck oxygen during the air journeys. At Srinagar the Prime Minister of Kashmir and the Resident met them, and took them through streets lined with people to see them pass. Their faces, reported Pethick, showed neither welcome nor hostility, but just curiosity. In the 'English' climate the almond blossom was recently over, and hawthorn and fruit trees were in flower. 'It is very lovely.' He described the Shalimar gardens with their streams running down in cascades. 'One of them has twelve terraces and a cascade above each.'

At an official luncheon on Easter Sunday, 'the Maharajah and Stafford talked fishing for one and a half hours'. The Maharajah was then Sir Hari Singh, whose enthusiasm for fishing, recalls Earl Alexander, caused him to stock the streams and rivers of Srinagar with British trout. 'He kept pools of trout at different stages of development, and the Mission members were given huge trout to eat at mealtimes.'

New efforts at agreement followed the return of the Mission to Delhi on April 24th. In Kashmir its members had decided to suggest the formation of an interim Government as a new line of approach, but this plan was rejected by both sets of Indian leaders.

'Hotting up. Politics corresponding', Pethick reported tersely to Emmeline from a temperature of 107 degrees. He added that an old friend, Meliscent Shepherd of the Association of Social and Moral Hygiene who had spent twenty years in India, had shared with him that morning's pre-breakfast walk.

On April 27th he wrote to the Presidents of both Congress and the Muslim League saying that the Mission had decided to make one more effort, and invited each side to send four negotiators to meet them. As a *rendezvous* he suggested Simla, in the hope that the cooler air and remoteness from the capital might help agreement. Both Congress and the Muslim League criticized the scheme, but the one appointed Azad, Nehru, Patel and Abdul Ghaffir Khan as representatives, and the other agreed to send Jinnah, Liaquat Ali Khan, Mahommed Ismail Khan and Abdur Rab Nishtar.

The next day Pethick endeavoured to console Emmeline for his absence on the May dates that they both specially valued.[1] 'Just in case I am whisked off to Simla in a hurry I send you

[1] The significance of these dates suggests that May 12th was the day he first proposed to Emmeline, and May 26th the day that they became engaged a year later. The remains of a rose found among his papers, given to him by Emmeline on May 26, 1901 and still vividly pink, indicates that the second date is correctly ascribed.

greeting for our 12th May. The only time we have been physically separated for that season was in 1930 when you were in South Africa . . . But of course we are not really separated for where our heart is there is our treasure also.'

Reaching Simla on May 1st before the Tripartite Conference opened, Pethick reported 'a most wonderful place'. Snowy mountains divided them from both Kashmir and Tibet; from his verandah in Viceregal Lodge perched on the top of a 7,000 feet hill, he could see a panorama which stretched from 50 to 150 miles. They had come part of the way by plane and then 94 miles by car. The last 55 miles were a steady climb and most of the cars had broken down.

The previous night, he said, he had dined with Jinnah and his sister, who closely resembled each other. 'They both look very tall but that is because they are thin with aquiline faces. In reality they are only 5 feet 9 inches and 5 feet 4 inches . . . In spite of all the beauty here I wish I was with you for our festival . . . The political situation has moved slowly forward to a climax which I can't predict.'

On May 2nd cars, rickshaws and ponies brought the members of Congress and the Muslim League to join the Mission at Simla. 'One day', wrote Pethick, 'I will tell you all the behind-the-scenes details of the Alice-in-Wonderland croquet party which it involves.' ('As soon as one part of the apparatus seems all right another part has walked off', he had explained to his secretary Esther Knowles in an earlier letter.) 'I am still clinging to the hope that I may be back on 26th May but . . . it may well be that I shall have to stay in India right into June.' Meanwhile it was consoling to describe a troop of monkeys seen jumping from branch to branch of the tree-tops when he was out for a walk. 'One, a young mother, had a baby tucked under her arm but jumped with the rest.'

Pethick opened the Conference on May 5th with a short address, but after two days of discussion the gulf between the parties remained as wide as ever. To his secretary he wrote that the result of all their talks was quite unpredictable. 'At times I am fascinated by the psychological aspect of it all but the stakes we are playing for are very high.'

He now sent the Presidents of Congress and the Muslim League a list of suggested points for constitutional agreement, but Jinnah found 'many objectionable features', and Azad pointed out that some of the suggestions were opposed to their views. One day Pethick sat in conference for nine hours on end, but could nevertheless write to Emmeline on May 8th: 'In spite of the anxiety, of the awe-inspiring consequences of what we say or do, there is a thrill almost amounting to enjoyment in grappling with these tremendous forces, in trying however imperfectly to ride the whirlwind. And there is a sense too that we are but the instruments of Powers far greater than ourselves, whose Will will in the end be done.'

Next morning the Conference adjourned for two days so that Nehru and Jinnah could talk together. The resumed meeting was not successful, and they adjourned again so that each party could provide a statement of its attitude to the points still outstanding. The subsequent long memoranda showed that, though both sides had modified their views, the gap remained too wide to be bridged.

'Our political weather', wrote Pethick on May 10th, 'is subject to the same rapid changes as the physical weather in the English climate. Sun and storm follow one another at short intervals. Yesterday morning it looked as if the Conference could not fail to break down; by evening it had come out full sunshine but this morning there are dark clouds again . . . Even if it fails we shall have made some headway and you would be astonished if you knew what amount of agreement we had secured.'

But on May 13th, disappointed though not yet disillusioned, he was obliged to report: 'So we didn't get agreement though we made substantial headway'. On the previous day the Conference had disbanded, for though friendly feelings were expressed by all three participants, it was clear that further discussion would serve no useful purpose. The Mission announced that, though an agreed plan had not been reached, their work was far from over. They returned to Delhi promising to issue a statement defining the next steps to be taken. On May 15th, replying to a letter sent when hopes were still high, Emmeline was writing optimistically from Fourways: 'I am thrilled to know that we may have you with us again on May 26th'.

The promised statement,[1] issued on May 16th, was a long and

---

[1] See Appendix 2 for the summary of these proposals, which tried to achieve a compromise between unity and partition.

careful document which announced that, as the main political parties had failed to reach agreement, the Mission had decided to set up an Interim Government which would carry on the administration of British India until a new Constitution could be formed. Detailed recommendations followed outlining the possible shape of this Constitution which Pethick summarized two years later in his essay on Gandhi. Finally the Mission begged all Indians to consider carefully the alternatives of violence, chaos and even civil war which might succeed the rejection of their proposals.

Pethick followed the publication of this statement with a broadcast 'to the world' of which Emmeline subsequently wrote: 'You might have been speaking to us in the next room. The manner as well as the substance was perfect. I am so glad that you spoke not only very clearly, articulating every word and syllable, but also slowly so that those to whom the language was not their mother tongue could follow and understand. As you will know the reception of the Plan in this country has been marvellously restrained.' Prophetically she concluded: 'My personal feeling is that it is "too good to be true" and that the present moment is the calm before the storm'.

Pethick's broadcast began by referring to the passionate desire in Indian hearts for independence and the readiness of the British Government to accord it, 'within or without the British Commonwealth, in the hope that out of it would spring a lasting and friendly association between our two peoples on a footing of complete equality'. He continued by summarizing the obstacles confronting the Mission and their endeavours to create agreement, and went on to analyze their view of the Muslim claims.

'While we recognize the reality of the fear of the Muslim League that in a purely unitary India their community with its own culture and way of life might become submerged in a majority Hindu rule, we do not accept the setting up of a separate Muslim sovereign state as a solution of the communal problem.' Such a state, he continued, would contain a substantial minority of other communities; it would also endanger the country's defence by splitting the Army in two. Their own recommendations secured the advantages of a Pakistan without the dangers inherent in the division of India. After describing their proposals and announcing the suggested Interim Government, he concluded with what seemed to him the fundamental issue. 'The future of India and how that future is inaugurated are matters of vital importance not only to India herself but to the whole world. If a great new sovereign state can come into being in a spirit of mutual goodwill both within and without India, that of itself will be an outstanding contribution to world stability . . . But the constitution for India has to be framed by Indians and worked by Indians when they have brought it into being. The responsibility and the opportunity is theirs and in their fulfilment of it we wish them godspeed.'

A debate in the House of Commons coincided with this broadcast, in which the Prime Minister read the Mission's statement, and Winston Churchill described it as 'an able but melancholy document'. On May 17th a broadcast by Lord Wavell commended the statement, and on this and the previous day two Press conferences elucidated it for over 100 Indian and foreign pressmen. Sir Stafford Cripps conducted the first; at the second, according to a day-by-day account of the Mission's work subsequently published by two Indians, Anil Chandra Banerjee and Dakshima Ranjan Bose, 'Lord Pethick-Lawrence, speaking easily and with even temper, answered scores of questions'.

One question put to him inquired whether he agreed with Mr Churchill's notion of losing the Empire. Characteristically he replied: 'Nothing can redound more to the highest traditions of liberty which prevail in my country than if, as a result of our labours, we have in the years to come a sovereign country here in India whose relationship with ours is one of friendliness and equity'.

'His knowledge of the different and often baffling aspects of the plan was precise and sound', wrote B. Shiva Rao in his obituary article, 'and he never permitted any opportunist approach to any problem as an easy way out. No step could be taken and no decision adopted without his careful scrutiny and assent.'

The numerous authorities on the transfer of power agree that, though the prolonged conferences might have appeared sterile, they had materially altered British-Indian relations since the Indians were at last convinced that the British meant to withdraw. Controversy might continue but suspicion decreased; the Anglo-Congress relations especially improved, though those with the Muslim League remained difficult because Jinnah suspected a British 'deal' with the Congress leaders.

To begin with Mahatma Gandhi, who had begged the Mission to present their document in the form of a proposal rather than the language of an award, reacted favourably to the statement; the Mission, he said at his prayer meeting on May 19th, had produced something of which they had every reason to be proud. Next day he wrote in *Harijan* that it was the best document the British Government could have produced in the circumstances. 'It reflects our weakness, if we could be good enough to see it. The Congress and the League did not, could not, agree. We would grievously err if, at this time, we foolishly satisfy ourselves that the differences are a British creation.'

He went on however to illustrate Pethick's comments on his subtlety by saying: 'My compliment . . . does not mean that what is best from the British standpoint is also best, or even good, from the Indian. Their best may possibly be harmful.' But as Jinnah, though critical, persuaded the Muslim League on June 6th to accept the Mission's statement as a basis for discussion, a widespread hope grew in both India and Britain that a way of reconciling the divergent claims of the two main parties had at last been found.

CHAPTER 23

Ordeal by Frustration

Would the Indian parties accept the suggested Interim Government? Would they agree to discuss the proposed Constitution? Would they, at worst, reject both schemes, or perhaps react positively to one?

More vividly and truthfully than any official document, Pethick's letters reflect the tensions and anxieties of the Mission in the exhausting tropical heat as they waited for the Indian leaders to give them the answer to these questions. The burden lay heavily upon them all, but heaviest upon him who was the Mission's official leader.

One major problem for Pethick—as for his predecessors in delicate negotiations, such as Simon and Cripps—was the sensitiveness and liability to misunderstanding of Indian psychology. So often, words and actions intended as friendly gestures seemed to become causes of stumbling. With his direct, lucid mind and relatively simple temperament, Pethick sometimes found the subtleties of Gandhi and the hostile responses of the easily-affronted Jinnah almost more than he could bear. He was constantly bewildered and distressed by the fact that his honourable good intentions seemed so often to offend rather than pacify these extremely complicated human beings.

On May 18th he brought Emmeline face to face with realities up to date. 'I have had to say to myself that it is no good letting my heart or my head be obsessed with the idea that I want to be home for 26th May. I came out here to do a certain job and I have just got to stay till it's finished; and that's that. As soon as it is finished I shall come home as fast as I can to be with my old love again, and the day I come back whatever it be according to the calendar will be our 26th May, our forty-fifth anniversary.'

He continued more cheerfully. 'My life here is full of colour and experience. Colour on the physical plane: the powerful sun, the flaming trees, the flashing birds, the darting chipmunks and lizards. The trees are red (gold Mohur), gold (Cassia Sistilla), and apple-blossom-tinted (Cassia Nodosa). Colourful personalities—Gandhi, Nehru, Jinnah, Wavell, to say nothing of people like Meliscent Shepherd, Mrs Naidu, Agatha Harrison . . . So far in all the "changing vicissitudes of this mortal life" I have been upheld to keep my balance and my health, remembering that it is not I that am doing it but He. So my beloved I am patient and I am sure you will be also to await the day of our reunion when it comes in His good will . . . Our D Day has come and gone and we are waiting the result . . . so far it has been sunny weather. All this may be dashed at any moment but let us at any rate bask in the sunshine while it lasts.'

At evening he was obliged to record a setback. 'As I anticipated some clouds have darkened the sun and Jinnah threatens not to give us an answer for three or four *weeks!* I really don't know what to make of it. But there are still many encouraging signs . . . At the moment it looks as if Congress will come in.'

One minor encouragement was the decision of the Standing Committee of the Chamber of Princes to accept the Memorandum on States' Treaties and Paramountcy presented to them by the Mission on May 22nd; these, they found, provided the necessary machinery for the attainment of India's independence, which they supported, and a reasonable basis for their own participation. On the next day Pethick, stirred by a communication from Emmeline, began for the first time to disclose his latent yearning to return home.

'Your dear letter of May 18th brought tears to my eyes. You mention in it the fact that the aeroplane for our return journey was ordered to be here on May 20th. How I wish that . . . there was any real likelihood of our leaving in a few days. It is unfortunately far otherwise . . .

'But darling we have just to bear this separation. I recognized to the full when I left home that I was in the hands of God and that His good pleasure must be fulfilled. I must not even in thought go back on the consecration and I know you would not wish me to do so. The difficulties of this job do not grow less and the subtleties of the Indian mind if anything increase.'

He concluded, however, by referring to a new setback for which Hindu subtlety was not responsible. 'Poor Stafford has had to go to hospital. He expects to be away a week. His eagle mind has used up the energies of his body.'

In the event Sir Stafford was absent much more than a week; he was not able to join the other members of the Mission for lunch until June 21st. His indisposition began when he fainted in Simla after a morning call on Gandhi; he had overestimated his ability to climb the steep roads, and walked back too quickly. Throughout the last month of the Mission's work he was periodically ill. One senior member of the Mission believed that he did too much, saw too many people, and associated too closely with the Congress leaders at the expense of the Muslims; 'he spoke to Jinnah like a prosecuting counsel'. But Pethick was in no two minds about the value of his energetic colleague in dealing with the many legal dilemmas involved.

'I miss the counsel of Stafford Cripps terribly', he told Emmeline some days later. Meanwhile he had written her on May 23rd that he looked like sitting around for a fortnight, waiting for Jinnah to consult his followers. 'It is a bit outrageous but if only it works out all right in the end, what is a mere fortnight in the life of a nation?'

The day before, Emmeline was writing from Peaslake: 'You will hardly be surprised that as the days of our month of May draw towards the end, I become sentimental with the longing to welcome you home again. I realize that it is necessary to play the game of Patience right to the very end. The report in *The Times* this morning of the indisposition of Sir Stafford Cripps gave us all a shock. Apart from our great concern on his behalf, I realize what an extra burden of responsibility and work it throws on his colleagues.'

But she added two days later: 'I am much too keen on the success of your Mission to wish you to leave it a moment sooner than is expedient. And I am so thankful for your continued health and serenity that there is an undercurrent of music in all the days in spite of the fact that once or twice recently another theme is blent with the main melody. But now that I know that the month of May is definitely out of reach I shall settle down again.'

On May 25th the Viceroy and the Mission put out a further statement after considering Jinnah's communication of May 22nd and a resolution of the Congress Working Committee dated May 24th.

'The position is that since the Indian leaders, after prolonged discussion, failed to arrive at an agreement, the Delegation put forward their recommendations as the nearest approach to reconciling the views of the two main parties. The scheme stands as a whole and can only succeed if it is accepted and worked in a spirit of co-operation.'

Pethick's letter to Emmeline on May 26th began with a purely personal interlude, and went on: 'Our political barometer continues to go up and down. At the present moment after a severe depression it has appreciably risen . . . Cripps is in hospital but is improving and hopes to be out in a few days. Alexander has gone off to the south on an Admiralty mission. Jinnah is still at Simla and his Muslim League does not meet till June 3rd. The Congress have adjourned and departed so I and the Viceroy are left alone.

'I have told them to have an aeroplane standing by by June 10th but I am afraid that doesn't mean I shall get off by then. Still the time is coming when I shall have to say to the parties *not* that "my patience is exhausted" but "time gentlemen please". It may be the only way to get them to decide anything.'

On the same day Emmeline was writing: 'This is our May 26th. I woke early with thoughts of you . . . My memory goes back to forty-five years ago—how very definitely and clearly certain moments in one's life stand isolated as if they were moments ever-living, regardless of the passing of time . . . And now we are together again in a different way and there are still chapters to be written to our life . . . I gather from the broadcast last night as well as from *The Times* yesterday morning that you have reached that dead point of seeming frustration which we knew had to come.'

In the meantime Gandhi and the Working Committee of Congress had closely scrutinized the Mission's statement of May 16th, which Gandhi in a *Harijan* article on June 2nd still described as 'a brave and frank document'. Nevertheless it seemed to him to have three vital defects: First, the formation of a popular government at the centre should have preceded the statement; secondly, the question of paramountcy remained unsolved; and thirdly, it visualized the retention of troops during the interim period. 'A nation that desires alien troops for its safety, internal or external, or has them imposed upon it, can never be described as independent . . . It is in effect a nation unfit for self-government.'

Other communities besides the Congress found defects in the Plan. The Sikhs, corresponding with Pethick through their chief spokesman Master Tara Singh, reported that 'a wave of dejection, resentment and indignation has run through the Sikh community', since 'the Sikhs have been entirely thrown at the mercy of the Muslims'. The Scheduled Castes Federation led by Dr Ambedkar also found fault with the statement; so too did the Anglo-Indians.

On May 28th Pethick had written to Emmeline: 'I am so glad that you feel just as I do about my coming home. The job comes first, second, third and all the time. But when it is done—so far as it can be done—all my mind and heart will be in coming home and seeing you again.'

Sir Stafford, he added, was now back with his colleagues, 'but with a long way to go yet'. His wife was coming out to take him home by ship, and passages had been booked for them on a vessel sailing from Bombay on June 16th; by that time he hoped that their job would be done.

'These people here keep on keeping us waiting in turn and then are inclined to grumble at us for the delay. I suppose we must remember that we have been keeping them waiting in a sense for the last fifty years! I think on the whole we make progress though sometimes there is a great slip backwards which seems to retrace the forward steps of many days. Through it all I do not forget that we can only do our best with the parts that are given to us, it is the Great Dramatist who decides whether the play is to have a happy ending.'

On the same day Emmeline was writing: 'What a heavenly little letter this morning. Yes, I had adjusted my mind at once (or nearly at once) to the continued separation—knowing and rejoicing in the spirit with which you have accepted from the first your task in the present Government . . . Much as I miss you I would not have you cut short by a day or an hour the time required . . . I share your conviction that results—important as they are—are beyond our calculation or our will, but honesty of purpose and faithfulness to every demand are the supreme factors within the compass of our purpose and determination.'

Three days afterwards he thanked her for her patient acceptance of the frustrating delays. 'Your spiritual support means a great deal to me in these days when I have to call on all my spiritual resources in order "neither to fail nor falter nor regret". I find it is not enough to have patience. I have also to have unfailing goodwill to those who try my patience and at the back of it all to retain that reliance on the wise purpose of the Designer of all things. And so I pray that courage, endurance and wisdom may continue to be vouchsafed to me, and that all my works may be "begun and continued and ended in Him".'

In a few days, he thought, he might be able to 'trouble' Sir Stafford Cripps again 'with some of the conundrums which confront me morning noon and night. We have to get agreement on lots of things and a failure to get it on any one of them may mean a breakdown with consequences which humanly speaking are pretty serious . . . The weather is rather trying with maximum between 100° and 108° and minimum between 80° and 85° . . . After a talk with Stafford who is much better Sudhir Ghosh came to see me, a young man of twenty-nine who acts as "Mercury" to Gandhi. We had a delightful talk. I have seen him many times before and am very fond of him.'

On June 4th the Viceroy wrote to Mr Jinnah: 'You asked me yesterday to give you an assurance about the action that would be taken if one party accepted the scheme in the Cabinet Delegation's statement of May 16th and the other refused. I can give you on behalf of the Cabinet Delegation my personal assurance that we do not propose to make any discrimination in the treatment of either party; and that we shall go ahead with the plan laid down in the statement so far as circumstances permit if either party accepts; but we hope that both will accept.'

On June 6th, following Jinnah's advice, and in spite of a protest about the Mission's conclusion regarding Pakistan[1] as 'unwarranted, unjustified and unconvincing' . . . and an 'affront offered to Muslim sentiments by a choice of injudicious words', the Muslim League accepted as a whole the scheme outlined by the Mission, and agreed to join the constitution-making body.

'The two parties, like boxers,' writes Percival Spear, 'were now

---

[1] 'We are unable to advise the British Government that the power which at present resides in British hands should be handed over to two entirely separate Sovereign States.'

circling each other searching for weak spots. The worried umpire, who wanted them to shake hands, was beginning to lose control of the situation.' Two days earlier the umpire-in-chief had written anxiously to his wife: 'My labours here continue unabated. The days that lie immediately ahead are likely to be days of crisis and anything may come out of them.' In reply to this, hardly less weary of crises than he was, she commented on June 5th: 'I begin to feel like a train that has lost its engine and is waiting in a siding.'

The previous day he had repeated: 'Our climacteric can be expected in about six days. We may get full agreement. We may get rejection by both parties. We may get any one of various gradations between the two . . . They have been printing stories here of my intention to *retire*, but I have said nothing whatever to justify this; I think it originates with *The News of the World*.' He continued two days later by telling her of a dream that for once had diverted his mind from the Mission's problems:

'It is certainly very hot—112° maximum in the day is bad enough, but 93° minimum in the night is worse, in spite of air-conditioning and fan. Last night I was a little restless and about four o'clock I went into my bathroom and got into a bath of what does duty for cold water (a few degrees below blood heat). I dozed off and dreamt that you and I were driving down from Mascot to Dorking Station in a horse-drawn fly. We agreed that at our age (our present age) there was something to be said for this placid method of progression. This pleasant little dream so soothed me that when I got back into bed I slept peacefully.'

He concluded with regret: 'I have no fresh news to give you . . . I have purposely allowed our intention of leaving about June 15th to leak out as I think it may help the parties to take definite decisions . . . Apart from being homesick I confess to being a little weary, but I can certainly stick it out another ten days or fortnight or even a little longer if really necessary.'

CHAPTER 24

The Price of Achievement

On June 8th Pethick thankfully reported to Emmeline the Muslim League's acceptance of their plan; Congress, he added, might well do the same and yet there might be a clash about the Interim Government on the question regarding parity of numbers between the two bodies. 'If there is not agreement there will still be some arguing to be done and an agreement of sorts may or may not be reached in the end . . . Our present view remains that we ought not to stay much longer.'

Less calmly he continued three days later: 'Oh, my dear, we struggle on. We are at the last main fence but whether we get over it or fall at it I can't say. It is touch and go.' The following day he sent her a longer letter which graphically defined the cost of the negotiations in human terms.

'The situation is very critical. And this afternoon it looked for a while as if a decision would almost certainly be reached in some thirty-six hours and could scarcely be other than a rejection. For a moment I had a sensation of relief. As one who has kept for a long while a weary vigil at the bedside of a beloved sick relative and there are signs that the end is approaching. And then came the reaction as I thought of the terrible time ahead if the calamity in fact materialized. And so I stifled back my desire for personal escape and thanked God that while there was life there was still hope. And it may be . . . but can it . . . and will it? Can we in very truth claw back victory out of the mouths of the hounds of defeat? It may mean abandoning any hope of getting back before the end of June. It may mean failing in the end after it all. But as in the poem John X. Merriman gave us:

> 'Great is the facile conqueror,
> But he who unhorsed
> And covered o'er with blood and sweat
> Fights on, is greater yet.'

'Everyone here takes the situation differently. Alexander is frankly angry but will play the game by his colleagues even at great personal inconvenience. Cripps refuses to be discouraged. He has postponed his passage home. The Viceroy is the soldier fighting gallantly a rearguard action. Gandhi in his own peculiar way is at the moment fighting three-quarters on our side. Several others desperately want a peaceful settlement, and with them are many of the general public. But there are many reckless men and women who eagerly hope for a breakdown and a return to revolutionary activities. And there are many who blame everyone but themselves and reserve their choicest epithets of abuse for the Mission.'

His only breaks in the day, he said, were short walks at 7 a.m. and 7 p.m. and an occasional game of billiards.

'Otherwise I just work and negotiate and discuss and read the papers. But I pray that I do so to the glory of God.'

That same day the Viceroy invited Nehru and Jinnah to a joint consultation, but Jinnah declined. The Viceroy then saw Nehru, and made new proposals which were unacceptable. Nehru then put forward further suggestions which the Viceroy felt impelled to reject since they were unlikely to command Jinnah's agreement. He next suggested an Executive Council of thirteen members, but Congress turned down the formula on which this was based. A complete deadlock had therefore been reached, and in order to precipitate a decision the Viceroy issued a new statement on June 16th announcing that 'no useful purpose can be served by further prolonging these discussions'. Since it was essential that a strong and representative Interim Government should be set up, he proposed to issue invitations to fourteen named persons to serve on it. Of these, five were Hindu members of Congress, five members of the Muslim League, and three representatives of minorities (Sikhs, Indian Christians, and Parsees). Nehru and Jinnah both appeared on the list.

Paragraph 8 of the statement ran: 'In the event of the two major parties or either of them proving unwilling to join in the setting up of a Coalition Government on the above lines it is the intention of the Viceroy to proceed with the formation of an Interim Government which will be as representative as possible of those willing to accept the statement of May 16th'.

Jinnah interpreted this paragraph to mean that if Congress

rejected the Interim Government proposals but the Muslim League accepted them, the Viceroy would be obliged to form a government which would inevitably consist mainly of Muslims, although it would be unrepresentative and hence unworkable. This paragraph was the basis of his subsequent accusation that the Viceroy and the Mission had been guilty of bad faith.

Pethick wrote on June 17th to Emmeline: 'With the publication of our statement yesterday the political barometer has risen somewhat but at any moment may go down again'. If she had heard nothing further by the time his letter reached her, she must take it 'either that they were still haggling about it or that one or other of the parties has turned either the long term or the short term scheme definitely down. I hope that in any case we may not have to stay here many days longer, but if necessary we may have to do so . . . It is getting damp and sticky and the monsoon may break before we leave. The swimming pool is full of hot water and it is not easy to swim in it.'

His letter of June 19th outlined a new source of discouragement which for him was peculiarly disappointing.

'At the moment Gandhi is being very awkward. He suffers from high blood pressure and when he gets an idea he won't let go of it even if it goes contrary to what he has been urging up to the day before. He prefers theoretical perfection as he sees it and is not really interested in the practical considerations of government which involve mutual accommodation. At the moment, almost for the first time in its history the Congress High Command having been converted by him to support our interim scheme, are refusing to "right about face" at his suggestion and wreck it. Whether they will stand firm on this remains to be seen.'

In a broadcast made (September 14, 1954) from the perspective of his last decade, Pethick reached his final judgment on the Mahatma.

'I did not find Gandhiji a very easy person with whom to negotiate a political settlement. Where he considered a matter of principle was at stake he was very unwilling to make concessions. Even when in verbal discussion he appeared to have conceded a point I frequently discovered afterwards that his interpretation of our talk was not the same as mine. Some little word or phrase he had used which seemed unimportant at the time, I found later rendered the concession nugatory.

'On the other hand Gandhi was most generous in attributing good motives to those who differed from him. Another part of his endearing qualities was his unbounded faith in the possibilities of ordinary men and women. There was no height of nobility or sacrifice which he would hesitate to demand from them. And it was wonderful how often they responded to his faith in them. But this too had its dangerous side for he did not always seem to me to realize that governments in the exercise of their responsibilities must sometimes use compulsory powers to restrain wrongdoers from doing harm to others.

'Gandhi was known as a Mahatma on account of his ascetic life and his great spiritual faith which he drew from Hindu, Christian, Muslim and other religious sources. He was a great man too in the mundane sense because he won the allegiance of tens of millions of his fellow men and women and was rightly accounted one of the architects of Indian independence. I treasure his memory not only for these qualities but as that of a firm personal friend during the major part of a long life.'

After the statement of June 16th had been issued, Jinnah decided to reserve his decision until Congress, which was debating it at great length with Gandhi, had come to a conclusion. At first it appeared as though they would accept the statements of both May 16th and June 16th; Pethick records in *Mahatma Gandhi* that the *Hindustan Times*, which was closely in touch with Congress, published a cartoon showing the Cabinet Ministers packing up to go home above the caption: 'All's well that ends well'.

But optimism was premature; the new hope of an agreed settlement foundered upon yet another rock. For one of the proposed Hindu members of the Interim Government suggested by the Viceroy, Gandhi and the Congress—which throughout its history had contended that the central Government of India should be constituted as a *de facto* Cabinet 'with full power' and that the minorities should be represented in proportion to population—proposed to substitute a Muslim who was not a member of the Muslim League. They might, Pethick thought, have this time made an exception in their historic practice had not their determination been hardened by acrimonious Press articles on both sides and by Jinnah's public pronouncement that the Muslim League would never tolerate such an arrangement.

Knowing that an Interim Government could not function without a measure of initial goodwill, the Mission felt compelled to reject the Congress proposal.

On June 20th Pethick's letter to Emmeline showed for the first time a measure of exasperation created by extreme fatigue, and by the tendency of the wrangling parties to argue as though all eternity was before them while he and his colleagues were growing daily more conscious of urgent work piling up at the India Office, the Admiralty, and the Board of Trade.

'Whatever happens (and the political barometer is standing pretty low at the moment) these people are not going to get me down. Neither am I going to admit that the Mission has been a failure or that our work has been in vain. The goodwill we have shown will live on and bear fruit even if they curse us by bell book and candle when the time comes for us to depart . . . I think it most improbable that I shall be back before the end of June.'

Responding immediately to the note of unwonted impatience in his letter, Emmeline sought to show him the Indian scene in the largest perspective that she could visualize.

'I agree with you that neither you in your big mission nor I in my domestic sphere or in sympathy with you can afford to let anybody "get us down". Now is the moment when we must make practical use of all our philosophy and all our faith . . . Your problem in India is the problem of the whole world today. There is unrest, revolt, suspicion, hatred everywhere. There was a long article on Burma in *The Times* today. The problems there are being intensified by what is happening in India.'

She concluded by telling him that the Surrey countryside was covered with wild roses. 'I never see them without thinking of you.'

But already, in his next two letters, he had apologized for his momentary lapse from iron control.

'The political barometer has gone so up and down that I really don't know from day to day what the final result will be . . . It is now as certain as anything can be that the Congress will reject the plan for an Interim Government. What they will do about the Constituent Assembly is at the moment of writing still in doubt. But my hopes are not very high . . . People start coming to interview me at 7 a.m. and the last doesn't leave much before midnight. And nothing whatever comes of it! And the heat is stifling.'

On June 25th Maulana Azad, the President of Congress, finally conveyed to the Mission their decision on its statements of May 16th and June 16th. This was not, however, a downright acceptance like that of the Muslim League, but involved an 'interpretation'[1] of some of the main suggestions. It nevertheless contained the words: 'While adhering to our views, we accept your proposals and are prepared to work them with a view to achieve our objective'.

The Mission decided that this constituted an acceptance, though qualified, and Pethick was able to give Emmeline some definite news at last.

'Congress today turned down the plan for Interim Government but accepted the long-term plan for Constitution-making. The result though not so good as at one time seemed possible is a considerable achievement for which I am profoundly thankful.'

In the light of this Congress decision the Viceroy, notwithstanding his letter of June 4th to Jinnah which had contained the qualifying clause 'as far as circumstances permit', did not continue the attempt to form an Interim Government. Instead, since the verbal combatants were now all exhausted, he announced the formation of a Caretaker Government of officials which would function during the elections for the Constituent Assembly, and carry on until the prospect of creating an Interim Government representative of both main parties appeared more encouraging.

When Jinnah learned of this decision he strongly dissented from it, and did not conceal his opinion that the new arrangement constituted a breach of faith. He had been prepared to enter an Interim Government if Congress had accepted the May 16th statement free from 'interpretations', but felt that if they took office without commitment to the Mission's actual version, the document would be worthless to the Muslims. He therefore maintained that the Congress reply was not a true acceptance, and thus only the Muslim League was entitled to enter the

[1] i.e. suggested modifications relating to the powers of the Constituent Assembly, the procedures for its election, the residuary powers vested in the provinces which appeared to the Congress to infringe 'the basic principle of provincial autonomy', and the 'vague' provisions regarding the appointment of representatives for the Indian States.

Interim Government. According to the strict letter of the documents he had a clear technical case, but the one-sided Government which he visualized (as he must certainly have known) would have been an absurdity, calculated to produce an explosion.

The June 26th statement by the Viceroy and the Mission concluded with a hopeful endeavour to paper over the cracks.

'In leaving India the members of the Cabinet Mission express their cordial thanks for all the courtesy and consideration which they have received as guests of the country and they most sincerely trust that the steps which have been initiated will lead to a speedy realization of the hopes and wishes of the Indian people.'

The long ordeal of anxiety and suspense, endured through the hostile heat of a tropical summer, was over at last—not happily, as Pethick had once thought possible, but usefully and without total disaster. On the foundations that the Mission had laid, the independence of India would eventually be built. They had brought India's future from the clouds of speculation into the daylight realm of reality, and they had at last convinced the Indian leaders that a British Government really intended to keep its pledge. Henceforth, in the words of Mr V. P. Menon, 'it was not to be so much a struggle to wrest power from the British, as a dispute as to how that power, once inherited, should be shared by the parties concerned'.

On June 27th, Pethick sent Emmeline his final letter from India; she would have heard, he wrote, that they were leaving on the 29th, and he hoped that she would be glad to see her husband, who longed overwhelmingly to be with her. 'He has nearly reached the limit of human endurance. I cannot assess how far we have succeeded or how far we have failed. I am afraid that humanly speaking the failure (in spite of first appearances) greatly exceeds the success. But that may prove too pessimistic a forecast . . . It may be that in the mercy of God what looks like failure may prove the road to success.'

The great trouble in India, he concluded, was suspicion, which caused the Press to rush into torrents of abuse on behalf of those who did not get what they wanted, 'and the still small voice of reason and moderation is unheard in the babble of conflicting claims'. Fortunately he was to survive to see a day when no cloud of suspicion would darken India-British relations, and each country would look for friendship and support to the other.

For Pethick the heralds of that calmer time had appeared even before he left India. 'I have made some charming friends', ran his last sentence to Emmeline, 'in particular Rajagopalachari,[1] who has written me a most *affectionate* letter to say goodbye.'

This warm communication from a distinguished Indian leader began a correspondence which lasted to the end of Pethick's life. But just before the Mission finally departed, he received another affectionate letter which went far to redeem his sorrowful sense of frustration and disappointment.

'My dearest Pethick', wrote Sir Stafford Cripps on June 29th, 'I just feel that I could not leave India without expressing to you as the leader of our Mission the intense admiration and gratitude that I feel for all you have done.

'It has not always been easy in this intemperate climate to hold together the team but your courtesy, fairness and deep sincerity have overcome any obstacles that there might have been. Our common affection to you has been a binding force for the whole of our team.

'In the conduct of our negotiations you have made a wise mixture of caution with enthusiasm for the cause of Indian Independence and a determination not to let your patience become exhausted, even though you yourself were feeling physically exhausted.

'It has been a tremendous privilege and joy to me to be associated with you in this historic enterprise and I believe that you can be satisfied with the contribution that you have made to World History.

'Though it is true that the results are those of the team it is to you that the major share of the credit must justly be given. Your unremitting labours, the high trust in which the Indian leaders held you and your convincing sincerity have created an atmosphere of trust amongst the Indian people different to anything known from the earliest times of British occupation.

'The superficial and partisan attempts to discredit your work are not I am convinced reflecting anything but the anger of disappointed politicians.

[1] Prime Minister of Madras, Finance Minister, Home Minister, and Governor-General in succession. After his retirement, founded the new Swatantra Party in 1959 at the age of eighty-one. An authority on Socrates and Hinduism.

'Our "home life" here in Willingdon Crescent, a most important factor in our work, has been happy and restful because of the kindliness of the "Father" of our party.

'We have all learnt to love our leader with unrestrained affection and I regard it as the highest privilege that I should have been allowed to serve under and with you during these last three and a half months.

'May God Bless and keep you to see the fulfilment of your labours.

Stafford.'

CHAPTER 25

Rough Road to Independence

As Pethick has explained in his study of Gandhi, the Mission left a confused pattern behind it in India.

'Both the major parties had accepted the proposals of May 16th for a long-term settlement, and were prepared to take part in the election of members of the constitution-making body which was already in progress. But no representative Government had been set up or was in immediate prospect.'

The Congress leaders, including Gandhi, were at last convinced of the Mission's sincerity. At the all-India Committee meeting in Bombay—where Nehru, who had been elected Congress President two months earlier, took over this position from Azad—they decided, after prolonged discussion, to endorse their Working Committee's support of the Mission's proposals. Eventually the elections to the Constituent Assembly produced 275 Congress members and 73 representatives of the Muslim League.

Back in England, Pethick had little time to relax amid the wild roses in his Surrey garden; on July 18th he reported on the work of the Mission to the House of Lords while Sir Stafford Cripps spoke in the House of Commons.

Pethick began by describing the marked diversities of race, religion, language and culture in the great Indian sub-continent. 'No wonder it is, then, that Indian statesmen are keenly conscious of their responsibilities and take divergent views as to the precise constitutional future of that country . . . While the Congress has always stood for one United India, the claim of the Muslim League has been for the division of India into Hindustan and Pakistan. Therefore, while the first task of the Mission was to convince Indians of the sincerity of the British people in offering them independence within or without the British Commonwealth according to their choice, their second task was to bridge the apparently unbridgeable gap between the rival views of the two great Indian parties.'

They had been, he claimed, entirely successful in their first objective, but the main difficulty in achieving the second 'lay in the fact that not only were the major parties differing in their views of the future constitutional structure of India, but this divergence prevented them from agreeing on a Constitution-making machinery'.

He went on to summarize 'the very welcome spirit of accommodation' at the Simla Conference which had led the Mission to put out their Statement of May 16th, with its proposals for a constituent assembly. That Statement had on the whole an excellent reception, though both sides criticized some of its proposals. On June 6th, in spite of its criticisms, the Muslim League had accepted the scheme; 'this was a great step forward, and I pay tribute to the courage and statesmanship of Mr Jinnah that, in advance of the Congress, he should have advocated in his Council and carried through that body acceptance of our proposals'. The Congress had finally accepted on June 26th; 'thus we have secured in the end the acceptance of both the major parties'.

He added that the elections then in progress seemed likely to return some of the best human material in India to the Constitution-making body. 'If my expectations in this respect are fulfilled, a most valuable start has been made to the creation of a constitutional structure for the future of India. It is on a free consensus of the many diverse elements of the Indian people that the success of the new constitution will depend.'

Pethick then turned to the less satisfactory results which had followed the negotiations for an Interim Government. No agreement on this had been achieved either at Simla or in Delhi; 'we reached a complete deadlock and it seemed the only possible way to break it was for the Viceroy, in consultation with the Mission to choose a suitable Interim Government on a basis of six Congress, including one from the Depressed Classes, five Muslim, one Sikh, and two others — one a Parsee and one an Indian Christian'.

The Congress, he continued, though troubled by the type of parity still remaining between the Muslim League and the Caste Hindus, might have consented to this arrangement had there not been, unfortunately, a widely published disclosure of certain letters written by Mr Jinnah at that moment, the most important of which contained a sentence saying that the Muslim League would never accept the appointment of any Muslim by the Viceroy other than a Muslim Leaguer . . . 'The Congress has always insisted on the national character of their organization and this is fully demonstrated by their nomination of personnel in the Provincial Assemblies. It was made clear to Mr Jinnah that neither the Viceroy nor the Mission could accept his claim to a monopoly of Muslim appointments.'

By that time it was too late to accept much alteration of the Viceroy's plan. In their statement of June 16th, the Mission laid down the course they intended to pursue if neither of the major parties felt able to accept a Coalition Government on the basis proposed.

'If either opposed it, the whole basis of the Coalition fell to the ground. In this event our statement of June 16th stated that the Viceroy would seek to form an Interim Government which would be as representative as possible of all those willing to accept the statement of May 16th. When the Congress ultimately came to their final decision to accept the May 16th statement, while unfortunately rejecting the Interim Government, they quite clearly became equally eligible with the Muslim League for inclusion in such a representative Government.'

He added that when the Congress refused to work the scheme of June 16th, it could not be pursued. 'The situation now is that the Viceroy will proceed to act on Paragraph 8 of the statement of June 16th after a very short delay.' Nobody, he continued, had desired a 'Caretaker Government' of officials, but no other solution was possible. 'The next stage will be for the Viceroy to resume negotiations at the earliest moment with the two major parties for the formation of an Interim Government.'

In spite of Pethick's friendly reference to Jinnah's statesmanship, neither his speech nor the simultaneous explanation given by Sir Stafford in the Commons convinced the President of the Muslim League that the Viceroy and the Mission had not gone back on their undertakings. Ten days after Pethick's statement in the House of Lords, he persuaded his Council to withdraw their acceptance of the Mission's proposals, and instead proclaimed a 'Direct Action Day' for August 16th.

When the day came, the combination of processions, meetings and bitter propaganda in the major cities precipitated riots which lasted for four days. Owing to their dire consequences in Calcutta, the main border city where Hindu and Muslim areas meet, nearly 5,000 persons lost their lives and about 15,000 were injured. This massacre came to be known as 'the great Calcutta killing'. In the opinion of one historian,[1] 'these fearful events marked the real end of united British India'.

Early in September new rumours of Pethick's impending retirement brought an anxious telegram from the Viceroy. This he felt compelled to refer to the Prime Minister, assuring him that he had never said anything either in public or in private to justify such reports. Had the Mission to India been as successful as many people thought it, he might have asked to be relieved of his burden, but to lay it down now with such grave issues still unsolved would, he felt, be running away.

As he relinquished the opportunity of escape, did he criticize himself, recapitulating the events of the past few months, for failing to do the impossible and to solve the insoluble? A letter to his secretary, Esther Knowles, written at this time, suggests that perhaps he did.

'With regard to India I don't know what to say to you. On the one hand all sorts of people praise me. But I am conscious of my own and the Mission's shortcomings in the past and great difficulties in the future. I know that the right thing is to put aside all regrets as to the past and all fears as to the future, and face up to the task now with such judgment and wisdom as I possess. The result is out of my keeping.'

Time brought a measure of philosophy towards even the consciousness of failure, and in his essay *If I Had My Time Again*, published five years later, he was able to take a realistic view of personal self-criticism: 'I have come to recognize that such mental self-flagellation is a form of vanity and does positive injury to the tissues of the brain. To make mistakes is part of the law of being of all living things who mainly progress by trial and error. Our personality has to learn wisdom by making mistakes. The fool is not the man who makes many diverse mistakes but he who goes on making the same mistake over and over again.'

His correspondence at this time included letters from both Jinnah and Nehru, to whom he had written after leaving India. Jinnah's letter, though cool, was courteous and referred appre-

[1] Percival Spear. *India* (1961).

ciatively to A. V. Alexander; but it seems unlikely that Pethick, always so scrupulous in his standards and practice, ever wholly recovered from the accusations of bad faith so publicly handed out both to himself and to the Viceroy. Among the many famous statesmen, both British and Indian, on whom he wrote and broadcast between his retirement from the India Office and his death, Jinnah is a notable omission. But the only published criticism of him that he appears ever to have permitted himself occurs very briefly in his book on Gandhi, after he has described the Muslim League's withdrawal of their previous acceptance of the Mission's proposals and the programme of direct action: 'These were grave decisions'.

Nehru's cordial letter probably recalled a comment made by him to Pethick during the Cabinet Mission: 'I know you think that we are difficult people to pin down to an answer, but you must realize that if you and we do come to an agreement, you are laying down a burden and we are picking it up'. In a subsequent essay contributed to *A Study of Nehru*, edited by Rafiq Zakaria and published in 1959, Pethick wrote: 'He is today by far the most outstanding personality in his country and is esteemed, obeyed and loved by the vast masses of the people. Nevertheless, powerful as he is, he remains in theory, in practice and, I am convinced, at heart a democrat . . .

'The great majority of my countrymen and countrywomen are not familiar with the details of the internal political and economic condition of India and her people. Their interest in Nehru is mainly concerned with his pronouncements and activities in the field of foreign affairs. They include, of course, some who have accepted rather grudgingly the metamorphosis of our Empire into the Commonwealth as well as those who, like myself, regard this transformation as the highest expression of British democracy.

'It is perhaps not surprising that the former are the more vocal and in consequence it is their criticism, often ill-informed and unjust, which is reproduced in India as the British reaction. But in fact this is not true. The great majority of the British people do not expect or wish India's Prime Minister to be a yes-man dutifully reflecting all the views and actions of the leaders who at any particular moment hold the reins of Government in the United Kingdom . . .

'We are entitled freely to express our reactions to what he says or does. But in both cases it must be the criticism of friends and not of enemies anxious to score off one against the other. That is the essence of our common tradition, and knowing Jawaharlal as I do I am confident that as an Asian democrat and a lover of the British people he will uphold that tradition to the mutual benefit of the Commonwealth and to the greater good of human understanding throughout the world.'

During the autumn of 1946, events heavy with consequences for India's destiny moved uneasily on. In July the Viceroy had made new efforts to form an Interim Government. Jinnah declined the invitation, and Lord Wavell eventually accepted a list presented by Nehru consisting of seven Congressmen, one Indian Christian, one Sikh, one Parsee, and two non-League Muslims. He explained in a broadcast that participation was still open to the Muslim League.

On September 2nd this Government took office, and thereby made Indian history. Though nominally 'The Viceroy's Executive Council', it was widely described as 'the Cabinet'. Nehru was thenceforth known as 'Prime Minister', though he was not officially entitled to this description until August 1947. This Government was immediately confronted with the massacres in Bihar and Bengal which followed 'Direct Action Day' in Calcutta. Both Hindus and Muslims were the victims, each charging the other with aggression.

Owing to these events the Viceroy persuaded the Muslim League to join the Interim Government, and Jinnah finally nominated five members of whom one was the future Prime Minister of Pakistan, the courteous and responsible Liaquat Ali Khan. In November, while Gandhi was personally labouring for reconciliation in the disturbed provinces, four members of the Interim Government, Nehru and Patel from the Congress and Liaquat and Nishtar from the Muslim League, visited Bihar and Bengal. For the time being their presence averted further disaster.

In spite of its participation in the Central Government, the Muslim League remained adamant in its refusal to join the Constituent Assembly, due to meet on December 9th, and in the hope of reaching a solution, Prime Minister Attlee invited Nehru, Jinnah, Liaquat and Balder Singh (representing the Sikhs) to meet him in London, But agreement proved to be unattainable, and on December 6th the British Cabinet issued a statement which took a significant step towards Pakistan:

'Should a constitution come to be framed by a Constituent Assembly in which a large section of the Indian population had not been represented, His Majesty's Government would not contemplate—as the Congress have stated they would not contemplate—forcing such a constitution upon any unwilling parts of the country.'

On December 9th the Constituent Assembly met, but an atmosphere of unreality pervaded a gathering in which the Muslim League was represented by empty chairs. After a short session the Assembly adjourned without any achievement except a declaration of independence, moved by Nehru, which was not put to the vote.

CHAPTER 26

India's Tryst with Destiny

When 1947 began, the main fact on the Indian political horizon appeared to be the implacable hostility between the two leading parties. Nobody could then have prophesied how the year would end.

The British Government tackled the deadlock by issuing, on February 20th, a new and sensational declaration.

'The Cabinet Mission which was sent to India last year spent over three months in consultation with Indian leaders in order to help them to agree upon a method for determining the future constitution of India, so that the transfer of power might be smoothly and rapidly effected. It was only when it seemed clear that without some initiative from the Cabinet Mission agreement was unlikely to be reached, that they put forward proposals themselves . . .

'Since the return of the Mission an Interim Government has been set up composed of the political leaders of the major communities. With great regret His Majesty's Government still finds differences among Indian Parties which prevent the Constituent Assembly from functioning as it should . . .

'The situation is fraught with danger and cannot be indefinitely prolonged. His Majesty's Government therefore announce their definite intention to transfer power into responsible Indian hands not later than June 1948 . . .

'It will be the wish of everyone in these islands that, notwithstanding constitutional changes, the association of the British and Indian peoples should not be brought to an end, and they wish to continue to do all that is in their power to further the well-being of India.'

This announcement, fixing for the first time a date by which a decision of some kind would have to be reached, startled both Britain and India. Opposition speeches were made in both Houses of Parliament criticizing the statement on the ground that the date selected was far too early, and only Lord Halifax, in an address illuminated by his knowledge of India's problems, prevented the Lords from recording their disagreement. In India an unwonted sense of urgency failed to diminish the discord between Congress and the Muslim League, but made relevant to the needs of the time the dynamic methods of the new Viceroy, Lord Mountbatten, who succeeded Lord Wavell in March.

Reinforced by his royal birth, military prestige, handsome appearance, and the resilient vigour of early middle age, Lord Mountbatten and his elegant, intrepid wife were brilliantly to reap where those who had borne the burden and heat of the earlier day had sown. 'How much India and Pakistan owe to this wise Viceroyalty it is impossible to overstate', said Pethick five years later in a broadcast on Sir Stafford Cripps, whose persuasions he held largely responsible for Lord Mountbatten's acceptance of the position.

On April 2, 1947, Pethick wrote to the Prime Minister to say that he had now reached the end of his tether. He had still not wholly recovered from the gruelling ordeal of the Cabinet Mission; one of his secretaries has stated that, though he lived for another fourteen years, he never did get back the stamina which had been his before those months in India. During that period he had spent himself regardless of his health and well-being, and it was not of his health that he was thinking now, but of the interests of the India and Burma Independence Bills soon to be considered. He was already seventy-five, and felt that a younger man with a less exhausted and more agile mind should pilot these important measures through Parliament.

This time, with warm expressions of gratitude for his courage and endurance, he was permitted to retire, and Lord Listowel took his place as Secretary of State.

He went to the Isle of Wight for a short overdue rest, but the feeling of regret which dominates a letter to Esther Knowles written from Ventnor on May 4th seems to justify a doubt whether his strong sense of dedication to India might not have induced him to retain his office for another four months had he realized that independence was so near.

'I have had lots of very friendly and much too complimentary letters from all sorts of people about my retirement', he wrote. 'I should have liked to have seen the Indian problem solved or on the way to solution during my term of office but it has eluded me, and I have had to lay my burden down with no solution in sight.'

He was now technically free, but the drama to which the Cabinet Mission had so substantially contributed was still being played out, and deeply concerned him. On April 21st the rough road took another dramatic turn when Nehru conceded publicly that the Muslim League could have Pakistan if it wished, so long as it did not include areas where the majority had no desire to belong to it. The new Viceroy, quickly perceiving the total dilemma with his swift and fresh mind, decided that there was no alternative to partition; any attempt to impose unity would cause, in Nicholas Mansergh's words, 'the bloodiest civil war in the history of Asia'.

Against a background of increasing communal riots, Lord Mountbatten concluded that even the date of June 1948, which the British Houses of Parliament had criticized as too early, would be too late for the welfare of India. At the beginning of May he drew up a scheme for a compromise settlement, which visualized the creation of Pakistan if demanded by the Muslim representatives in the Muslim majority provinces. After Congress, the Muslim League, and the Sikhs had provisionally concurred, he flew to London, put his plan before the British Government, and returned to India with their approval.

'The only alternative to coercion is partition', he said, and in the end even Gandhi, the prophetic champion of a united India, was compelled to agree.

On June 3, 1947 the British Government put forward its compromise plan based on Lord Mountbatten's statement, and a few weeks later the Indian Independence Act embodied in legislative form the scheme of June 3rd. It provided for the creation of two independent Dominions, to be known as India and Pakistan, on August 15, 1947. Lord Listowel presented this measure in the House of Lords, and Pethick supported him with the same consecrated and single-minded devotion that had gone into the work of the Cabinet Mission.

'British Imperialism, sometimes labelled Colonialism, is dead', writes Dr G. P. Gooch in his essay on Pethick. 'Lord Pethick-Lawrence was one of our Elder Statesmen who drove the nails into its coffin.'

In Delhi, on the eve of the transfer of power, Nehru, sensitive, imaginative, and deeply responsive to the challenge of history, spoke memorable words to the assembled Members of the new Indian Parliament.

'Long years ago we made a tryst with destiny, and now the time comes when we shall redeem our pledge, not wholly or in full measure, but very substantially. At the stroke of the midnight hour, when the world sleeps, India will awake to life and freedom . . . It is fitting that in this solemn moment we take the pledge of dedication to the service of India and her people, and to the still larger cause of humanity.'

On the stroke of midnight his hearers dedicated themselves, 'in all humility', to the service of India, 'to the end that this ancient land attain her rightful place in the world and make her full and willing contribution to the promotion of world peace and the welfare of mankind'.

Simultaneously in Karachi, the middle-sized port encompassed by the desert and the sea which ten years later would have grown into a modern capital, a new State, with Jinnah as its first Governor-General, came into being. And to the British Commonwealth of Nations, hitherto European in their outlook and their blood, were added two new States in which peoples of other colours and cultures would enrich the older and narrower tradition. They were the first of many by which the Commonwealth would be transformed in the next two decades.

This coming change was not yet fully realized when in London, on August 15th, Indians and their British friends gathered at the offices of the respective High Commissioners to unfurl the flags of the two new Dominions. The presence of both High Commissioners at both ceremonies seemed at that moment a favourable augury for happier future relations than those which had challenged Pethick and his colleagues.

On August 26th, he wrote a friendly letter to the new Premier of Pakistan, Liaquat Ali Khan.

'Now that the excitement and the bustle are over, I write to send you my heartfelt good wishes in the stupendous task which you have undertaken. It is with profound thankfulness that I realize that the destinies of your people numbering far more than those of my own country are under the guidance of yourself whose calm judgment and wise and kindly statesmanship I learnt to respect during our association.'

Nearly ten years afterwards, on January 16, 1957, he broadcast a talk on Liaquat in the 'London Calling Asia' programme of the BBC which underlined this feeling of appreciation and friendship.

'He was a most likeable man with a high code of honourable conduct from which I never knew him to depart. His was no easy rôle as politician and statesman in the critical days of the late 'forties of which I am speaking. The situation demanded calmness and courage, and he had both qualities in a high degree. I remember so well the three-sided talks in Delhi and Simla in the spring and summer of 1946 . . . Liaquat, while adhering loyally and firmly to his leader, Mr Jinnah, never failed to state his case with courtesy and moderation.

'I recall too how in November of the same year when feeling was running high in Bengal between Hindus and Muslims, Liaquat went, together with Pandit Nehru and two other members of Congress and the League, into that province to reason with the inflamed populace. Only by their persistent and combined efforts was the tension reduced and bloodshed averted . . . Unhappily these friendly and conciliatory interchanges did not find favour with all of his co-religionists. An extreme and fanatical band of his critics threatened him with personal violence; and the day came when one of them made a successful attack upon his life. On hearing of the tragic assassination I was filled with deep grief. For myself I had lost a dear friend. His country had been deprived of a wise and devoted public servant.'

With characteristic and appropriate concern for a valiant woman, he concluded: 'Above all I felt for the Begum, who during his life stood so splendidly by his side and rendered him invaluable help by her ability and charm in his political and social activities. We are all grateful to her that having put aside her grave personal sorrow she has consented still to serve her country as Ambassador at The Hague.'[1]

Many tragedies awaited both the new peoples — massacres, migrations, the misery stretching over weary years of homeless refugees; the assassination of Gandhi by one frenzied nationalist and of Liaquat by another. But achievements lay ahead of them too—of a kind that belonged to the logic of history, yet could not have been foreseen by those who took part in the Cabinet Mission.

[1] Today (1963) Begum Liaquat Ali Khan is Ambassador in Rome.

Pethick's letter to Liaquat Ali Khan appeared to be an act of magnanimity to an opponent, however friendly, whose party had outwitted the conscientious umpire. After the long and wearisome negotiations the victory seemed to lie with Jinnah, but by one of the major ironies of history, it was to prove a victory which benefited those amongst whom he had so persistently contended.

Towards the end of the section called 'Modern India' in his long and careful history, Percival Spear has produced in reply to his own question 'Was partition inevitable?' the following judgment:

'There is another point to remember before too much regret is felt for the lost unity of India. The federal provisions of the Cripps and later proposals[1] so reduced the powers of the central government that it is very doubtful if the great developments of Nehru's India would have been possible under them. It is probable that the centre would have been weak, and political energy spent by the communities in jostling for position instead of reorganizing the country. Industrial development would have waited on party tactics, and five-year plans on political polemics. Only a joint directorate of the two parties could have achieved the kind of development which has actually occurred, and of that there was never any sign. However much partition may be regretted in principle, it was perhaps necessary, on this account, in the larger interests of the country.'[2]

That is one constructive reply to the sense of failure which dominated the Cabinet Mission in 1946-7, and undermined even Pethick's hopeful confidence. He and his colleagues had convinced both the major Indian parties that Britain was ready and willing to transfer power — an effect largely produced by Pethick's simple but shrewd sincerity. They had demonstrated that a loose Federation was not a possible form of compromise between unity and partition. By their inevitable failure to achieve such a compromise they had convinced the British government and Parliament of the necessity of partition and made possible the instructions to Lord Mountbatten to 'divide and quit'. These results compelled Congress (other than Gandhi) to accept partition as unavoidable.

[1] i.e. those of the Cabinet Mission.
[2] This view is still not acceptable to many Indians.

The creative achievements of modern India in the past fifteen years have grown out of the Mission's work, which eventually made it possible for Prime Minister Nehru to tell the Indian nation in a Delhi address from the ramparts of the Red Fort on August 15, 1962, that the average life-span of people in India had increased from thirty years before Independence to fifty at the present time.[1]

In fact, therefore, the Mission did not fail. It facilitated a settlement which, after much tribulation, worked effectively for both the new Dominions, and seems likely to endure.

[1] This result was largely due to the improvement in India's standard of living, but also to the conquest of malaria and the development of antibiotics by scientists working in many countries.

CHAPTER 27

A Partnership Ends

For the next seven years Pethick sailed contentedly in calmer waters, finding much pleasure in the fellowship of the House of Lords, and great enjoyment from the Debates in which he took part with quiet assurance. Only at the end of this peaceful period had he again to face anxiety—this time the inevitable consequence of the passing years.

His speeches—normally two or three in each Parliamentary session—ranged over the wide variety of subjects of which he had special knowledge. A study of Hansard over these years shows that he spoke on the Criminal Justice Bill (a plea for the abolition of capital punishment), Foreign Affairs, Indian affairs, British nationality, Colonial policy, women peers, and electoral reform. In a short tribute on September 12, 1950, to the memory of Lord Hailsham, he recalled that the father of the 1963 Minister for Science had preceded him as Captain of the Oppidans at Eton in 1885.

But his best energies were reserved for the debates on Economics; he joined in every review of 'the economic situation', as well as speaking on its more detailed aspects such as the Iron and Steel Bill (1949), Government accounts (1950), the cost of living (1950), and the Finance Bills of 1951 and 1954. So valuable did his unofficial rôle as Economics tutor to the House of Lords become, that after his death his colleagues found it difficult to fill his place.

Outside the House his time was occupied by the continuous demand for his services; he gave useful short addresses all over the country, and contributed articles to numerous magazines, many of them relating to Indian politics or Oriental philosophy. Several of these publications, such as *Vedanta for East and West, The Middle Way, Forum,* and *World Faiths*, were not widely known and had small circulations, but it was never his habit to refuse a request owing to its modesty. If the assignment was valuable to somebody somewhere, he accepted it and carried it through with a good grace.

He had time now to pay more attention to his own neighbourhood of Shere, which included the hamlet of Peaslake. In 1948 the parish held an Exhibition to make the population—half country people and half city men commuting daily to London—into a united community. During the pleasant autumn of that year he wrote a letter to Esther Knowles in praise of October, which he described as 'a month of quiet fruition'.

'The turbulent rush of bursting life of the spring is long gone by, the fierce heat of the summer and its storms of shattering rain have subsided. The harvest is gathered in and counted. But the sun can still be warm and the days are long enough to provide a nice balance between light and darkness. I find the same quiet contentment in the October of life. Gone are the unbridled passions of youth, the overmastering ambitions of middle age. A mellow acceptance of being remains positive, responsive, vigorous and even stimulating.'

From now until the end of his life, he found great satisfaction in his membership of the International PEN, which he had joined in 1945 after an invitation from its President, Sir Desmond MacCarthy, to attend a dinner given in his honour. After his retirement as Secretary of State he attended PEN functions whenever he could, and in August 1950 managed a brief visit to that year's PEN Conference at Edinburgh in spite of a serious accident to Emmeline.

'She and I all through our life have been most resolute in not interfering with one another's engagements', he wrote to the Secretary, Herman Ould. Two years later, after Herman's death, a letter to the Assistant Secretary, Maureen Kilroe, described a visit he had paid to Herman in hospital.

'I told him that the one thing in my life which had given me unalloyed satisfaction was my association with the PEN.' He therefore recorded much gratification from the PEN's invitation to him to be a vice-president of the English Centre. From that time onwards, he became a friend and correspondent of the new secretary, David Carver, and in later years attended PEN Conferences in Vienna and London, and gave a tea party for the PEN at the House of Lords. One of his Conference speeches dealt with the topic—vital especially to the literary *emigrés* from

N

Eastern Europe who had joined the English Centre—of Writers and the Idea of Freedom.

'It is the province of statesmen', he said, 'to deal exclusively with the outward expressions of freedom because it is over these alone that they are in a position to exercise any measure of control. But the concern of writers is with the heart of freedom within individuals for, unless this is possessed, the outward expressions of it will lose the greater part of their value . . .

'One of the primary duties of rulers is to protect their subjects from foreign aggression and civil rapine . . . But outside their province are the more subtle psychological fears and anxieties—the fear of making mistakes, the fear of running counter to conventional opinion, the fear of being misunderstood, the fear of sickness, suffering, old age and death. Only the resolute spirits of men and women can give them freedom from such fears as these.'

This last passage involved more than a detached reference to the sources of mortal fear, for over every pleasant activity since Pethick's departure from the India Office a shadow had lengthened.

'E.P.L. gets very easily overtired even when she is only happily sitting and talking to friends and relatives', he had written to Esther Knowles from Ventnor in May 1947. Emmeline was then nearly eighty, and even her vitality was subject to the laws which set a term to human life.

In July 1950 she fell in the garden and fractured her leg. Weeks in hospital followed when the bone was 'pinned', and then months of convalescence in which Pethick hardly left her side except for his work in the House of Lords. During her final months he never travelled further than London for more than a day or two at a time.

On June 7, 1951, Emmeline wrote to Mary Mazzoletti: 'I am getting stronger every day but I am still very crippled and not able to walk more than a few steps . . . I realize that it takes a very long time to recover one's power after an operation. I have not been in London for about a year and do not know when I shall see my London home again. At present the flights of stairs up to my flat make the idea impossible. I must try to get back some of my powers before October of this year, because on October 2nd my husband and I celebrate our fiftieth wedding anniversary and I hope, dear Mary, you will be able to come.'

A PARTNERSHIP ENDS

Eventually she managed to travel to London for their golden wedding, which involved a dinner party given for them in a Strand restaurant by the Women's Freedom League and the Suffragette Fellowship. The guests numbered 124, and 264 names were recorded for the gifts presented to them; these included several leading Indians, such as G. D. Birla, Rajkumari Amrit Kaur, Krishna Menon and C. Rajagopalachari. Significantly among the English names was that of Mrs H. McCombie, known to the Suffrage movement as Helen Craggs.

At the high table Emmeline and Pethick sat together—she spare, straight and fragile, Pethick with his blue eyes still flashing keenly—and listened to congratulatory speeches by Sylvia Pankhurst and Krishna Menon, then High Commissioner for India. Afterwards Pethick told a reporter that he had married his wife because she smoked cigarettes, could get off buses when they were moving, and didn't wear gloves when she went for a walk. These habits were all symbolic of the 'liberated' woman fifty years ago.

A month later Pethick wrote to Mary Mazzoletti from Fourways: 'We had the last of our golden wedding celebrations last Tuesday. We had it in this house and it took the form of a party for our Peaslake friends. We invited a hundred, seventy-five accepted, and sixty-five came.'

In January 1952 Emmeline commented to the same correspondent: 'Isn't it wonderful that we should have been given so many years of love and friendship?' But by April the sense of enjoyment had faded, though Pethick always took care to make her the centre of their household and, so far as it was still possible, caused each day's events to revolve around her. Exasperated by her immobility and by the deafness which had begun to be a serious handicap about the time of the Edinburgh election in 1935, she often found her mind reverting nostalgically to the splendid days of the Suffrage movement and could not always share Pethick's Prospice-like faith in the great mystery of absorption into the Central Life.

In April 1952 that Central Life summoned to itself a younger and more vigorous comrade. The death of Sir Stafford Cripps, after a long and heroic battle for health in a Swiss clinic, caused Pethick to reflect upon the impact of his former colleague's brilliant personality on others, and the refutation given by the spiritual faith which illumined his inner life to the popular judgment of politics as invariably sordid and opportunist. A leaflet commemorating Sir Stafford, preserved among Pethick's papers, quoted the words of William Penn: 'This is the comfort of friends, that though they may be said to die, yet their friendship and society are in the best sense ever present because immortal'.

In a broadcast in the 'London Calling Asia' BBC programme on April 22nd, Pethick spoke of Sir Stafford's 'formidable' championship of his own unconventional opinions, his sturdy defence of his adopted political faith, and his clarity and resourcefulness in approaching intricate problems. Vividly he recalled his friend's dynamic contribution to the work of the Cabinet Mission.

'Then came the time for the Mission to prepare its most important memorandum setting forth its views . . . Cripps volunteered. In one hour he brought to me the finished work—some 3,000 words written out in his own neat handwriting, in his usual red ink, covering ten closely packed foolscap pages. It was this document which with only minor alterations we finally adopted.'

Pethick concluded by referring to Sir Stafford's deliberate self-sacrifice in the public cause.

'As he had done all his life he overworked himself—starting his labours each day long before the world as a whole had awakened from sleep. And so at last his body which he had so rigidly forced to do the bidding of his mind in the service of his country refused any longer to obey him. We mourn his loss today—sustained by our love of his courage, his sense of humour, his courtly kindliness and the Christian virtues which were the mainstay of his life.'

Emmeline had always hoped that she too would die before Pethick; without him, she repeated, she would feel like a train which had lost its engine. The time was now coming near when her wish was to be fulfilled. Between December 1953 and February 1954, several letters to Pethick's old friend Isabel Seymour described the series of heart-attacks which preceded their final parting.

'In these circumstances', he wrote on December 18th, 'the glamorous baubles of Christmas which have delighted me from childhood up to advanced years are in this present year without their traditional attraction. But the celebration of the Festival of Birth with all its outward manifestation of light, of flowers, of birdsong, of human fellowship, remains undimmed if, perhaps, at the moment less appreciated.'

He went to great trouble to make Christmas enjoyable for Emmeline, with the tree, and presents, and guests to drink her health, taken up to her room, and they agreed that it had been one of the best Christmasses of their lives. A third heart attack in January and a fourth in February made it quite clear that they would not share another.

'We took every care', he wrote to Isabel, 'to see that she suffered no pain, and were successful . . . So we live on from day to day and almost from hour to hour. May we all stand together, resolute, loving, calm and triumphant . . . I have counted twelve crocuses out in the garden.'

During the last weekend of her life, Emmeline asked Stella Newsome of the Suffragette Fellowship in a brief moment of consciousness: 'And how does the fight for equal pay go on?' She died on March 11, 1954, aged 86, and was cremated at Woking on March 16th. At the service the organist, at Pethick's request, played the funeral march from Wagner's opera *The Ring* which he and Emmeline had once heard in Bayreuth, and many times listened to at Covent Garden. For him it had no equal in music, since it was not a sorrowful dirge but a march of triumph well fitted to celebrate the life of a hero.

Some years earlier, after the death of their old friend Mary Neal who had lived with them at Peaslake during the war, Emmeline had given the funeral address. Pethick now decided to pay the final tribute to his wife himself, and the words he spoke were long remembered by those who were present.

'My very dear friends, we are about to commit to the flames the body of the woman who was known to the world as Emmeline Pethick-Lawrence. All of you have come here because you knew and admired what she *did* in her public life. But many of you have come also because you were privileged to love her for what she *was* and to be loved by her in return.

'In the few words that I am going to say to you, I shall not attempt to separate the two because in everything she did and was she was essentially human.

'Before I married her she once said to me: "Never forget the baby and the sinner". She was thinking primarily of herself, but her words applied equally to her own attitude to all mankind. She never thought of men and women as units to be expended in a political battle. They were always to her individuals to be loved for their weakness as well as for their strength.

'She had a great and abiding sense of justice; at whatever cost to herself she was prepared to resist tyranny. At all stages of her life she was a champion of the weak against the strong. As a child she was a rebel at school against harsh and cruel rules. At home as the eldest of the family she upheld her younger brothers and sisters against the misuse of parental authority. As a Sister of the West London Mission she was the friend and uplifter of the outcast. In later life she stood out against class injustice and racial prejudice. Her fight for the equal sovereignty of women is written into the annals of our country's history. She risked her life to call a halt to oppression in Ireland. She loathed war and pleaded for justice to beaten foes. She espoused many lost causes and turned them into winning ones.

'By her spiritual power she planted in the hearts of friends and foes the seeds of a new sense of human dignity and of a new approach to the problems of public and private life.

'But of the many victories she won, the greatest of all was the victory over herself — over her fears, her limitations and her frailties. Her first term of imprisonment as a Suffragette was a fiasco. She just could not face it. To my intense alarm she decided to make a second attempt. Undaunted she went in and undefeated after serving her sentence she came out—not once but many times. She faced the hunger strike and forcible feeding.

'So it was throughout her life, and so was it in the days of its approaching end. I do not think she was ever afraid of death, but she resented the intrusion of death's heralds on her activities. Pain, weakness, loss of independence, irked her and for a time broke down her composure and her gentleness. But before the end came, she had won this battle too. Serene, loving and utterly happy, she welcomed the coming of death's last herald, and in her sleep she awaited and received the Majestic Presence who gave her rest.'

CHAPTER 28

The Long Afterglow (1)

It had always been part of Pethick's philosophy that whatever misfortunes befell the individual — disappointment, as in his early struggles to enter Parliament; painful responsibilities, as in the Cabinet Mission; even the loss of those nearest and most dear, such as he was now enduring—life was there to be lived, and in all circumstances must be carried on with the utmost resourcefulness that a man or woman possessed. His Trinity College contemporary, Bertrand Russell, had embodied the same philosophy in his book *The Conquest of Happiness*:

'All our affections are at the mercy of death, which may strike down those whom we love at any moment. It is therefore necessary that our lives should not have that narrow intensity which puts the whole meaning and purpose of our life at the mercy of accident.'

By April 27th he was back in the House of Lords with a full-length speech on his favourite topic, the economic situation, which he followed in May and July by addresses on the Rents Bill and the Finance Bill. On May 14th, feeling that memorial services were solemn and cold, he arranged a 'feast of joy over a great life' at the Central Hall, Westminster, with his old friend A. V. Alexander—now Viscount Alexander of Hillsborough—in the chair. The seven speakers, who included Sybil Thorndike, Sylvia Pankhurst and Dr Edith Summerskill, spoke of Emmeline in the spirit of *The Times* obituary which had said of her: 'She was indeed in the main stream of Victorian philanthropy, but she brought an individual touch and a sense of mission to the work which gave it permanence and something of greatness'.

Later in the year he found deep satisfaction in another obituary article which Christabel Pankhurst had contributed to the American weekly magazine, *Equal Rights*. After her parting with the Pethick-Lawrences in 1912, Christabel had refrained from any approach until her letter to Emmeline in 1922; after that a casual correspondence continued for the rest of her life. By 1954 she gave only occasional lectures and was enjoying a final period of leisure in California. She now wrote of Emmeline:

'Of all the treasurers of any movement, Lady Pethick-Lawrence was surely the best . . . Friends of the cause saw with delight—and foes with dismay—the enthusiastic response to her appeals . . . Yet that was only one part of the magnificent service given by Emmeline Pethick-Lawrence, from the hour she joined us, to the votes for women cause—service which was in fact a continuation of her lifelong work for women and girls.

' "It's women for women now", was the watchword that she coined and often used. It bespoke the loyalty of women to women which animated the Suffragette pioneers of those days and was called forth by them in countless other women—as never before in history. Indeed it was this loyalty of women to women which, more than anything else, finally won the vote, which was the key to all other needful reforms and to the recognition of women's equal human status.'

One of the friends whom Pethick had invited to address Emmeline's memorial meeting was Agatha Harrison, the Quaker interpreter of India, who first went there as a member of the Royal Commission on Labour in 1930, and later became secretary of the India Conciliation Group, and a friend of C. F. Andrews, Mahatma Gandhi and the Nehru family. For many years she visited India regularly, and in 1948 had supplied Pethick with material for his essay on Gandhi. Together they had grieved the following spring for the death of Sarojini Naidu, whose last service to Pethick had been her Foreword for this book.

A few days after writing him a letter in praise of Emmeline, Agatha went to Geneva with a colleague, Gerald Bailey, for that year's Asian Conference. There she died suddenly. Instead of hearing her pay a last tribute to Emmeline, Pethick spoke with Krishna Menon and Reginald Sorensen at a meeting called to commemorate her by the India League on May 31st.

Throughout that spring he tackled the letters which had descended upon him like leaves in a frosty autumn; his Indian correspondents included Mrs Pandit, Chakravarti Rajagopalachari, and the High Commissioner, Mr Kher, who conveyed a personal message from Jawaharlal Nehru. Not for Pethick was the lazy newspaper announcement which responds with formal printed words to the sympathy of friends who have been moved to write in intimate terms. He answered every communication himself, often in manuscript. He also arranged to sell 'Fourways' and simplify his complex routine. Only in a letter to Isabel Seymour in April did he give verbal form to the ordeal of those months, and to the hope which they had not extinguished.

'I have written hundreds (of letters) with my own hand and hundreds by dictation to so many dear friends, that I am not quite sure what I have written to you already . . . Now that I have a little time to think and feel I find myself dazed. It is like being present at a violin concerto with the violinist absent. I eat and drink and work and play and go through the motions of my accustomed life, but there is something missing.

'My religious faith, as you know, is different from yours. I have no knowledge or experience or inner light which enables me to predicate what happens to the individual after death. It lies entirely beyond my ken. But when I look out upon this shatteringly wonderful universe I am driven more and more to feel that the Central Life from which it all emanated has some good purpose in creating it and in particular in creating me and Emmeline, and that that good purpose cannot remain unfulfilled.'

The following year Pethick contributed his recollections of Olive Schreiner to the 1955 Centenary meeting organized by the PEN, with Vera Brittain in the chair, and Daisy Hobman and William Cooper as his fellow speakers. Two months later, during that spring's General Election, he supported one of the youngest Parliamentary Labour candidates, Shirley Catlin, sixty years his junior, at modest meetings in the Essex townlets of Holland-on-Sea and Walton-on-Naze. A night in a small country hotel offered little comfort to an octogenarian, but the candidate typified the future political young woman of whom he and Emmeline had dreamed, and for whose sake they had gone to prison twenty years before her birth.

A year later, Pethick shared the indignation which she and other representatives of Socialist youth felt during the Suez crisis; for him as for them, the Government's intervention in Egypt seemed to resurrect the nineteenth century imperialism which they had thought was dead. In 1933-4 he had visited Egypt with Emmeline, where he had made contact with Nahas

Pasha and other Wafd leaders, 'and came to the conclusion that they were ready to accept a reasonable settlement with the British, which would even include the vexed questions of the Canal and the Sudan'. The Anglo-Egyptian treaty had followed, but now the clock had been put back.

Rumours that Nehru was considering the withdrawal of India from the Commonwealth reached Pethick, to his perturbation, and in November he wrote an anxious letter to the Indian Prime Minister begging him not to desert those British people who were trying to redeem the Commonwealth from the 'disgrace' which had befallen it. Reassurance soon came from Mrs Pandit, then the Indian High Commissioner in Britain.

'It has been heartening to us in India to realize that the UK Government's action in Egypt did not have the support of a large number of people of all groups in this country. I think my brother has made it clear that India would not wish to leave the Commonwealth and that he believes that our continuing membership is of benefit not only to ourselves but to the United Kingdom.'

Three months afterwards, Pethick's friends were startled by the unexpected receipt of a printed card.

'Lord Pethick-Lawrence and Mrs Duncan McCombie[1] were married in London on February 14, 1957.'

To the many friends who sent congratulations, he explained: 'I have known Helen ever since some forty-five years ago I bailed her out as a Suffragette. She has the vitality and sense of humour of much younger women and as I, at eighty-five, keep up most of my activities we hope to have several years before us of happy companionship.'

There had been only casual contacts between Pethick and Helen McCombie after the suffrage movement until her son was wounded in the Second World War and she sought his help in approaching the Ministry of Pensions. At this time Helen was living in the country and lunched with him occasionally when she came up to London. She spent much of her time with her married daughter and grandchildren in Canada, and with her son in the United States, but returned to London on a visit in 1956 just when Pethick was becoming steadily more conscious of his solitude. Emmeline had always said that she did not want

[1] *Née* Helen Craggs, the daughter of Sir John Craggs.

him to endure this if she departed first; he had been accustomed to discuss his day's work with her, and public engagements did not fill the gap.

Helen McCombie, as the widow of a doctor twenty years her senior, who had her own means and a house in Belgrave Road, needed a good deal of persuasion. Eventually she agreed on the understanding that she would be free to spend long periods overseas with her children.

This second marriage, above all else, represented an affirmation; it was a positive action which typified Pethick's belief in the triumph of life at any age and stage. He would accept death when it came, but he did not propose to die in advance or allow his friends to kill him with their solicitude. Helen now brought him companionship, liveliness, and the interest of exploring a new personality; she also recreated in those final days the suffrage movement which meant so much to them both. He had brilliantly explained it in a long letter to Professor G. M. Trevelyan, the Master of Trinity, written in October 1949, after a dinner-table discussion the previous June.[1]

Helen's connection with woman suffrage went back to her schooldays at Roedean, where the headmistress was then the celebrated Penelope Lawrence.[2] When Helen bade her goodbye Miss Lawrence said: 'Do you realize that when you go out into the world, you will not have the right to vote as men do?' Helen commented: 'Why ever not? Why shouldn't I?' So Miss Lawrence advised her discreetly: 'If you want to know more about it, go and see the people at Clement's Inn.' She took the advice, and became a militant.

The publication that spring of Roger Fulford's book *Votes For Women* was naturally of great interest to both Pethick and herself. In his story Roger Fulford treated Pethick with respect and clearly admired him, but the review which Pethick wrote for *The Women's Bulletin* stopped short of enthusiasm.

'In my opinion', he said of the book, 'its main defects are three. First, there are many inaccuracies . . . Secondly, there is at times a lack of proportion arising from the limited sources of information on which he has drawn . . . he seems to be quite unaware of the wide extent of the educational propaganda and

[1] See Appendix 1.
[2] She had no connection with Pethick's family.

the vast sums of money spent in promoting it by militants and non-militants alike. Thirdly, many of his judgments are prejudiced by his obvious partisanship in favour of the Liberal Governments of the day. Gladstone—and Asquith—must both bear a heavy responsibility for forcing women into revolutionary courses.

'These grave defects could have been guarded against and prevented if Mr Fulford had seen fit to take the usual course of consulting some at least of the leading protagonists of the conflict who are alive today before committing himself finally to print. As a consequence his book cannot be more than a partial and provisional presentation.'

That autumn, before fulfilling some self-imposed obligations to the memory of the Suffragette leaders, Pethick made a final visit to India, which Helen had never seen. This time he was fêted, entertained and garlanded; they stayed with the Prime Minister, and from Delhi were escorted to Agra, where he looked for the last time on his beloved Taj Mahal. They went also to the palaces of Jaipur, the Elephanta Caves in Bombay, and the Caves of Ajanta and Ellora which were new to them both.

'Wherever we went our slightest wish was anticipated and met', Pethick wrote to Mrs Pandit on his return. 'I spoke at a great number of meetings and gave two broadcasts. What was perhaps the most moving experience of all was the continued friendliness of all the people, high and low, whom we encountered in the course of our visit.'

In the East old age is still respected, but Pethick knew now that his years were not alone responsible for the reverence that he received; he was valued and acclaimed because he was recognized as one of the makers of the new India. He realized at last that the Mission which he led had not failed; it had been involved in the travail of a new Dominion struggling to come to birth, but without its work the long-delayed Independence would not have been achieved.

The plan of the Great Architect had differed from his own, but he had been, none the less, its consecrated instrument. When he reached the mortal hour of departure which could not now be long delayed, the esteem of modern India's creators would be his memorial.

CHAPTER 29

The Long Afterglow (2)

Between March 1958 and June 1961 the three Pankhurst sisters died in succession, Christabel in California, Sylvia in Ethiopia, and Adela in Australia. At the end they were separated, as they had always been psychologically, by the width of the world.

As one by one they vanished from the scene of their strenuous and revolutionary labours, did Pethick ever reflect on the words of seventeenth-century Henry Vaughan the Silurist:

'They are all gone into the world of light,
And I alone sit lingering here . . . '?

If so, he showed no sign of it in the numerous tributes by which he gave life to the memory of his friends. 'Lingering' was hardly a word which had ever described his attitude, and in any case he was now no longer alone; he had Helen, nearly twenty years his junior, to keep the outlook of a later decade constantly before him.

Though he and Emmeline had always shown consistent kindness to Sylvia and her son, it was Christabel, the symbolic modern girl of his youth, whose achievements really concerned him. Christabel's life had ended at Santa Monica, where as she slowly withdrew from public obligations the small pleasures brought by everyday life—her garden, the Pacific Ocean, and the rich sunsets of that lovely land—gave her great satisfaction. 'She had no illness; she just left us', wrote her lifelong friend Grace Roe.

Though she had died so far away, her London friends arranged a memorial service at St Martin-in-the-Fields, and asked Pethick to give the address.

'It was a formidable task', he then said, 'that Christabel undertook when she set out to rouse women to a sense of their own worth and dignity and to make use of this new-found resolution to break down the walls of prejudice and opposition . . . The result was very much what might have been anticipated. The world lifted an eyebrow and smiled derisorily. How absurd it was to imagine that this silly and rather disreputable escapade would promote the cause of women. Of course it could only have exactly the opposite effect . . .

'But Christabel thought otherwise. And we, looking back over the fifty years of intervening history, are forced to the conclusion that the world's forecast of the future was wrong and that of the young girl was right.'

The following day, in an article published by *The Catholic Citizen* called 'Christabel Pankhurst—The Girl who slew the Dragon', he commented on a controversy which even in the nineteen-sixties has not died: 'Some people still maintain that it was not the Suffragettes with their militant tactics who won the vote but the quiet progress of persuasion aided by the spectacular services rendered by women to their country during the war of 1914-18. They seem to forget that when Christabel flung down her challenge the peaceful campaign for women's enfranchisement was at its lowest ebb . . . But the controversy is not really very important. Genius is its own defence and its own glory. Its fruits remain an everlasting memorial.'

Directly the service of commemoration was over, he began the endeavour to have Christabel's name added to the monument to her mother in Victoria Tower Gardens. With characteristic magnanimity, he never hesitated to give the Pankhursts all the credit for the achievements of the Suffragette movement and to understate his own contribution. But for him Christabel's book *Unshackled*, which for all its emotionalism and episodic treatment probably gives the most authentic account, might never have been available to the public.

The discovery of this manuscript added a dramatic little episode to the sensational history which the book related. For years an impression had prevailed that some time or other Christabel had written a story of the militant campaign, but she died without disclosing the existence of such a book or leaving any instructions referring to it. Grace Roe searched through her papers but found nothing; then she remembered that a mutual friend possessed several boxes which had once belonged to Christabel. She obtained permission to examine them, and in one, amid a quantity of valueless papers, discovered a substantial typescript. It had apparently been written some twenty years earlier, and 'collateral letters' suggested that Christabel had not wished it to be published until after her death.

Grace Roe brought the manuscript to England, and asked Pethick to see it through the Press. Uncertain of its quality he hesitated at first, but a glance through the material reassured him. Christabel had revised the manuscript so carefully that the text went to the publishers almost unaltered, but she had not chosen the title, which he supplied. He also contributed a Preface describing the discovery of the document, and a Postscript summarizing the long-range consequences of the suffrage movement.

'The essential thing is that women are free today, as never before in human history, to order their own lives . . . But is that to be all? Does their responsibility end there? Have they any new contributions to make to the problems that all down the ages have beset mankind? . . .

'No one knows the answer to this question. Only the future will give it, as one by one the scrolls of human destiny are unwound. But all those still living today who paid the price for women's freedom wait and watch anxiously for the answer and pray that it may be one for the healing of mankind.'

In the volume he published many photographs showing the Suffragette pioneers in action — Annie Kenney, Mrs Despard, Keir Hardie, George Lansbury, the Pankhurst sisters with their mother, and himself and Emmeline formally dressed on their way to the Law Courts. He repudiated, as his secretaries testify, all photographs showing Christabel in later life, and as frontispiece chose a picture of her wearing the flower-decked picture hat that he gave her, with a ribbon tied under her chin and a bunch of daffodils in her lap.

Two years before the end of his own life, this book had taken him back to the political struggles which preceded his long history as a Labour politician and the leader of a Cabinet Mission, and reminded him of the price that he himself had paid for the women's vote. No doubt too he carried to his grave a new memory of the fresh-faced girl with the soft mouth and impudent nose who had so much attracted him in his early middle age.

For the remainder of his time he still laboured to vitalize the memory of those who had served the suffrage cause. In July 1959 his friend Lord Kilmuir unveiled the memorial to Christabel at the foot of her mother's statue, and the following May he himself addressed a crowded meeting in the Manchester Free Trade Hall before unveiling a tablet which commemorated the first militant protest by Christabel and Annie Kenney in that same hall in 1905. During the spring of 1961 he took the chair at memorial meetings for Monica Whately and Charlotte Marsh, the cross-bearer at the funeral of Emily Wilding Davison, and, more cheerfully, organized an evening party at the House of Lords to celebrate the fortieth anniversary of the Six Point Group.

On July 27th he made his last speech in the House of Lords, a closely-argued criticism of the measures suggested by the Chancellor of the Exchequer for dealing with current economic problems.

'Although in his ninetieth year,' Lord Stonham wrote in *The Shield* for October 1961, 'no one imagined when the House rose in August that he would be leaving us so soon.'

'I have argued, and some of my colleagues in another place have argued,' said Pethick, 'that we are lagging behind in the matter of planning. I see no forward step by the Chancellor of the Exchequer to set the economy in greater motion by planning. I see none of that. On the contrary I see the same old dope, the same old quack medicines put forward as those that have been in the offing all this time, and which, in my opinion, have not succeeded in their purpose.

'That brings me to my last point, and it is one at which Members opposite will not be surprised. I think we are today in the position of having to face this business for a long time. We have got to stiffen the backs of the people of this country. We must make them realize that if they want to be a great nation, they must be worthy of being a great nation. They must be prepared to make sacrifices, and they must pull themselves together and work harder. But you cannot do that all on one side. If you are going to do that, you must make an appeal to people all round.

'Now the noble Viscount[1] cannot get away from the fact that in the Budget as a whole an enormous reduction of taxation was made in respect of the earned-income surtax payer, and that has

[1] Lord Hailsham, who had spoken before him supporting the Chancellor's proposals.

TRY, TRY, TRY AGAIN

[By courtesy of the Hindustan Times]

(*above*) Pethick and Helen Pethick-Lawrence at Guildford after their marriage in 1957

Pethick and Emmeline two years before their Golden Wedding

remained in the minds of the working people of this country as a very unfair division of release from taxation . . . The Government cannot expect to have a united people behind them while they limp under that cloud of unfair discrimination by way of relief to one certain class of the population and handicap on the other.'

A month earlier he had sent his final letter to Isabel Seymour, in a handwriting at last beginning to lose its solid geometrical vigour. He wrote to her, as he had so often written, of the purpose of life and the nature of God—who was for him a mathematician, a scientist, a composer, a dramatist and a doctor, as well as a father and a lover.

'To me *you* are an aspect of God, so was Emmeline and so was Christabel, and so also are Helen and Esther and Gladys and so also are every bird and beast and flower and every living thing, and also every minutest particle of this wonderful universe.

'My approach to God can only be through every faculty of mine with which he has endowed me. Body, mind, spirit are to me not disparate and separate realities, but different aspects of one eternal Reality.'

With humility he added: 'My mind is quite incapable of grasping the *nature* of life after our presence in this particular state in which we exist here on earth. The only prayer that I can formulate is that no wantonness of mine may impede or mar the purpose of God.'

CHAPTER 30

Requiescat

The last chapter of Pethick's autobiography sought to explain his quest for 'conscious union with the Great Spirit who founded the laws of life'. More concisely, he embodied the same sequence of ideas in the final paragraph of his essay, *If I Had My Time Again*: 'For years I sought in vain for this sublime thought which would satisfy at the same time my reason, my emotions, and my consciousness of a spiritual world behind the world of sense. I find it now in contemplation of the wonderful universe around me and of my own essential union with the Central Fount of Life which is at once its source and its substance.'

He would certainly never have called himself a poet, yet his most successful attempt to put this philosophy into words occurred in some unusual stanzas entitled 'A Cosmic Hymn', which *The New Statesman and Nation* published on November 21, 1949. According to one of his last letters to David Carver, he wrote these verses in Ireland in 1948. A note from Chakravarti Rajagopalachari, to whom he also submitted them, commented that 'the hymn is Vedanta pure and complete'. Possibly his intensive contacts with the Indian mind during 1946 showed their most constructive results in this poem:

> 'Thou art the source and substance of all cosmic life.
> We are Thy creatures and the instruments of Thy creation.
> Time and Space are the garments Thou has chosen
> In which to manifest Thyself in this our universe.
> All things that have breath partake of Thy spirit;
> All matter is the embodiment of Thy being.
> There is no portion of Space that is without Thee,
> And no moment of Time without Thy presence;
> And where Time and Space are not, there also art Thou.
>   * * * *
> I am a petal on Thy flower; I am a babe in Thy bosom;
> Through Thy umbilical cord I draw my sustenance.

Because I am one with Thee there is nothing beyond or outside
  of me;
All knowledge and all sensation are available to me.
But in this casket of my body I undergo separation;
I am subject to the limits of birth and life and death.
Thou hast entrusted me with the awesome gift of free choice,
So that I love and hate, I heal and hurt, I kill and I make alive.
Thou hast sent me forth on a high adventure
To experience and explore for Thee the working of Thy law.
When my mission is accomplished and my scroll complete,
Thou wilt break this casket and gather me again unto Thyself.'

In September 1961, the scroll was complete and the casket ready to be broken. At the end of the Parliamentary session, Pethick and Helen went to Gloucestershire to spend a weekend with Dame Isobel Cripps. There he felt suddenly so tired that he could not keep awake, went to his bed to rest as soon as he returned home, and never effectively rose from it again.

Pethick had always enjoyed magnificent health; his one continuous plague was arthritis, which from a quite early age caused the stiffness of his movements though it never interfered with his skill in games. His only serious illness, about five years before his death, took the form of a slight stroke which he overcame by relentless will-power. One morning he was dictating to his secretary when the newspaper fell from his hand and he became suddenly silent. For a few days his speech was impaired, but he would not allow the fact to be disclosed and managed to fulfil all his commitments. The chief difficulty was a large party, at which he was host, in the House of Lords; he solved this problem by keeping his secretary beside him to maintain the conversation and confining his own remarks to monosyllables.

His powers never deserted him again and he was not actually ill now; the trouble, said his doctor, was only old age and weariness which had at last overtaken him. He had greatly looked forward to celebrating his ninetieth birthday on December 28th, when the Fawcett Society had planned to give him a public dinner for which many friends and organizations had already taken tickets. To Esther Knowles he remarked with uncharacteristic wistfulness: 'I *would* have liked to live till my birthday party'. And she, with the courage of long association, compelled him to face the fate now so swiftly approaching.

'But supposing you don't? Are you ready, P.L.?'

And with quiet acceptance he replied: 'Yes, my dear—absolutely ready. I've had nearly fourscore years and ten; I've been a very fortunate man.'

He had always insisted that in the event of grave illness he would go to hospital and cause no personal trouble, and on August 6th he was taken to the Manor House Hospital where so many Labour leaders had looked their last on life. He asked to see Grace Roe and his cousin Dora Durning-Lawrence, but as consciousness faded he wanted no one with him but Helen and the two devoted secretaries who had so long taken the place of daughters.

If he suffered nobody knew, for he never complained. Within a few days he passed into a coma from which he did not awaken. He died on September 10th, six weeks and three days after his last speech in the House of Lords; in his sleep, like Emmeline seven years earlier, he awaited and received the Majestic Presence who gave him rest.

He who had spent so much of his time and strength in commemorating others was now to be widely remembered. After the cremation service at Woking where the small chapel was filled though the holidays were not yet over, the House of Lords paid its tribute to him at the first meeting of the new Session on October 17th in an atmosphere of emotion usually reserved for those who die in youth.

Half the members of that House seemed again to be present at the Memorial Service in St Margaret's, Westminster, on November 2nd—not cold and solemn, as he had feared for Emmeline, but crowded with friends and colleagues who brought there a sense of achievement and triumph. When Lord Attlee read the familiar Lesson from the Book of Wisdom—'The souls of the righteous are in the hands of God and there shall no torment touch them'—it seemed to many of those present to be unusually appropriate. In his address Lord Alexander referred to their association during the Cabinet Mission, and quoted F. W. H. Myers in recalling Pethick's imprisonment for the suffrage cause:

> 'Whoso hath felt the Spirit of the Highest
> Cannot confound nor doubt Him, nor deny.
> Yea with one voice, O world, though thou deniest
> Stand thou on that side for on this am I.'

'It is not for us', he added, 'to seek what was the exact faith or philosophy to which Fred Pethick-Lawrence gave most allegiance, but his character speaks for itself, and maybe we can decide, as instructed in the Church of England Prayer Book as we contemplate the life of a great and good man, "to amend our lives according to His most Holy Word".' He concluded with Whittier's lines:

> 'And now he rests; his greatness and his sweetness
> No more shall seem at strife
> And death has moulded into calm completeness
> The statue of his life.'

That Christmas Pethick's friends received as usual a card 'from Lord and Lady Pethick-Lawrence'. It showed a Chinese design of white roses by Chen Pan Ting, with a quotation in Chinese characters of which the translation ran: 'All the flowers of all the tomorrows are in the seeds of today'. Inside the card was a printed message from Helen.

'When my husband was dying, he expressed the wish that the Christmas cards we had chosen a month before should be sent out as usual. They are indeed his goodbye greeting to you.'

On July 7, 1962, in response to an Appeal for permanent memorials to Pethick and Emmeline, two final gatherings of friends filled the modern Village Hall at Peaslake and the Pethick-Lawrence House (a local community centre) in Dorking. Many telegrams from relatives and colleagues who could not be present included a cable from Helen in California.

At the first ceremony Edith Summerskill, after paying tribute to their memory, unveiled the portrait of Pethick and Emmeline painted by a Surrey artist, John Baker of Epsom. At the second Lord Longford (Frank Pakenham), who had known Pethick well only since they served together in the House of Lords but had come to regard him as a close and dear friend, uncovered a tablet on the front of the house, and indoors unveiled a portrait, also by John Baker, which showed Pethick sitting alone with his hands folded in characteristic fashion over his knee.

Outside the two halls the Surrey lanes were rich and somnolent after one of the rare warm days of a chilly summer; in the hedgerows Pethick's cherished wild roses, delayed by the long cold spring, traced delicate patterns of pink and white. Knowing that they would not forget Pethick and Emmeline, the friends who passed from these meetings into the Peaslake lanes and the Dorking streets quietly dispersed, and returned home to continue their varied occupations.

Life, as Pethick had always insisted, went on.

APPENDIX 1

TO PROFESSOR G. M. TREVELYAN, O.M. FROM LORD PETHICK-LAWRENCE

3rd October, 1949

My dear Master,

You may remember that when I had the honour of dining in Trinity last June I mentioned to you that I should like some day to have a talk with you about the woman's militant movement for the franchise at the beginning of the century. Thinking it over I have come to the conclusion that it will probably suit you better if I put what I have to say in writing.

I must begin by apologizing for troubling you at all about the matter but as you know I have been for a great part of my life a propagandist and I am still incorrigible in my old age. I do not like to think that you, our foremost British historian, should have, as it seems to me, the wrong slant on this movement which I hold to have been of considerable historic importance. The fact that I played a prominent part in it myself entitles me to speak on its behalf though I am free to admit that it also entitles you to charge me with bias. But then you have said (and I agree) that even an historian is none the worse for bias.

My case is: (1) That any section of the community that has no political rights should endeavour to win them by reason and argument, but that if prolonged peaceful agitation fails to influence those who have the power, then it has no alternative but to use extraordinary and extra-legal methods unless it is prepared to acquiesce in its own subjection.

(2) That such methods should be designed so as (*a*) to arouse the largest number of the unenfranchised section to a consciousness of their subjection, (*b*) to create the greatest difficulties for the Government, and (*c*) to win the support of the bulk of the population by casting odium on the Government for its repressive counter measures.

(3) That the militant suffrage agitation acted broadly on these lines (though it naturally made some mistakes), and that it was instrumental—though not exclusively—in creating a situation from which there was no escape except by conferring a measure of enfranchisement on women.

I do not think you will substantially disagree with me on either of the first two points which are borne out by countless examples, the latest of which come from Asia—India and Indonesia, in the former of which I was acting for the Government—but I gather that you do not accept my version of the facts as to the third. It is to this point therefore that I will specially devote myself.

I was brought up, like you, in the Liberal fold and I still think that we owe much of our national democratic heritage to the great Liberal statesmen of the nineteenth century. Nevertheless I think that the Liberal Party bungled the case of the women and of the working man, and lost its prestige and pre-eminence by so doing. By the time that the militant suffrage movement began women had grown tired of asking politely for the vote and being fobbed off it by discreditable political devices; and some younger spirits had become rebellious.

The militants directed the spearhead of their attack upon the members of the Liberal Government because they were the most vulnerable, in that it was contrary to Liberal principles to deny enfranchisement to a section of the community which paid taxes and was subject to the laws made by a Parliament in which they were not represented. In the earlier stages of the agitation they abstained from violence and concentrated on questioning Cabinet Ministers, campaigning against Liberal candidates at by-elections and committing technical breaches of the law. As a consequence they were subjected to considerable violence at the hands of stewards at meetings and of the police in the streets and they suffered terms of imprisonment.

I think it is indisputable that in this way they succeeded in rousing the sympathy of a very large number of their own sex. Many thousands enrolled themselves in the militant organizations. They included such prominent women as Dr Garrett Anderson, the Mayor of Aldeburgh; Mrs Saul Solomon, widow of the Cape Premier; Lady Constance Lytton, and leading actresses, novelists and others. Funds were contributed running into hundreds of thousands of pounds. The paper *Votes for Women*, the weekly organ of the movement, had a circulation of 30,000 to 40,000. About a thousand women served terms of imprisonment. Moreover after militancy began (and in my opinion, and in the publicly expressed opinion of Mrs Fawcett, the leader of the 'constitutional' suffragists, largely in consequence of it) the membership of the non-militant suffrage societies showed a marked and rapid increase.

They succeeded also in directing the attention of the general public to the question. At one time from 100 to 200 meetings were being held every week, some of them vast open-air demonstrations, others in the largest halls of the country which were packed to overflowing. I do not suggest that all the members of the audiences were supporters though many were, but there was little or no hostility; and in the street demonstrations the crowds were mostly sympathetic. In fact in the so-called 'raids on Parliament' the women counted on the crowd to protect them from the police.

APPENDIX 1

How far electors were influenced at by-elections to vote against Liberal candidates by Suffragette orators and canvassers can never be proved one way or the other but the Press frequently alleged that they were, and there is no doubt that Cabinet Ministers were greatly embarrassed and hard put to defend their attitude. Naturally, as is always the case when coercive action is taken by a Government, British public opinion reacted against the Government.

During this period of the agitation there was a growing feeling among all parties in the House of Commons that the question of woman suffrage ought to be treated seriously and sympathetically, and in 1910 an all-party committee devised a compromise proposal which came to be known as the 'Conciliation Bill'. In order not to prejudice the chances of this compromise the militant societies were asked to desist from any militant action. They agreed; and for several months they carried out strictly constitutional and non-provocative activities. But in the end the Liberal Government made it quite clear that they would have nothing to do with the Conciliation Bill and Mr Asquith remained adamant in his opposition. Militancy was therefore resumed in all its forms. Women continued to go to prison in increasing numbers and suffered violence in the streets and at Liberal meetings for their insubordination.

It was then that some militant women decided upon a change of tactics in the direction of actual violence against property. They were influenced to take this course (1) by the preference for being arrested quickly rather than after being knocked about, and (2) by the taunts levelled against them by Cabinet Ministers that their rebellion was trumpery and not of the same account as the riots indulged in by men agitators in the nineteenth century. The form of violence adopted was that of breaking windows. At first the leaders of the militant movement opposed and tried to restrain women from taking this course, but later they recognized it and organized it. A great shop-window breaking raid took place in London and created a sensation. The Government took action by arresting the leaders of the militant movement on a charge of conspiracy. I was one of those leaders and I made a speech in the dock at the Old Bailey in my own defence. I enclose with this letter, a verbatim report of it which you may feel disposed to read (*not* the biographical note which precedes it, which has no relevance to the present issue). It gives a number of further facts which I have not repeated in this letter. The trial, which was given immense prominence in the Press, ended in our conviction, the jury appending a sympathetic rider, and we were sentenced to nine months' imprisonment. At the same time several hundreds of the rank and file of the movement were also imprisoned. After serving part of our sentence the prisoners adopted the hunger strike. Some of us were forcibly fed and then released.

Subsequently there was a division in the leadership. Mrs Pankhurst decided on new and more violent tactics which did not appeal to my wife and myself, and we parted company. The Government also adopted new tactics and instead of applying forcible feeding to hunger strikers, took powers in a special Act of Parliament—the Cat and Mouse Bill—to release them and to rearrest them when they had recovered their health. The agitation continued with increasing bitterness on both sides up to the outbreak of the First World War.

Meanwhile on the purely political side there had been many developments. Supporters of woman suffrage did not succeed in inducing Mr Asquith to support a woman suffrage measure. Instead, he promised that the Franchise Bill which would be introduced to extend the male franchise would be open to amendment to include women. In the event the Speaker ruled that the Bill could not be so amended. This created an *impasse* in which it became evident that though the supporters of woman suffrage were not strong enough to insist on the passage of a Bill to enfranchise women, they were strong enough to prevent the passage of a Bill to enfranchise more men from which women were excluded.

The external war brought a truce to the domestic militant campaign and during the war women rendered great services to the nation. When in the middle of the war a new registration and franchise reform measure became necessary a Speaker's conference was constituted to frame the basis of its provisions, and a partial enfranchisement of women was included among them and was accepted as a reasonable compromise and as such was enacted.

I am in no doubt that the women's war service reconciled a large number of doubters to the inclusion of women in the future lists of electors. But I equally have no doubt that the prominence given to the question by the pre-war agitation made it impossible to ignore their claims and that, without it, gratitude to women for their help in critical hours might easily have fizzled out, without the accordance of any tangible recognition of their right to participate in the future governance of their common country.

APPENDIX 2

Outline of a constitution for India drawn up by the Cabinet Mission on May 16, 1946. From *Mahatma Gandhi* by H. S. L. Polak, H. N. Brailsford and Lord Pethick-Lawrence, pp. 270-1.

'The statement began with a recital of the facts as disclosed by the preliminary interviews, and an expression of opinion that neither the proposals of the Muslim League nor those of the Congress would meet the case, stating the considerations on which that conclusion was based. It proceeded to draw the outline of a constitution which all parties might be willing to accept.

'It envisaged three tiers. At the top there would be a Union of India, embracing both British India and the states. This Union would deal with foreign affairs, defence and communications and have power to raise the finances requisite thereto. The Union would have an executive and a legislature, and in the latter any question raising a major communal issue would require a majority of the representatives of each of the two major communities.

'The bottom tier would be occupied by the provinces and the states, in whom would vest all residuary powers.

'The provinces would be free to form groups with executives and legislatures. Such groups, if formed, would constitute the intermediate tier and would determine the provincial subjects to be taken in common.

'For the purpose of bringing some such constitution into being the statement recommended for acceptance the setting up of a constitution-making body. This would be elected by the members of the provincial legislatures. To each province would be allocated a number of representatives proportionate to the population of the province and voting would be by communities—general, Muslim and Sikh— the 'general' to include all persons who were not either Muslims or Sikhs. The states would be invited to send representatives to the constitution-making body in numbers proportionate to their total population.

'The procedure on the constitution-making body would be that after a preliminary meeting of the entire body, the provincial representatives would divide up into sections—Section "A" consisting of Madras, Bombay, United Provinces, Bihar and Orissa; Section "B" of the Punjab, North-West Frontier Province and Sindh; Section "C" of Bengal and Assam. These sections would settle the constitutions of the provinces in their section, and would also decide whether a group should be formed and, if so, with what subjects it should deal. Finally, the whole of the members of the constitution-making body should reassemble to settle the Union constitution.

'The statement made also certain other recommendations: (1) Resolutions either changing the basis of the proposed constitution or involving a major communal issue should not be accepted by the constitution-making body unless agreed to by each of the major communities. (2) After the constitution had come into operation, any province, by a vote of its legislature, would be free to opt out of the group in which it had been placed. Further, after ten years it could claim a reconsideration of the terms of the constitution. (3) On the attainment of independence by British India, paramountcy over the states would neither be retained by the British Crown nor transferred to the new government. (4) An Advisory Committee should be set up to report to the constitution-making body as to the rights of citizens, minorities and tribal and excluded areas, and how best these should be included in the constitution.

'After making an appeal to all Indians to accept the proposals made to them so as to avoid the danger of violence and to secure a settlement by consent, the statement concluded with the following words:

' "We hope that the new independent India may choose to be a member of the British Commonwealth. We hope, in any event, that you will remain in close and friendly association with our people. But these are matters for your own free choice. Whatever that choice may be, we look forward with you to your ever-increasing prosperity among the greatest nations of the world and to a future even more glorious than your past." '

APPENDIX 3

Books and Documents consulted for Part III

1. ANIL CHANDRA BANERJEE and DAKSHINA RANJAN BOSE (News Editor, The *Jugantar*, Calcutta; and Lecturer in History, Calcutta University). *The Cabinet Mission in India.* A. Mukherjee & Co., Calcutta. 1946.
2. JAY PARVESH. *India Steps Forward* and *The Story of the Cabinet Mission in India.* Indian Printing Works, Lahore. Oct. 1946.
3. EARL MOUNTBATTEN OF BURMA. *Time Only to Look Forward.* Nicholas Kaye. 1949. (Speeches by Rear-Admiral the Earl Mountbatten of Burma as Viceroy of India 1947-8.)
4. H. S. L. POLAK, H. N. BRAILSFORD and LORD PETHICK-LAWRENCE. Foreword by H. E. Mrs Sarojini Naidu. *Mahatma Gandhi.* Odhams Press. 1949.
5. ALAN CAMPBELL-JOHNSON. *Mission with Mountbatten.* Robert Hale. 1951.
6. E. W. R. LUMBY. *The Transfer of Power in India 1945-47.* George Allen & Unwin. 1954.
7. V. P. MENON. *The Transfer of Power in India.* Longmans, Green. 1957.
8. NICHOLAS MANSERGH. *India, Partition and Independence.* (Survey of British Commonwealth Affairs, R.I.A.A. Oxford University Press. 1958.)
9. ED. RAFIQ ZAKARIA. *A Study of Nehru.* Times of India. 1959.
10. PERCIVAL SPEAR. *India, A Modern History.* University of Michigan Press. (University of Michigan History of the Modern World. 1961.)
11. EARL ATTLEE, K.G., P.C., O.M., C.H. *Empire Into Commonwealth.* Oxford University Press. 1961.
12. B. R. NANDA. *The Nehrus. Motilal and Jawaharlal.* George Allen & Unwin Ltd. 1962.

13. *India Office Library Pamphlets*
Statement of the Policy of H. M. Government made by the Secretary of State for India on June 14, 1945.
Speech by Secretary of State for India in House of Commons, June 14, 1945.
Statement by Cabinet Mission and the Viceroy, May 16, 1946 (from Documents and Speeches on British Commonwealth Affairs 1931-52. Ed. Nicholas Mansergh).
Statement by Cabinet Mission and Viceroy, May 17, 1946.
Cabinet Mission 1946. Correspondence with Congress Party and Muslim League, May 20th - June 29th.
Statement by Cabinet Mission, May 25, 1946.
14. Correspondence between F. W. and Emmeline Pethick-Lawrence, March-July 1946.

INDEX

Aberdeen, South (by-election), 80
Abinger Hatch Hotel, 31, 33
Abyssinia, 109, 110
A Call to Women (E. Pethick-Lawrence), 56
Adam Bede, 27
Addams, Jane, 78, 85, 86
Adjar (Madras), 127
Aga Khan, 142
Agadir, 68
Agra, 22, 140, 154, 204
Ahimsa, 112
Ajanta Caves, 204
Albert Hall, 54, 58, 60, 67
Alden, Percy, 20, 21, 24, 25, 30, 37
Alexander, A. V. (Earl Alexander of Hillsborough), 26, 31, 79, 147, 150, 153, 154, 156, 165, 170, 182, 199, 212-13
Allen & Unwin Ltd., George, 80n
Ambedkar, Dr., 142, 166
Amery, Leo, 134
Amritsar, 130
Andrews, C. F., 200
Angell, Norman, 79
Anglo-Indians, 166
Arkus, 106
Armageddon, 68
Armistice, 85
Armistice Day (1918), 83
Arnold, Sydney (Lord Arnold of Hale), 80
Asian Review, 153
Ashwell, Lena, 78, 121
Asquith, H. H., 46, 52, 56, 58, 61, 64, 69, 81, 87, 90, 204
Astor, Nancy Lady, 91
Ataturk, 106
Atomic Bomb, 123-4
Attlee, C. R. (Earl), 76, 104, 113, 123, 124, 127, 130-3, 144, 147, 148, 160, 181, 183, 186, 212
Australia, 22, 43
Authors, Society of, 76
Azad, Maulana, 144, 148, 156, 158, 174, 178

Baghdad, 150
Bailey, Gerald, 200
Baines, Mrs (Suffragette), 55
Baker, John, 213
Baldwin, Stanley, 88, 93, 97-8, 110, 111, 130

Balfour, A. J., 41
Balkan Wars, 68
Banerjee, Anil Chandra, 160
Bank of England, 93, 99, 100, 103
Barnett, Canon S. A., 23, 37
Barrie, J. M., 54
Battersea North, 83, 84n
Battle of Britain, 117-18
Bayreuth, 197
B.B.C., 24, 54, 59, 124, 189, 196
Belgium, 117
Benares, 22
Benés, Eduard, 88
Bengal, 128, 134, 135, 138, 139, 183, 189
Benn, Wedgwood, 142
Bermondsey Settlement, 23
Besant, Annie, 60, 127, 136, 141n
Besant and Rice, 27
Bevan, Aneurin, 76, 118-19, 119n
Bevan, Aneurin (Michael Foot), 118-19, 119n
Bevin, Ernest, 76
Bihar, 183
Billington-Greig, Mrs Theresa, 51
Birla, G. D., 195
Birmingham, 52
'Black Friday', 56, 62
Blackwell, Alice Stone, 86
Blavatsky, Madame, 127
Boggart Hole Clough, 47
Bolpur, 138
Bombay, 22, 127, 137, 141, 178, 204
Booth, Charles, 23, 36
Booth, General, 51
Bose, Dakshima Ranjan, 160
Bose, Sir Jagardis, 140
Bose, Subhas Chandra, 139
Botha, General, 39
Boulogne, 66-7
Bournemouth Labour Party Conference (1940), 75, 117
Bow Street Police Court, 55, 59, 60
Brahmo-Samaj, 22, 135
Brailsford, H. N., 37, 54, 56, 79, 145n
Brandeis, Justice Louis, 86
Britain in Pictures, 42
Brittain, Vera, 201
Brixton Prison, 60, 63, 64, 76
Bryce, James, 36
Brynner, Yul, 89
Buddha, 112-13
Buddhism, 76

223

Budget (1930), 98, 100
Bulawayo, 39
Bunting, Sir Percy, 137
Bunting, Sheldon, 137
Burma, 123, 130, 132, 134, 173
Burns, John, 23
Butler, R. A., 148
Buxton, C. Roden, 80
Buxton, Mrs C. R., 85
Buxton, Noel, 37

Cabinet Mission, 8, 97, 108, 140, 143-77, 185, 186-7, 189-90, 191, 196, 199, 204, 207, 212
Calcutta, 22, 138, 139, 181, 183
'Calcutta Killing', The great, 181
Cambridge, 17, 18-20, 21, 36
Campbell, A. Y. G., 137-8
Campbell-Bannerman, Sir Henry, 24, 36, 46
Cannon Row Police Station, 50
Canterbury, Archbishop of, 150
Cape Colony, 35
Caretaker Government (Britain), 134
Caretaker Government (India), 174, 180
Carlyle, Thomas, 42
Carnegie Hall, 78
Carver, David, 193, 210
'Cat and Mouse' Act, 53
Catholic Citizen, The, 206
Catlin, Shirley (Mrs Williams), 201
Cause, The (Strachey), 48n, 94
Caxton Hall, 50
Ceylon, 22
Cecil Houses, 93
Cecil, Lord Robert, 54
Chamberlain, Austen, 129
Chamberlain, Joseph, 35, 36
Chamberlain, Neville, 110, 111, 113
Chelmsford, Lord, 129
Chen Pan Ting, 213
Chesterton, Mrs Cecil, 93
Children of Gideon, 27
China, 22
Chorlton v. Lings, 61
Christ, Jesus, 153
Christianity, 112-13
Christians, 152, 170
Churchill, Winston, 41, 53, 75, 88-90, 92, 98, 117, 132, 160
Citizenship of Women, The (Keir Hardie), 38
Civil Disobedience, 42

Civil Disobedience Campaign (India), 93, 129-30, 131
Clement's Inn, 33-4, 41, 48, 59, 67, 80, 203
Cleveland Hall, 27
Clifton-Brown, Colonel (Lord Ruffside), 75, 120, 122
Club, 1917, 80
Clynes, J. R., 90
Cole, Margaret, 106
Coleridge, Audrey and Phyllis, 63
Coleridge, Lord (Justice), 61
Collective Security, 109-10
Conciliation Bill, 56, 58, 62
Congress, Indian National, 127-191
Conquest of Happiness, The (Russell), 199
Conscientious Objectors, 110, 116
Conscription, 76
Conservative Party, 41, 96
Contemporary Review, The, 20n, 43, 137
Cooper, William, 201
'Cosmic Hymn', 77, 210-11
Courtney, Kathleen (Dame), 79
Courtney, Leonard, 37
Credit Anstalt Bank (Vienna), 99
Criminal Justice Bill, 192
Cripps, Dame Isobel, 211
Cripps, Sir Stafford, 89, 99, 107, 108, 113, 123, 133, 143, 147, 150, 154-5, 156, 160, 162, 163-7, 170, 176-7, 178, 180, 186, 190, 195-6
Cruickshank, Joan (Duval), 109, 140
Cullen, Miss (Suffragette), 48
Curzon, Lord, 128

Daily Herald, 31
Daily Mail, 52
Daily News, 54
Daily Telegraph, 80
Dalton, Hugh, 76, 106, 117
Darjeeling, 139
Darling, Mr Justice (Lord), 71
Davison, Emily Wilding, 71
Degrees for Women, 85
d'Egville, Sir Howard, 136
Delhi, 22, 140, 151, 156, 158, 179, 187, 189, 191, 204
Denbigh, 41
Denmark, 43, 117
Despard, Mrs Charlotte, 50, 51, 83, 84n, 207
De Wet, General, 39

INDEX

Dimitroff Committee, 108
'Direct Action Day', 180, 183
Dorking, 33, 72, 80, 168, 213-14
Downing Street, 59, 124
Dublin (St Patrick's), 84n
Durning-Lawrence, Dora, 212
Durning-Lawrence, Sir Edwin, 18, 31, 35, 60
Duval, Victor, 52, 54
Drummond, Flora, 49, 98

Echo, The, 30, 37-9
Eden, Anthony, 110, 119, 122
Edinburgh, East, 109, 116-17, 122, 123, 143
Edward VIII, 111
Edwards, Clem, 41
Edwards, Joseph, 37
Egypt, 38, 201-2
Elephanta Caves, 204
Eliot, George, 27
Ellis, Havelock, 76
Ellora Caves, 204
Elmy, Mrs Wolstenholme, 53
Empire Into Commonwealth (Attlee), 131
Empire Parliamentary Association, 136
Equal Franchise Bill (1928), 93
Equal Rights, 199
Esperance Girls' Club, 27-8
Esperance Social Guild, 38
Eton, 18, 19, 99
Evening News, 144
Everest, Mt, 139

Fabian Society, 80
Fawcett, Dame Millicent, 42, 43
Fawcett Society, 211
'Fight the Famine Council', 85
Finance Bills (1951 and 1954), 192, 199
Finland, 43
First World War, 32, 68, 70, 72, 76-83, 115, 129, 136
Fletcher, Sir William Morley, 19
Foot, Michael, 118, 119n
Forcible feeding, 63
Forum, 192
Forward, 138
Fourteen Points, 79
'Fourways' (Gomshall), 87, 119, 120, 121, 144, 149, 155, 158, 201
Free Trade, 89, 99
Free Trade Hall (Manchester), 208
From Fear Set Free (Sahgal), 106n
Fulford, Roger, 7, 46, 50, 54, 94, 203-4

Galsworthy, John, 54, 76
Gandhi, Mahatma, 42, 52, 128-31, 133-4, 135-7, 140, 142, 145, 145n, 147-8, 152-4, 161-5, 167, 170-2, 178, 183, 187, 189, 190, 200
Geneva, 113-14, 200
General Elections: 1906, 24, 40-41, 127-8; February 1910, 49; November 1910, 56, 58; 1918, 81, 83-4; 1922, 87-8; 1923, 88-90; 1924, 91; 1929, 96; 1931, 104-5; 1935, 109; 1945, 122, 123, 127, 134, 144; 1955, 7, 201
General Strike, 92
George V, 56, 111
George VI, 111
George, Lloyd, 30, 31, 37, 39, 45, 55, 58, 71, 79, 87
German Republic, 85
Germany, 77, 83, 85, 99, 111, 128
Ghose, Sir Charu, 136
Ghosh, Sudhir, 167
Gladstone, Herbert, 53, 55
Gladstone, W. E., 35, 36, 41, 43, 44, 61, 62, 69, 127, 204
Gokhale, Gopal Krishna, 128
Gold Standard, 99, 100, 101, 103, 108
Gollancz, Victor, 100, 106, 106n
Gooch, Dr G. P., 18, 19, 20, 31, 36, 37, 43, 52, 68, 81, 187
Gosbank, 106
Government of India Act (1935), 131-2
Green Lady Hostel, Littlehampton, 28
Greenwood, Arthur, 113-14, 117
Grey, Sir Edward, 40, 52, 78
Grey Eminence (Huxley), 121
Grinko, 106
Groom, Gladys, 118, 209

Hague, The, 78
Hailsham, Lord, Jnr., 192, 208
Hailsham, Lord, Snr., 192
Hamilton, Cicely, 98
Hammond, J. L., 37
Hanover (S. Africa), 39
Hansard, 192
Harcourt, Lewis, 71
Hardie, Keir, 23, 38, 41, 44, 207
Hardinge, Lord, 128-9
Hardy, Thomas, 54
Harijan, 161, 165
Harrison, Agatha, 147, 152, 163, 200
Harrison, Frederick, 37
Harrison, Irene, 147
Hastings (constituency), 81

Harwich Division of Essex, 7
Healy, Tim, 60, 62
Henderson, Arthur, Jnr., 121
Henderson, Arthur, Snr., 103, 107
Henley, W. E., 76
Hertzog, General, 39, 97
Hill, Alderman Alfred, 88
Hillman, Sidney, 86
Hinduism, 112, 127
Hindus, 132-191
Hindustan, 148, 178
Hindustan Times, 172
Hindu Weekly Review, 136, 143
Hiroshima, 124
Hitler, Adolf, 108, 109, 111, 112, 115
Hoare, Sir Samuel, 110, 132
Hobhouse, Rt. Hon. C. E. H., 59, 60, 71
Hobhouse, Emily, 36
Hobhouse, Stephen, 59
Hobman, Mrs D. L., 86, 201
Hodder & Stoughton, 124n
Holland, 117
Holland, Canon Scott, 37
Holloway Prison, 49, 53n, 56, 60, 64, 72
Holmes, Justice Oliver Wendell, 86
Holmwood, The (Surrey), 33, 38, 65, 67, 87
Holtby, Winifred, 100
Household Means Test (Bill to abolish), 117-18
Housman, Laurence, 76, 108, 110
How-Martyn, Mrs Edith, 51
Hughes, Hugh Price, 27
Hughes, Mrs H. P., 27
Huxley, Aldous, 121
Hyde Park, 43, 55

Iceland, 43
Independence Bills, India and Burma, 186
Independents, 146
In Darkest London (Mrs Cecil Chesterton), 93
India, 21, 22, 76, 77, 92, 97, 105, 123, 127-91, 204
India (Spear), 181
India Conciliation Group, 200
India League, 200
Indian Independence Act, 187
Inner Temple, 24n
International Suffrage Congress (Istanbul), 105
Interparliamentary Union, 91-2
Ireland, 198, 210

Iron and Steel Bill, 192
Irwin, Lord (Halifax), 130, 131, 132, 139, 186

Jacobs, Dr Aletta, 78
Jaipur, 204
Jallianwallah Bagh, 130
Japan, 22, 109, 123-4, 128, 134
Jebb, Eglantine, 85
Jinnah, Mohammed Ali, 129, 134, 145, 146, 147, 148, 153, 154, 157, 158, 161, 162, 163, 164, 165, 167, 170, 172, 174, 179, 180, 181, 182, 183, 188, 189, 190
Johannesburg, 39

Kabul, 139
Kaiser, The, 68, 72, 83, 85
Kaiser-i-Hind, The, 140
Kanchenjunga Range, 139
Karachi, 150, 188
Karma, 112-13, 115
Kashmir, 155-6, 157
Katherine House, Fitzroy Square, 27
Kaur, Rajkumari Amrit, 195
Kenney, Annie, 40, 46, 52, 53, 207, 208
Khan, Abdul Ghaffir, 156
Khan, Liaquat Ali, 147, 156, 183, 188-9, 190
Khan, Begum Liaquat Ali, 189, 189n
Khan, Mahommed Ismail, 156
Kher, Mr (High Commissioner), 200
Khyber Pass, 139
Kiev, 106
Kilmuir, Lord, 207
Kilroe, Maureen, 193
Kingsley Hall, Bow, 131
Kingsway (WVSU headquarters), 67
Knight, Mrs (Suffragette), 46
Knowles, Esther, 38, 118, 157, 181, 186, 193, 194, 209, 211
Krause, Judge (South Africa), 111

Labour Manual, The, 37
Labour Party, 20, 24, 41, 44, 87-124
Labour Record and Review, The, 38
Labour Representation Committee, 24
Lady Into Woman (Vera Brittain), 48n
La Follette, Senator Robert, 86
La Follette's (magazine), 86
Lahore, 140
Lambeth North, 35, 36
Lang, Anton, 111
Lansbury, George, 54, 64, 110, 136, 207
Lansdowne, Lord, 80

INDEX

Laval, Pierre, 110
Law, Bonar, 88
Lawrence & Co., Sash-makers, 17
Lawrence Alfred, Jnr., 18, 35, 37, 39
Lawrence, Alfred, Snr., 18
Lawrence, James, 18
Lawrence, Miss Penelope, 203
Lawrence, William, Jnr., 18
Lawrence, William, Snr., 17, 18
League of Nations, 85, 86, 129
League of Nations Union, 110
League of Young Liberals, 26
Leeds Assizes, 55
Lees-Smith, H. B., 117
Leicester West, 84, 88-90, 91, 96, 109, 136
Leningrad, 106
Liberal Party, 24, 36, 40-41, 49, 87, 96
Liberal Unionism, 35
Life and Labour of the People (Booth), 23, 36
Lincoln's Inn, 80, 87
Lincoln's Inn Fields, 87
Linlithgow, Lord, 132
Listowel, Lord, 186-7
Lodge, Sir Oliver, 54
London Museum, 47, 48, 53n
Longford, Earl of (Frank Pakenham), 213
Low, Sir David, 110
Lucknow, 22, 140
Lutyens, Sir Edwin, 33
Lytton, Lady Constance, 49, 53
Lytton, Lord, 54, 56

Macarthur, Mary, 84n
MacCarthy, Sir Desmond, 193
Maclean, Sir Donald, 99
MacDonald, Ramsay, 26, 37, 79, 84, 88, 91, 101, 102-3, 104, 131
Macmillan, Chrystal, 79
Madras, 22, 136, 137, 138
Maison Esperance, 28
Malaviya, Pandit, 142
Malleson, Miles, 76
Manchester, 40, 41, 47
Manchester College, Oxford, 36
Manchester Guardian, 111
Manchester University, 45
Manchuria, 109
Manor House Hospital, 212
Mansergh, Nicholas, 132, 132n, 187
Mansfield House Settlement, Canning Town, 20-25
'March of the Women' (Smyth), 61, 98
Markevicz, Countess, 84, 84n

Marsh, Charlotte, 208
Marshall, Professor Alfred, 20, 21
'Mascot, The', 33, 38, 87, 168
Masterman, C. F. G., 36
May Report, 99, 100
May, Sir George, 99
Mazzini, Joseph, 36
Mazzoletti, Mrs Mary, 119, 194, 195
McKenna, Mr (Home Secretary), 53
Menon, Krishna, 195, 200
Menon, V. P., 147, 154, 175
Men's League for Woman Suffrage, 54
Men's Political Union, 54
Merriman, John X., 39, 169
Messel, Rudolph, 106
Middle Way, The, 192
Militancy, technique of, 53ff
Mill, J. S., 42, 43, 45
Minerva Club, 93
Minto, Lord, 128
Mitchison, G. R., 106
Mitchison, Naomi, 106
Montagu, Edwin, 129
Montagu—Chelmsford Report, 130
Montagu, The Hon. Lilian, 28
Montagu, The Hon. Marian, 28
Moore-Guggisberg, Decima, 120
Moral and Social Hygiene, Association for, 91, 121, 156
Morel, E. D., 79, 80
Morley, John, 36, 128
Morley-Minto Act, 128
Morrison, Sybil, 115
Moscow, 106
Mosley, Sir Oswald, 100
Mountbatten of Burma, Earl, 186, 187, 190
'Mud March', 50
Munich crisis, 112
Murray, Professor Gilbert, 54
Muskett, Mr (prosecutor), 55
Muslim League, 128, 154, 155, 156-7, 159, 161, 167, 169, 170, 171, 172, 174, 178, 179, 180, 183, 184, 186, 187
Muslims, 129-91
Mussolini, 109, 110, 111, 115
Muzoomdar, Mr, 22
Myers, F. W. H., 212
Mysore, 138

Nahas, Pasha, 202
Naidu, Mrs Sarojini, 137, 142, 145n, 152, 163, 200
National Government (1931), 99, 102, 103, 131-2

National Government (1940), 75, 117
National Liberal Club, 59
National Union of Women Teachers, 8
National Women's Peace Party of America, 79
Nazi movement in Germany, 20, 85
Nazi-Soviet Pact, 114
Neal, Mary ('Sister Mary'), 37, 38, 39, 53, 120, 197
Nehru, Jawaharlal, 92, 127, 130, 133, 146, 154, 156, 158, 163, 170, 178, 181, 182-3, 184, 187, 188, 189, 190-1, 200, 202, 204
Nehru, Motilal, 92-3, 130, 142
Nehru, A Study of (ed. Zakaria), 182
Nevinson, H. W., 54
New Fabian Research Bureau, 105, 106
New India, 136
News of the World, 168
Newsome, Stella, 197
New Statesman and Nation, 210
New Zealand, 22, 43
Nijni Novgorod, 106
Nishtar, Abdur Rab, 156, 183
Noordam, The, 79
Norman, Montagu, 99
Normanton, Helena, 120
Norway, 43, 117
Nottingham Castle, 59

Oberammergau, 121
Observer, The, 104
Odhams Press, 18n, 145n
Old Bailey Conspiracy Trial, 8, 61-3, 144
Old Square, Lincoln's Inn, 80, 118, 124
Orange Free State, 39
Ossinsky, 106
Ould, Hermon, 193
Oxford House, 23
Oxford University, 19, 85

Pakistan, 128, 146, 147, 147n, 148, 150, 153, 154, 155, 159, 167, 178, 184, 186, 187
Pandit, The Hon. Mrs Vijayalakshmi, 92, 143, 145, 200, 202, 204
Pankhurst, Adela, 45-6, 47, 49, 205
Pankhurst, Christabel, 32, 33, 34, 40, 45, 49, 50-55, 59-60, 66-9, 70, 83, 84n, 93, 95, 199-200, 205-7, 208-9
Pankhurst, Mrs Emmeline, 34, 42, 44, 45, 47, 49, 50-51, 53, 58, 59, 60-62, 66, 67, 93-4, 97-8, 209

Pankhurst, Dr Richard, Jnr., 98
Pankhurst, Dr. Richard, Snr., 61
Pankhurst, Sylvia, 28, 32, 33, 44-5, 48n, 49, 53n, 94, 98, 195, 199, 205
Parmoor, Lady, 89
Parry, Sir Hubert, 54
Parsees, 170
Passmore Edwards, 37
Patel, Sardar, 147, 156, 183
Peace Ballot, 110
Peace News, 115
Peace Pledge Union, 110, 115
Peach, Harry, 89
Pearce, Mabelle, 27
Pearce, Dr Margaret, 25
Pearce, Mark Guy, 27, 30, 32
Pearl Harbour, 133
Peaslake, 72, 87, 115, 164, 193, 197, 213-14
P.E.N., The, 76, 193-4, 201
P.E.N. News, 35
Penn, William, 196
Peshawar, 139
Pethick, Harold, 66
Pethick, Henry, 31
Pethick, Tom, 26
Pethick, William, 30
Pethick-Lawrence, Emmeline
  Militant leader, 7
  Correspondence with F.W.P.-L., 8
  Influence on F.W.P.-L., 20
  First meeting with F.W.P.-L., 25, 28
  Family background, 26
  Letter to Vera Brittain, 26n
  Marriage, 30, 31
  Honeymoon, 31
  Appearance, 33
  Plaque at Clement's Inn, 34
  Friendship with Keir Hardie, 38
  First visit to South Africa, 39-40
  First meeting with Mrs Pankhurst, 44
  Becomes WSPU Treasurer, 44-67
  Arrested and imprisoned, 49, 55, 58-9, 60
  Association with Women's Freedom League, 51
  Old Bailey trial, 61-3
  Severs connection with WSPU, 66-70
  Contests civil action for window breaking and addresses jury, 71
  Supports pacifism, 77
  Helps to found Women's International League for Peace and Freedom, 77-9

Fights Rusholme Division of Manchester, 1918, 83-4
Visits Zurich for WILPF, 85
Assesses Suffrage issue, 95
Visits South Africa, 97
Pays tribute to Mrs Pankhurst, 98
Travels in Middle East, 105-6
Publishes autobiography, 111-12
Visits Geneva, 113-14
Attitude to Second World War, 115-16
Retires to 'Fourways', 114ff
Silver Honeymoon visit to India, 136-42
Writes to Pethick on eve of Cabinet Mission, 148-50
Corresponds with Pethick while the Mission is in India, 150-73
Health fails, 194-6
Golden Wedding, 195
Last Christmas, 196-7
Dies at Peaslake, 197
Funeral service, 197-8
Commemoration meeting, 199
Memorial meetings at Peaslake and Dorking, 213-14
Writings: Contribution to *University and Social Settlements*, 25; *My Part in a Changing World*, 28, 32, 68, 71, 77, 98, 111, 115

Pethick-Lawrence, F. W.
Friendship with author, 7, 8, 26n
College life, 17, 18-20
Forbears, 17-18
Schooldays, 18-19
Travels round world, 21-2
First meeting with Emmeline Pethick, 25, 28
Tennis player, 26, 87
Courtship, 29-30
Edits *The Echo*, 30, 37-9
First Marriage, 30-1
Honeymoon, 31
Candidate for North Lambeth, 34-6
Contacts with Olive Schreiner, 35-6
Joins the Liberals, 36
Appointed 'Dunkin Professor', 36
Visits South Africa, 39-40
Attitude towards woman suffrage, 43-4
Meeting with Christabel Pankhurst, 45
Supports WSPU, 46-67
Begins 'Bailing Out', 50
Edits *Votes for Women*, 53ff
Defence of Mrs Baines, 55
Becomes Joint Treasurer for the WSPU, 55-6
Old Bailey trial, 61-3
Suffers forcible feeding, 63
Severs connection with WSPU, 66-70
Made bankrupt, 70-1
Contests civil action for window-breaking, 70-1
Becomes a conscientious objector, 76
Contests South Aberdeen as a 'Peace-by-Negotiation' Candidate, 80
Becomes Labour Candidate for Hastings, but retires from contest, 81
Witnesses triumph of woman suffrage, 81-2
Supports Emmeline in Rusholme Division, 1918, 83, 84
Opposes Treaty of Versailles, 85
Visits USA, 85-6
Contests South Islington, 87
Contests West Leicester and defeats Winston Churchill, 88-90
Studies the House of Commons, 91
Retains seat in 1924, 91
Celebrates his silver wedding, 92
Visits South Wales for Labour Party, 93
Appreciates changes wrought by suffrage movement, 95
Re-elected for West Leicester, 96
Writes poem to Emmeline, 97
Speaks at unveiling of Mrs Pankhurst's statue, 98
Becomes Financial Secretary to the Treasury, 96-102
Involved in 1931 economic crisis, 100-3
Loses office, 102
Defeated in 1931 Election, 105
Visits Middle East and Russia, 105-7
Returns to House of Commons as M.P. for East Edinburgh, 109-23
Letter to Emmeline on Munich crisis, 112-13
Visits Geneva, 113-14
Attitude to Second World War, 115
Correspondence with Vera Brittain about wartime suffering, 116
Publishes his autobiography, 121
Statement on Germany, 122

Statement on Britain's future (1945), 122
Becomes Secretary of State for India and for Burma, and receives a peerage, 123-86
Describes end of Second World War, 124
Entertains Gandhi during Suffrage campaign, 135-6
Silver Honeymoon visit to India, 136-42
Broadcasts to India, New Year 1946, 146
Appointed to lead Cabinet Mission, 147-8
Takes Mission to India, 150-2
Visits Kashmir, 155-6
Visits Simla, 156-8
Broadcasts to the world, 159-60
Struggles to achieve agreement, 160-74
Receives appreciative letter from Sir Stafford Cripps, 176-7
Leaves India, 178
Reports to House of Lords on work of Mission, 178-81
Retires as Secretary of State, 186-7
Becomes 'Economics tutor' to the House of Lords, 193ff
Work with International PEN, 193-4
Golden Wedding, 194-5
Broadcasts on Sir Stafford Cripps, 196
Arranges Emmeline's last Christmas, 196-7
Gives funeral address for Emmeline, 197-8
Arranges Commemoration meeting, 199
Speaks at Olive Schreiner Centenary and in General Election of 1955, 201
Reactions to Suez crisis, 201-2
Second marriage, 202-3
Last visit to India, 204
Memorials to Christabel Pankhurst, 205-8
Publishes *Unshackled*, 206-7
Last speech in House of Lords, 208-9
Expresses religious beliefs in A *Cosmic Hymn*, 210-11
Last illness and death, 211-12
Memorial service, 8, 212-13
Memorial meetings at Peaslake and Dorking, 213-14

Writings of: *Fate Has Been Kind*, 7, 29, 32, 43, 44, 85, 90, 108, 115, 117, 121, 135, 136, 142, 210; *If I Had My Time Again*, 18, 19, 31, 33, 69, 135, 181, 210; Local Variations in Wages, 19; The Heart of the Empire (essay on housing), 36; Women's Fight for the Vote, 42, 47; The By-election Policy of the W.S.P.U., 47; Women's Work and Wages, 47; Mr Asquith's 'Pledge', 47; Treatment of the Suffragettes in Prison, 47; A Levy on Capital, 80; Why Prices Rise and Fall, 86; The Gold Crisis, 100; Twelve Studies in Soviet Russia (contrib.), 106; Mahatma Gandhi (essay), 159, 172, 178, 182
Pethick-Lawrence, Helen (Mrs Duncan McCombie, née Craggs), 7, 50, 71, 195, 202-3, 202n, 204, 205, 209, 211, 212, 213
Polak, H. S. L., 145n
Poland, 113
Porchester Place, 86
Poverty in London, 22-3, 28
Prague, 113
Pressing Problems of the Closing Age (Christabel Pankhurst), 95
Princes, Indian, 152, 163
Prison and Prisoners (Constance Lytton), 53
Privy Council, 111
Punch, 67

Queen's Club, 80
'Quit India' Resolution, 133, 133n

Rahmat Ali, 147n
Rajagopalachari, C., 133, 176, 176n, 195, 200, 210
Ramkrishna Paramhansa, 127
Ranchi, The (P. & O.), 136
Rao, B. Shiva, 136, 143, 152, 160
Reading, Lord, 130
Reason, W., 24
Reform Bill (1832), 17, 59
Reform Bill (1918), 81
Reform Club, 71, 80
Reformers' Year Book, The, 37
Reichstag, 92
Reigate, 41
Rents Bill, 199
Rhondda, Viscountess, 98

INDEX

Richards, MP, Professor Robert, 146
Richardson, Mary, 71
Ring, The (Wagner), 112, 197
Roberts, Dr Harry, 42
Robins, Elizabeth, 50, 53, 60
Roe, Grace, 32-3, 70, 72, 205-7
Roedean, 203
Rokeby, Venus, 71
Roslyakov, 106
Rostov-on-Don, 106
Round Table Conferences (India), 104, 105, 131, 132, 140, 142
Rowlatt Acts, 129
Rowlatt, Judge, 129
Royal Aero Club, 80
Rusholme Division (Manchester), 83
Russell, Bertrand (Earl), 19, 54, 77, 199
Russia, 105-7, 128

Sahgal, Nayantara, 106n
St John, Christopher, 55
Salvation Army, 51
San Francisco, 22
Santiniketan, 138
Sapru, Sir Tej, 130, 142, 152
Scheduled Castes Federation, 166
Scott, McCallum, 37
Scrapbook for 1912, 59
Schreiner, Olive, 35, 36, 39-40, 56, 76, 79, 86, 201
Schreiner, Olive: Her Friends and Times (Hobman), 86
Schreiner, W. P., 35, 39
Schwimmer, Rosika, 78
Second World War, 77, 80, 85, 115-24, 132, 133
Sen, Keshab Chandra, 135
Sex Disqualification (Removal) Act, 85
Seymour, Isabel, 105, 115, 116, 121, 196-7, 201, 209
Sforza, Count, 119
Shalimar Gardens (Srinagar), 156
Sharboro, Mrs (Suffragette), 46
Sharp, Evelyn, 50, 59
Sharpeville, 130
Shaw, Bernard, 80
Shepherd, Meliscent, 156, 163
Shere, 87, 144, 193
Shield, The, 208
Sikhs, 146, 152, 166, 170, 183, 187
Silver Wedding (Pethick-Lawrences), 43
Simla, 134, 156, 157-8, 164, 179, 189
Simon Commission, 92, 130-1
Simon, Sir John, 162

Simon Report, 131
Singh, Balder, 183
Singh, Sir Hari, 156
Singh, Master Tara, 166
Sleem, 136
Smethwick, 83, 84n
Smilga, 106
Smillie, Bob, 23
Smuts, General, 97
Smyth, Dame Ethel, 55, 59, 61, 98
Snowden, Philip, 96, 99, 101, 103, 104
Socialism, 75-124
Socialist League, 107
Sorensen, Reginald, 200
South Africa, 30, 34-6, 39, 40, 86, 97, 128-9, 130, 135, 157
South African War, 30, 35, 39, 41, 43, 60
South African Women's and Children's Distress Fund, 36
Spanish Civil War, 111, 113
Spear, Percival, 147n, 167, 181n, 190
Spectator, The, 101, 104
Sphinx, The, 38
Srinagar, 155-6
Stalingrad, 106
Steyn, Jan, 39
Stocks, Mary, 106, 111
Stonham, Lord, 208
Stourbridge, 84n
Strachey, Ray, 48n, 94
'Street Bill, The' (1925), 91
Subjection of Women, The (Mill), 43
Suez crisis, The, 201
Suffrage Annual and Women's Who's Who, 69
Suffrage Movement, The, 32, 42, 43-72, 94-5, 135
Suffragette, The (Sylvia Pankhurst), 28, 32, 94
Suffragette Fellowship, 195, 197
Suffragette Movement, The, 33, 42, 43-72, 94-5, 135, 195
Suffragette Movement, The (Sylvia Pankhurst), 94
Summerskill, Baroness (Dr Edith), 108, 199, 213
Survey of British Commonwealth Affairs (Mansergh), 132
Swanwick, Mrs H. M., 79
Swaraj Parliamentary Party, The, 130, 137, 138
Swatantra Party, 176n

Tagore, Devendranath, 138
Tagore family, 22
Tagore, Rabindranath, 60, 130, 138-9, 140
Taj Mahal, 139, 140, 154, 204
Tawney, Professor R. H., 21
Testament of Youth (Brittain), 26n, 82n
Theosophical Society, 127
Thorndike, Dame Sybil, 34n, 199
Tibet, 157
Tigris, 150
Tilak, Bal Gangadhur, 128
Tillett, Ben, 23
Time and Tide, 100
Times, The, 54, 142, 165, 173, 199
Toynbee, Arnold, 23
Toynbee Hall, 23
Trevelyan, OM, Dr G. M., 19, 37, 120, 121, 143, 203
Trinity College, Cambridge, 19, 20
Tripartite Conference, 157
'Triumvirate, The', 51
Truman, Harry S. (Memoirs), 124n
Truro-Helston Division (Cornwall), 35
Tuke, Mabel, 59
Tunis, 150
Twain, Mark, 37

'Unconditional Surrender', 124
Under Six Reigns (Gooch), 81
Unemployment, 99, 108
Union of Democratic Control, 76, 79, 80
Union of Soviet Socialist Republics, 43
United Nations Demographic Year Book, 141n
United States, 22, 78-9, 86, 91-2, 99, 108
United Suffragists, 67, 77
University Settlements, 23
University and Social Settlements (W. Reason), 24, 25
Unshackled (Christabel Pankhurst), 45, 51, 69, 95n, 206-7
Untouchables, 152

Vancouver, 70
Vancouver Island, 66
Vaughan, Henry, the Silurist, 205
Vedanta for East and West, 192
Vereeniging, Peace of, 37
Versailles, Treaty of, 85, 98, 114
Verwoerd, Dr, 36
Victoria Tower Gardens, 97, 206

Vijagaragavacharga, Sir T., 136
Vivekananda, 127
Votes for Women (Fulford), 7, 46, 94, 203-4
Votes for Women (newspaper), 34, 53, 59, 60, 67, 71, 77

Walker, ARA, A. G., 97
Wallace Dunlop, Miss (Suffragette), 53
Wall Street crash, 97
'Jane Warton' (Lady Constance Lytton), 53
Wavell, Lord (Viceroy), 134, 144, 147, 148, 151, 154, 160, 163, 164, 165, 167, 170, 171-2, 174-5, 179, 180, 181, 182, 183 186
Webb, Beatrice, 23, 31
Webb, Sidney, 31, 54
West London Mission, 27, 32, 198
Weston-super-Mare, 26, 26n
Whately, Monica, 208
Whittier, J. G., 213
Why I Went to Prison (E. Pethick-Lawrence), 55
Wilkinson, Ellen, 110
Willingdon Crescent, 152, 177
Wilson, President, 79
Wimbledon (by-election), 54
Window-breaking, 55, 59, 62
Woolf, Leonard, 120
Woolf, Virginia, 120
Woman and Labour (Olive Schreiner), 40
Women's Bulletin, The, 203
Women's Emergency Corps, 78
Women's Freedom League, 51, 92, 195
Women's International League for Peace and Freedom, 77, 78, 79, 85
Women's Peace Crusade, 92
Women's Social and Political Union, 34, 42, 43-72, 77
Women's Suffrage (Fawcett), 42
World Faiths, 192
World Women's Party, 113
Wormwood Scrubbs, 63

Zakaria, Rafiq, 182
Zambesi Falls, 39
Zangwill, Israel, 50, 60
Zeppelin raids, 80
Zinovieff Letter, 91
Zurich, 85